Praisesong of Survival

Praisesong
of Survival

Lectures and Essays, 1957–89

RICHARD K. BARKSDALE

PREFACE BY

Dolan Hubbard

INTRODUCTION BY

R. Baxter Miller

UNIVERSITY OF ILLINOIS PRESS
Urbana and Chicago

Publication of this book was made possible in part by a grant from the Campus Research Board of the University of Illinois at Urbana-Champaign.

This book is printed on acid-free paper.

Library of Congress Cataloging-in-Publication Data

Barksdale, Richard K. (Richard Kenneth), 1915–
    Praisesong of survival : lectures and essays, 1957–89 / Richard K.
Barksdale ; preface by Dolan Hubbard ; introduction by R. Baxter
Miller.
        p.   cm.
    Includes bibliographical references.
    ISBN 0-252-01898-2 (cl) — ISBN 0-252-06286-8 (pb)
    1. American literature—Afro-American authors—History and
criticism.   2. Afro-Americans—Intellectual life.   3. Afro-Americans
in literature.   I. Title.
PS153.N5B29   1992
810.9'896073—dc20   91-881
                                                                    CIP

The following permissions have been given to use quotations from copyrighted works: From *Selected Poems* by Langston Hughes. Copyright © 1959 by Langston Hughes. Reprinted by permission of Alfred A. Knopf, Inc. From *The Panther and the Lash* by Langston Hughes. Copyright © 1967 by Arna Bontemps and George Houston Bass, Executors of the Estate of Langston Hughes. Reprinted by permission of Alfred A. Knopf, Inc. From *The Dream Keeper and Other Poems* by Langston Hughes. Copyright © 1932 by Alfred A. Knopf, Inc., and renewed 1960 by Langston Hughes. Reprinted by permission of the publisher. From poems by Margaret Danner. Reprinted by permission of Naomi Washington.

To my devoted wife, Mildred Barksdale,
and to my grandsons, Adam and Andrew Barksdale

Contents

Preface: Reflections on Richard K. Barksdale as Teacher, Mentor, and Scholar

Dolan Hubbard

> He was a scholar, and a ripe and good one;
> Exceeding wise, fair-spoken, and persuading:
> Shakespeare, *Henry VIII*, IV, ii, 51

I first met Richard Kenneth Barksdale in April 1982 at the Forty-second Annual Convention of the College Language Association in Charlotte, North Carolina. He had formerly served as president of this largest and most prestigious of African American literary organizations. He and Chester J. Fontenot, Jr., the delegation from the University of Illinois at Urbana-Champaign, greeted me warmly and welcomed me to the doctoral program in English where I began my studies that fall, specializing in African American literature. Instinctively, I felt that I had known this dean of African American letters all my life. He has been a kindred spirit since I first taught from his coedited anthology *Black Writers of America* while I served as a member of the faculty at Winston-Salem State University (1977–82). That early bond made for a smooth transition to the stately campus with its aura of hospitable friendliness that often proved to be misleading.

What I will most treasure from my association with Barksdale is that contact between him and the students was close and that he emphasized the development of the total person. Though he was perpetually busy with several projects and balancing the responsibilities of service to the university, he always maintained an open-door policy.

With his understated brilliance, polished elegance, disarming wit, dashing smile, and golden-throated baritone chuckle, Barksdale, master teacher, made you feel secure intellectually and emotionally in a rigorous doctoral program. With unaffected grace, he imparted knowledge.

He would regale us with stories about African American royalty in both the creative and performing arts and make these artistic innovators accessible to us, make us see their strengths as well as their weaknesses, and make us see talents such as Bessie Smith, Zora Neale Hurston, Louis Armstrong, Richard Wright, and Margaret Walker Alexander in their ritual context as they told the African American story. He wanted us to see the beauty as well as the ugliness of the enslavement of Africans in the United States—that we did not emerge from this harrowing experience as saints or sinners but as formidable characters in a still-unfolding drama.

It is a singular pleasure to have been invited to comment on Dr. Barksdale as teacher, mentor, and scholar. My pleasure in briefly recounting Barksdale's extraordinary legacy is tempered by the knowledge that his nearly half century's service to higher education cannot be compassed into a few pages. Let these jottings serve then, as Augustine says in the *Confessions,* as a sign pointing to a larger world.

After more than forty years of teaching, Richard K. Barksdale retired in 1985. Born 31 October 1915, in Winchester, Massachusetts, Barksdale is a Phi Beta Kappa graduate of Bowdoin College (1937); he earned a master's degree at Syracuse University (1938) and another at Harvard University (1947). He served in the army from 1943 to 1946, before being honorably discharged with the rank of Second Lieutenant. In 1951 he was awarded the Doctor of Philosophy degree from Harvard and became the second African American to take his degree from that institution in English literature. In 1972 Bowdoin College conferred upon him the honorary degree, Doctor of Humane Letters.

Professor Barksdale has published widely in scholarly journals, for instance, *Phylon, College Language Association Journal, Western Humanities Review,* and *Black American Literature Forum.* He coedited, with Keneth Kinnamon, the volume *Black Writers of America* (1972). A specialist on the Harlem Renaissance, he is the author of the critically acclaimed *Langston Hughes: The Poet and His Critics* (1977). Among his numerous professional affiliations and honors, he has served as president of the College Language Association (1973–75) and the Langston Hughes Society (1981–83). He was awarded the Langston Hughes Prize by the latter group (1986); the Therman B. O'Daniel Distinguished Educator Award by the Middle Atlantic Writers Association (1989); and the National Council of Teachers of English Black Caucus Distinguished Educator Award (1989).

Nearly always active in the affairs of higher education, he served with distinction as a member of the Advisory Committee, Mellon Humanities Program for Black Colleges (1975–79); the Graduate Record Examination Administrative Board (1976–78); and the University of Illinois Press Board (1982–86); and as a consultant for the National Endowment for the Humanities (1983); the Ford Foundation (1968–70); and the Commission on Higher Education, North Central Association (1973–86).

In much demand as an interpreter of the humanities, Barksdale has held several visiting professorships, among them the Langston Hughes Visiting Professorship in American and African American Literature, University of Kansas (spring 1986); Tallman Visiting Professor of English Literature, Bowdoin College (fall 1986); Visiting Professor in African American Literature, Grinnell College (April 1987); United Negro College Fund Distinguished Scholar, Rust College (spring 1988); and Visiting Professor in African American Literature, University of Missouri–Columbia (fall 1988). He is married to Dr. Mildred W. Barksdale, who has retired from her position as assistant dean, College of Liberal Arts and Sciences, University of Illinois at Urbana-Champaign.

At the University of Illinois, Barksdale came into his own as a man of letters on three fronts. First, free from his heavy teaching load and administrative responsibility in the historically black colleges, his scholarly production increased, as the record shows. He had cut his academic teeth while serving in the dual capacity as teacher and administrator in black colleges throughout the South—Southern University, Tougaloo College, North Carolina Central University, Morehouse College—and finally as dean of the graduate school at Atlanta University during 1967–71.

Second, his position at the University of Illinois enabled him to enhance his services to higher education in general and to expand his lifelong role as an unofficial "goodwill" ambassador for black academe in particular. In his position as acting head of the Department of English (spring 1974) and as associate dean of the Graduate College (1975–82), he put institutional teeth into engaging in meaningful dialogue with underrepresented constituencies and into the recruitment and retention of promising minority students. And finally, during his tenure at the University of Illinois, the Department of English produced nineteen African American doctorates plus two dissertations written by white students on black American literature topics. He personally directed seven of these dissertations.

A hallmark of his teaching is the belief that scholarship is most liberating when it has roots in society. He nurtured us, taking us as children and seeing us leave as young scholars. He reminded us of the incalculable contributions made to the Americas by Africans. He challenged us to be about the business of telling the American story in all its manifest dimensions. He insisted that we draw strength from our heritage, our voice, and our unique vision. He did not permit us to romanticize the African American experience, nor did he permit us to subscribe to narcissism, that because we are Americans of African descent, we have a monopoly on singing the blues. While he enhanced our skills in the art and craft of scholarship, he made us realize that intelligence is a tough taskmaster.

Richard Barksdale enabled us to discern significant relations among works of literature in the English, American, and African American traditions. He did not want us to be captive academics, limited to making linkage and establishing connections within the context of African American literature. I fondly recall his lectures to us; one could imagine the enormous sweep of his mind as he engaged in the process of historical meditation, as he revealed the complexity of the patterns of black life and culture. For example, one could not help but applaud Dr. B. for his magnificence in his rendition of Hughes's classic poem "The Weary Blues." I remember him for the dignity and ceremonial color he brought to Hughes's portrait of this debased African prince in the New World.

I realize now that behind Dr. Barksdale's gentility lay a most serious and crucial enterprise. Barksdale and his generation of intellectuals, on the cutting edge of scholarship, were in tune with the "shape of things to come." From their positions in the historically black colleges, they reaped the harvest of their years of figuratively laboring in the shadow of the academic vineyard. These intellectuals, who had in the main been trained at the predominantly white northern institutions, converted their alleged weakness into a strength as they prepared a generation of students to enjoin the battle against a rigidly segregated society on all fronts—politically, economically, and ideologically. The children of their students would come of age in the emotionally charged 1960s with the demand for black studies as a matter of course. They ushered in an era of sweeping policy changes that are still being felt today on the nation's college campuses. The intellectual arm of their project, the development of a body of African American literary criticism, is being carried out by a diverse group of scholars such as William Andrews, Houston A. Baker, Jr., Barbara Christian, Henry Louis Gates, Jr., Maryemma Graham, Trudier Harris, Joyce Ann Joyce, Deborah McDowell, R. Baxter Miller, Arnold Rampersad, Cornel West, and Susan Willis.

Barksdale's contribution to scholarship is at once a passionately argued defense of the kind of moral reflection associated with scholars as diverse as Matthew Arnold, W. E. B. Du Bois, Alain Locke, and T. S. Eliot, yet with an acknowledgment that the pragmatic legacy of them might be reevaluated in the light of the challenge posed by current critical theory. He provides a carefully delineated vision of what criticism actively engaged in society can accomplish.

As I reflect on what Barksdale means to hundreds of students and to me, I realize that our natural affinity for this grand old man of African American letters stems, in large part, from our somewhat similar backgrounds as young thinkers about scholarship. We were individuals from humble beginnings whose parents had little formal education, whose ability had been early recognized, and who had been nurtured by those unsung heroes of American education, by what surely seemed to be an army of black teachers diligently making bricks without straw. They challenged legions of students to reach for the stars. Like many of his students, Barksdale had made the improbable leap from being a stellar student in a provincial community to being a stellar thinker in the upper echelons of American higher education. In him, we saw ourselves and what we could become.

As one of the last of the great scholar-educators, Dr. Barksdale stands in a varied African American tradition that extends from W. E. B. Du Bois and Alain Locke through Benjamin Brawley, Benjamin E. Mays, Howard Thurman, Dorothy Porter, Sterling A. Brown, John Hope Franklin, and Ruthe T. Sheffey. Their rigorous training, fueled by the dynamic of an oppressed minority to prove its humanity, embossed their lives with what the Spanish philosopher Ortega y Gasset refers to as "nobility which is synonymous with a life of effort, ever set on excelling oneself, in passing beyond what one is to what one sets up as a duty and an obligation."

Guided by a rich humanistic tradition, these architects of African American scholarship created the moral and intellectual climate that led to the demise of American apartheid. They did not invent the African American conscience; but they unearthed new configurations of character and intent. The result is a genuinely consistent and integrated expression of the African American inheritance. Through the tradition of edification and uplift, Dr. Barksdale, you and your generation taught us the full meaning of Cervantes's wise perception: "The road is always better than the inn."

Richard Kenneth Barksdale, as exemplar and type, humanizes the world of the scholar. His life reflects a changed society in which, though class and privilege still count, those gifted with wit and intellect are not barred from competing and, indeed, making a contribution. His service to the humanities and to his profession has been his way of replenishing the well of learning. He has remained a gentleman in an age when that word has become an epithet of a bygone era. He is a beloved teacher, a valued colleague, a loyal friend, and the least selfish man I know.

Introduction

R. Baxter Miller

If we ought to forget a war which has filled our land with widows and orphans, which has made stumps of men of the very flower of our youth, which has sent them on the journey of life armless, legless, maimed and mutilated, which has piled up a debt heavier than a mountain of gold, swept uncounted thousands of men into bloody graves and planted agony at a million hearthstones—I say, if this war is to be forgotten, I ask, in the name of all things sacred, what shall men remember?

—Frederick Douglass[1]

Perhaps nowhere does Dick Barksdale conceptualize more brilliantly than in his insights about the triangle and the circle. For him, the geometric images provide provocative ways to read literary history. He explored the concept at first in "White Triangles, Black Circles," the presidential address delivered in New Orleans on Thursday morning, 10 April 1975, at the annual meeting of the College Language Association.[2] Later he would round out what he had begun:

In *The Song of Solomon*, Milkman matures and becomes responsible and accountable only when he flees from his present to search out his family's past, in a sense traveling back to events which occurred immediately after slavery and even crossing over imaginatively into slavery's time zone to imitate the ultimate in the search for circularity—a flight back to Africa like his slave ancestor, Solomon.

So *The Song of Solomon* ends, symbolically at least, in the same time zone in which *Beloved* begins—at that juncture in time when slavery's end was near and a quasi-freedom was about to begin—but at a time when slavery's ugly shadow was still everywhere. It was a time for black families, long broken and fragmented, to begin slowly to regather and rejoin and reunite and search, tediously, but with humble thanksgiving, for what might be the beginning of an unbroken circle.[3]

The image suggests a quest *for* human harmony but the sign *of* an unwritten faith.

The process of triangulation, on the contrary, implies inequality. In the art of gunnery, for instance, the weapon, target, and targeter take on a geometric design. Indeed, the principle may be behind even the "tremendous force that propels a swept-wing jet fighter through the upper air at speeds faster than sound." What has been a principle for the purpose of human destruction could become one for architectural design as well. For example, buildings based on the form of the triangle have "great strength and endurance."[4]

Barksdale communicates the angle by which mathematics, architecture, and historical memory contribute to the structure of human knowledge. For herein the principles of the triangle (material power) give meaning to the struggle for the circle (impractical idealism). Barksdale's own heart serves the idealism that, like his prose, implies great discipline. Though the triangle symbolizes inequity, the sphere represents symmetrical harmony. The circle communicates a spiritual and communal odyssey. While triangles imply some imbalances of sorts, circles "irradiate" the ethics of equality; while a few orbits may be sliced into matching halves or quarters of some rather appropriate design, spheres include the same number of degrees. And any point on the circumference is "equidistant from the center."[5]

Perhaps the hidden faith in the power of circles has an inverse logic: If there were slavery (triangle), there must be freedom (circle). If there are devils, there are gods. Because the history of slavery disrupts the flow in human community, the knowledge of history—which can restore the lost continuity—is redemptive.[6] While the literary historian seeks to record slavery, he intends also to reveal a focal point in this previously negative space and time. Indeed, the culture of African Americans appears almost as a remarkable light freed of its ghostly shadow, yet defined in such closeness to its origin.

These are the images of value that Barksdale writes and lives by, those that explain so subtly his unrelenting struggle with the proponents of postmodernism during his later years. Even theoretical historians such as Johann Gottfried von Herder (1744–1803)—whom Barksdale reveals as a supposedly empirical apologist for racism—show traces of self-interest and European self-empowerment in the world.[7] Despite his profound suspicions about critical theory, Barksdale understands intuitively the participation by even the literary historian within the academic rites of power.

Barksdale inquired about theories of race in his first published work, about Thomas Arnold, the eminent father of Matthew. That essay begins the present volume. Later in the book he explores in previously unpublished manuscripts the subject of nurturing and history in the novels of Toni

Morrison. Naturally he distrusts even those theorists who would propose that central values of power are only figments of the traditionalist's imagination. Eventually his words force us to double back along the road we have traveled. This movement is, I think, a spiral wherein history repeats itself while almost never turning completely over the same ground.

In his earliest work Barksdale saw himself rightly as a literary historian who questioned the Euro-American academic canons and the role of slaves as well as the descendants of slaves. He had turned to other disciplines, such as philosophy—especially to ethics and morality—and to anthropology. Finally, his literary history becomes a praisesong of his own survival.

The structure of his scholarly development began with the discordant history of race in a world that seemed to have ruptured irremediably the wholeness of humanity. What he has come gradually to accept, from 1968 until now, has been his own awareness of a power in spiritual idealism, such as Martin Luther King's. Even if the apocalyptic view of history were not truly empirical, at least it seemed to promise a kind of human community denied for the last four hundred years. Most recently Barksdale has safeguarded this covert hope as something to protect from academic expediency. He warns us, most of all, about the persistent endangerment of intellectual freedom in America.

It is important to appreciate Richard Barksdale for the scholar of Victorian literature he is. Intrigued by Frederick Faverty's "very fine" study of the ethnological tendencies of Matthew Arnold's father, he concedes that the theories of the elder probably influenced those of the famous son. Barksdale, agreeing that the progenitor Arnold spoke forthrightly on many problems of the Victorian, finds that both men "believed that separate racial types existed and that these types, over a period of time, developed certain distinctive traits which predetermined, to some extent, their historical development." To Barksdale, the Arnolds' success derives primarily from their reaffirming the ethics of Aristotle (384–322 B.C.) over the pseudo-modernist science of Herder.[8]

It was Aristotle who had provided the Arnolds (and Barksdale) with a theory of historical causality that they needed. In the *Politics*, Thomas Arnold believed, Aristotle had drawn upon knowledge of Mediterranean commonwealths and city states in order to suggest that racial differences involve those of conduct, behavior, and religion rather than confirming any real kind of dissimilarity in biological appearance. The senior Arnold had based his thought on a section explaining the way that differences in "conduct and moral outlook" were strong provocations of revolutions. To the Arnolds, Aristotle's theory of race implies a belief that enthnological assumptions are inseparable from historical facts. Thomas Arnold, believing that morality and religious practice were the only certainties of race that were justifiable historically, thought that in modern times these kinds of distinctions had taken on an "odious and fantastic character." This observation, once divorced from historical context, does not constitute a flat rejection of the racial theories widely endorsed by his own generation. But the elder Arnold's refusal to accept the traditional racism of the European nineteenth century was almost undeniable. To him, the proportionate power of races on earth shifted constantly, as did social fluctuations among classes in the world. The Gaul, for instance, who had been vanquished once by the conquering Roman, lived to see his former conqueror humbled and defeated. For Christianity would bring the decline of the empire from without just as well as decay and decadence would from within. As previous builders of a rich heritage with hero-kings—David, Saul, and Solomon—even the Jews could look forward to their inevitable downfall: "In the course of history, then, all of the races of the world were destined to enjoy a period of occasional ascendancy only to be leveled into insignificance by the on-sweep of historical events. For, if time were the great practical leveler, Christianity was the great spiritual leveller which would establish 'a happier system and better institutions' and eventually restore the 'original equality' of the races of mankind."[9]

In 1957, the year the Arnold essay was published in *Phylon,* Barksdale was using Aristotelian classicism as a way of deconstructing modernism (and eventually postmodernism). Almost always he would exploit literary history to test or authenticate the acceptability of a theory as well as an art. In order to get a handle on race and literature, he needed to retrace human thought to its origins, certainly to times before the Enlightenment— before modernism had fixed convenient stereotypes in Western thinking. Like a good postmodernist, he needed to look back past the structures that have now corrupted and institutionalized contemporary ideas. Each nation, Herder proposed, could be graded for what its race had contributed to history. Comfort was in making history a basis for comparative evaluations of ethnic groups. Indeed, Herder's assumptions about cultural nationalism provided a philosophical context for the designs of racial discrimination that became entrenched during the Victorian era. Barksdale wrote:

> Men came to believe that those races which had been historically unproductive could be quite justifiably subjugated by those races whose superiority presumably had been confirmed by their historical achievements. Thus it was that Christian white men condoned the Eighteenth Century enslavement of non-Christian black men, for enslavement was the historical destiny of a people who could show the world little *tangible* [my italics] evidence of cultural and industrial development. Thus it was, too, that the concept of *der ubermensch* developed to puff the racial arrogance of the Nordic peoples and

doom the race-conscious nationalities of Europe to an extended period of intermittent nationalistic wars.[10]

Today we know that Herder's own rather liberal thought reinforced at times the same hierarchy of power represented in texts of the Enlightenment. Now his position helps reveal the certain bond between history and literature, between literature and cultural politics. Conquerors and intellectual conquerors, in keeping with their own heritage, define cultural success by their own image of material wealth. A quest for either personal peace or world harmony is largely irrelevant.

Barksdale has distinguished himself through analysis of at least two kinds of written responses to history. Two of his favorite genres are comic forms and autobiographical narrative, for while the former is distant from impressionism aesthetically, the latter is intimately engaged with history. To Barksdale, the first art is consequently most akin to that of the literary historian—whose efforts probably surpass those of the more subjective literary critic and theorist—while the second art has more in common with the rhythmical beauty of poetry by Margaret Walker and Margaret Danner.[11]

Since the enforced slave trade from West Africa, as early as the seventeenth century, African Americans have employed many strategies of survival in the face of an often hostile white majority. When the tactics have been those of "physical confrontation and revolt," the unfortunate consequence has usually been the belligerent arousal of a "somewhat paranoid white majority." For example, the Nat Turner revolt of 1831 in Southhampton County, Virginia, like the urban riots in American cities in the late sixties, aggravated tensions in race relations. "In neither instance," Barksdale assesses soberly, "did a powerless black minority gain power or achieve any radical alteration in its relationship to a powerful white majority." Nat Turner's revolt proved fruitless until slavery ended eventually through armed conflict during a bloody Civil War. After the extensive urban riots of the 1960s, almost exactly a century later, most African Americans have remained confined to ghettoes wherein they continue to experience various kinds of racial discrimination. Though the tone and diction in this instance are clearly his, they are almost curiously militant for a scholar of his generation. A persistent kind of black anger, he says, found an outlet in the political activities of activist groups like those of the Black Panthers of the late sixties and early seventies, as well as in the early literature of confrontation by now maturing poets like Haki Madhubuti, Sonia Sanchez, and Nikki Giovanni. Comedy, in contrast to this anger, and as a kind of accommodation without dignity (as inherited from Booker T. Washington), becomes a more subtle offensive strategy. While lacking in the "self-destructive fury of the big-city black ghetto riot," the form might prove useful in transferring to black masses some political or economic power. Just as it provides the psychological inspiration and uplift of a good offensive strategy,[12] comedy expresses the *survival* value of a defensive strategy. Comedy as a literary form connects the survival strategies of nineteenth-century slavery with our strategies today. Comedy, in other words, marks the trace of our history and of our memory. Comic distancing happens when "autobiographers who have the gift of comic vision rise above racism's drab and cruel realities and inject a note that lightens the mood of the reader and lifts the tone of the narrative." Black autobiographers of this kind have been few. Not many of the nineteenth-century slave narrators, for instance, demonstrated comic techniques because the oppressive circumstances under which they had to survive were "so horrendous and dehumanizing." Indeed, comic distancing from the "daily routine of pain and suffering" that "all slaves had to endure" was too much to ask. Even the great autobiographers from the nineteenth century—Douglass, Payne, Washington, and John Langston—were too seriously engaged in recounting achievements to detach themselves from historical circumstances. It has been left, therefore, to the twentieth century to produce black autobiographers with comic vision. A few telling examples are Langston Hughes, Zora Neale Hurston, and Nate Cobb.

Almost never does Barksdale address directly an American preference for comedy as a desirable form for blacks. An interesting example derives from the Trueblood episode in Ellison's *Invisible Man*. Readers of the scene will probably recall the way that Norton, the white philanthropist who lusts subconsciously for his own daughter, becomes fascinated by Trueblood, a means for Norton to live out his own fantasy vicariously. Through comedy, says Barksdale, Ellison ridicules a Euro-American civilization that values repression of sexual activity more than the fulfillment of human dreams. The social inversion of placing a black man's "primitive" incest in the center of an "antiseptic" and "whitened" black middle-class college is as comic as Norton's own complicity with Trueblood's incident. Though the literary device of comic mockery offers, in this instance, "no radical alteration in the power relationships between a Black minority and a white majority," comic exposure of "social sin and immorality provides American citizenry with the opportunity for the kind of therapeutic laughter that can help to heal the long-festering wound of racism."

This intercultural therapy, I think, can persist only if the power relationships themselves are ultimately changed. For it takes only two qualifications—one each by Freudian and Marxist theory—for us to know that even great laughter is a substitute gratification for the freedom needed in the historical world. As comic figures in fiction, Ellison's Invisible Man and Hughes's Semple are spared the historical demands for them to *survive,* for each of them to come out of the figurative cave and descend the momentary mountain of fantasy. Does full awareness of the African American's plight leave the literary historian open to martyrdom, the forbidden alternative to survival? Is it possible to change the hierarchy of social power by a spiritual act of heroism as much as by a physical victory?

Barksdale achieves a kind of fusion especially when he writes so convincingly about Mark Twain and Langston Hughes. Though the Twain essay would appear in 1984, several years after most of the definitive chapters on Hughes in 1977, readers will likely find it sensible to consider the writings in proper chronology of the authors discussed. *Huckleberry Finn*, "by motive and intention," appraises the American scene of race in 1884 ironically. Today, teaching the book is difficult because irony as a narrative technique "involves a deliberate misstatement."[13]

What the able observation might take into account would be the formal limits to our ever being able to know an author's intent. Nor can we depend generally on the "American reading public" ("average reader," "American society"), which is composed variously of interpretive communities, to be universally agreeable in the appreciation of aesthetic values. Writers certainly create ironic texts to bridge the dangerous ground between the histories of their times and places, on the one hand, and the communities proposing to read those histories on the other. But the great dynamic of the space in between—the metaphors and voices of their own narrated experience, technique, and vision—would be indeed lost. It is the unpredictable inter-action between the historic text and the subjective reader of comic art that Barksdale distrusts. In other words, whose survival does Twain's text speak to?

Barksdale's own oblique answer was to spend the last fourteen or fifteen years writing about Langston Hughes.[14] To him, Hughes's greatest comic creation in poetry is Alberta K. Johnson, who is initially presented in *One-Way Ticket* (1949). As an obvious spin-off from Jesse B. Semple, a wonderful creation in prose, Madame emerged during the forties. Following experiences during the Depression of the thirties and World War II, Hughes began to develop a "comic vision—a vision that enabled him 'to play it cool,' to avoid personal and often emotionally eroding commitments and comment on everchanging social and political events. . . . *The Panther and the Lash*, published posthumously in 1967, is a somber volume of poetry. Its tone reflected the times. One guesses that Hughes knew that the Black man's gift for laughter still existed, but in that decade of war, riot, assassination, and bloodshed, the laughter was necessarily muted."[15] African-American comedy, like Hughes's, emerges from history and must eventually be read back into history.

Barksdale's purpose and method are historical, for he sets out to "assess what the critics have written in response to the poetry of Langston Hughes

over the forty-seven-year period of his literary career." In tracing Hughes's
development from the Jazz Age in the 1920s to the period of sit-ins and
urban riots during the 1960s, Barksdale leads his reader first through the
Depression of the 1930s, then the post–World War II era of the 1940s, and
finally to the age of be-bop as well as declining colonialism in the 1950s.
Barksdale emphasizes three major influences on Hughes, including intensive travel, productivity in many genres, and spiritual or psychic involvement
with Harlem. Hughes, he says, never joined the Communist party because
it limited freedom of speech and because Hughes could not abandon jazz,
which was disliked by the party. Barksdale disagrees with V. F. Calverton
(*Saturday Review,* 1940) and with Harold Cruse (*Crisis of the Negro Intellectual,*
1967). He believed that Hughes's work *did* develop beyond the 1930s, as
evidenced by a new experiment in fiction, a broadening of subject matter
from Harlem to Africa and the Black Diaspora, and a widening of political
scope that includes leftist issues and causes.

Barksdale, while acknowledging Hughes's early radicalism, avoids the
prescriptive approach of the Marxists and others in the Black Arts movement of the late sixties and early seventies. From Hughes's days of ambivalent
relationships ("The Negro Speaks of Rivers," "The Cat and the Saxophone")
he records the poet's reputation among black scholars of the time. His
inquiry leads through a general disaffection with the Negro intelligentsia
(*Fine Clothes to the Jew,* 1927) to the writer's final reappraisal by Alain Locke,
the only black critic with sufficient "temerity and esthetic insight" to question whether propaganda could be literature. In the twenties Locke agreed
with Keats that writing should serve beauty and truth (my extrapolation
here), but through the years his opinion changed: " . . . using the critical
criteria that bad propaganda can result in bad literature, Locke approached
Hughes's *A New Song.* "

Barksdale rates Jean Wagner's *Les Poètes Nègres des États-Unis* (1963) as the
"most extensive critical assessment of Hughes's poetry for all periods." He
finds that Wagner misreads Hughes's tone, while disagreeing with Wagner's
assertion that Hughes's religious and secular poems are similar in mode,
different in form. To Barksdale, Wagner misinterprets the "Glory Hallelujah"
section of *Fine Clothes to the Jew.* The French critic's mistake, in other words,
derives from the misbelief that blues and spirituals are the complementary
Gemini of each other. Barksdale cites an article published in *Phylon* (1947)
which portrays a preacher's censorship of Hughes for reading blues in a
church pulpit. The scholar concludes: "Wagner is certainly right in his
assertion that Langston Hughes was not, overtly at least, a profoundly
religious man. But he is wrong in his assumption that the poet did not
know the difference between a blues poem and a religious poem."[16]

Jazz, I would add, reexpresses the tones and forms of African American religions. Blues, on the contrary, assumes often the shape of lethargy or withdrawal by aesthetic distance. Barksdale knows that Hughes did not, as Wagner says, reduce problems of religion to problems of verse. In fact, Wagner sees Hughes's vision as moving from the abstract to the concrete, though Hughes often uses the tangible to suggest the intangible. So romanticists come to place Hughes in the transcendental tradition of Emerson, Thoreau, and Whitman. But Barksdale has almost always distrusted mystical inclinations both in poetry and in life. What is undeniable is that his *feel* (he would question the word) for his writer's world is unerring.

Understandably Barksdale's approach makes him seem a bit contradictory sometimes. Despite Wagner's success in giving Hughes's poetry the most thorough analysis to date, his central flaw came in taking a thematic rather than a chronological approach. Nevertheless, the French critic "is not hampered by extraneous concerns and is free to explicate the poems on the basis of actual content and not on the basis of assumed intent." In this instance, in other words, Barksdale favors an intrinsic approach. Elsewhere he defends Hughes against Owen Dodson's negative review of *Shakespeare in Harlem* (*Phylon,* 1941) by saying that these verses suit Hughes's intention and that they "become more meaningful" when viewed as a "pastiche of the big-city blues-songs born out of heartache" and "rising from the crowded streets of the black ghetto."

Barksdale points to new horizons. For more than forty years, evaluators of Hughes's poetry had seemed to be not literary critics but sociologists looking for a historical message. Hughes's own landmark essay, "The Negro Artist and the Racial Mountain,"[17] had challenged the very duality implied by politely academic truisms. Barksdale's great strength emerges from a historical understanding but also from a sensitive feel for the inseparability of black poetry and American history. He sees the Simple stories of the forties as Hughes's transition from the radicalism of the 1930s to what Arthur P. Davis calls Hughes's "cooly ambivalent vision," the detachment of the 1950s and 1960s. With Davis he views the comic link between Alberta K. Johnson in verse during the late forties and Jesse B. Semple in prose from the early forties until the middle sixties. Finally, Barksdale supersedes even Davis by stressing the need for scholars to analyze Hughes's comic vision.

Barksdale consistently questions the relative merit of the early, middle, and late Hughes. To him the verses from *Fields of Wonder* (1947), *One-Way Ticket* (1949), and *Montage of a Dream Deferred* (1951) take on a new meaning sixteen to twenty years later. His insight suits scholar as well as poet: " . . . he [Hughes] emerges as an artist who not only had the gift for trenchant analysis of the present but who, at the same time, could contemplate future vistas and read the voice of the future. In other words, even though he was the poet of rapid insight and fleet impressions, he rarely became so immersed in the particularities of a given moment that he forgot the future's debt to the present and the present's debt to the past."[18] Hughes, in other words, could read the spiral and circle of black American experience. The communal adventure, now shadowed by slavery, points toward an ideal of African American freedom kept alive by thinkers and dreamers still gifted with the imagination to see. What hopeful vision for human rights is grounded in slavery can finally be projected as coming true in the twenty-first century and beyond—but only through hope and will. The very affective distractions of "feeling," "hope," and "faith" are repressed from Barksdale's presumably empirical discourses about history; but they bolster his note of authenticity. In speaking at his retirement from the University of Illinois, he said that all of the noble ancestors of his long line still stood with him. They were there quietly and invisibly, too, when he wrote about Langston Hughes.

I have said that a deep appreciation for visionary expression has nearly always subsisted in Barksdale's uncompromisable insistence on the literal discourse of history. Perhaps nothing provides, more so than does Langston Hughes, an intriguing insight about the dualism of the literary historian. Hughes, Barksdale says, "broke the back of a tradition which sought to exclude secular folk material from the canon of black literature. And, in his use of the language of the black lower classes, Hughes prepared the way for the use and acceptance of the revolutionary black street poetry of the late 1960s." The scholar admires the quality that had helped Hughes, like Edward Shelton in *The Nigger,* to treat the theme of miscegenation on Broadway. Later, Barksdale reads the visionary parallels that bind Langston Hughes and James Baldwin, one of Hughes's least objective critics, with Martin Luther King, Jr.: "We now know that, just as the dancer can never become the dance, the dreamer can never become the dream. Once evoked or expressed, the dance and the dream drift off into a timeless life of their own, shorn of man's creative chemistry and no longer circumscribed by time, space, and place. Not so the dancer and not so the dreamer. Each remains in time's relentless grasp, subject to gravity's pull and to death's dissolution."[19] Baldwin (b. 1924) had a writer's affinity to Hughes yet an oral stylist's resemblance to King (b. 1929). Appreciating the range means respecting the scholarly world of Barksdale (b. 1915). The scholar, rather than encouraging us to journey into abstractions, must deal with Harlem within historical time. While the figure of the poet is that of an ascender into dreams, the image of the literary historian projects that of one who descends into "gravity's pull and dissolution."

I close with a balanced critique of Richard Barksdale's lasting achievement rather than with what even he himself would write or say. The significance of his work extends far beyond the thirty-four years of his opus. While his stance shows a strong preference for literal diction, the ultimate value of his posture comes through an intellectual freedom allowing us to challenge the reactionary tendency within modern theory itself. He warns his listeners that supposedly revolutionary dissent becomes institutionalized often as another form of cultural oppression.

Once, for example, he worried if his graduate seminar at Illinois would materialize or if the necessary population of students would be advised away from the course. Indeed, his own recommendation that his students "ignore deconstruction, post-structural textual exegesis, and continental hermeneutics" possibly helped give impetus to even his dubious detractors. "African American literature effectively," he has written, cannot "survive critical approaches that stress auctorial depersonalization and the essential unimportance of racial history, racial community, and racial traditions."

Somewhat correctly, he calls himself "old-fashioned" in this somewhat arbitrary context. We are, I would say, the producers of history just as we are the products of it. Though we seek objectively to erase our self-interest or imprint from the telling of history, our signature keeps alive the legacy of slavery as well as that of even the academy we tell about. The American need for racial comedy, in addition, reaffirms the power relationships established between literature, the telling of history, and the literary historians, who provide exposition about texts. Comic therapy represents an accommodation to the conservative prescribers of our thought far more than any proposition of fundamental change in the United States. Recognition of the subjective dimensions and political demands upon literary criticism and theory simply makes good sense. The poet and comedian, as evidenced by both Langston Hughes and William Shakespeare, are not always mutually distinct. Indeed, we may even argue that the coexistence of complementary manners and selves in one talent verifies the quality of genius. Finally, Barksdale confronts perhaps the most insurmountable obstacle faced possibly by every scholar, especially traditionalists: If history must be the final authentication for any critical position or method, how do we vindicate the theoretical forms of the future? Though Barksdale once criticized the poets of the sixties, for instance, rather strongly in 1969, why did he reverse himself as early as 1973?[20]

Nearly all of these friendly questions are strongly justified by systems of theory that have emerged after his days at Harvard during the late forties and early fifties. Though the popular Marxism of thinkers like Granville Hicks had wielded significant influence even earlier, during the Great Depression and beyond, the neo-Marxism of scholars like Susan Willis and Frederick Jameson has focused more today on the way that the academy commodifies creative and scholarly texts. New studies in semiotics could show the way that Barksdale's own kind of literary history is nearly always an implicit trace of courageous heart and basic decency hoped for in the world.

These human qualities he did not speak of. But a general sensitivity to the principles of reader-response criticism explains Barksdale's talent for researching history, for therein he sought new justifications to praise contemporary writing. While he has typically distrusted a method of myth in literary criticism, the theory of archetype helps explain the brilliance of his metaphors. Though the images of the triangle and circle are grounded in a detailed explanation of the African Diaspora, they demonstrate at once several patterns that extend across black American history. And while subsequent schools of theory have shown the limits of the historical position, the inquiries have almost certainly never dishonored it. Barksdale's own work is, indeed, an admirable example. His final complaint is probably not that postmodern theorists are jargon-ridden; it is instead, I think, that he has lived long enough to distrust any proposed fragmentations of African American dreams already deferred for a black community that still subsists at the margins of the mainstream.

Studies like Barksdale's evince the way that the literary historian provides that which is not only original but that which reveals the literary scholar as at once a product and producer of literary tradition. Hence, Barksdale began as a reliable recorder of cultural forms and values, but becomes both a sign and exemplar of them. Often he is not the anachronism he sometimes seems to be. His very life and scholarship are bound inextricably to the literary history told by him. He is no longer a detached observer of that history but an integral part of it, of the way the future of it will be written. What is most remarkable about the uniformly high quality of his essays is that he continues to engage with greater and greater sophistication the same critical and theoretical issues with which he began. But more than even Blyden Jackson, Saunders Redding, and George Kent—who were a few of his most renowned contemporaries—Barksdale reassesses the status of American literary history now.

Barksdale, bolstered by study on Euro-American aesthetics in the Victorian period and Gilded Age, came to read the struggle for Euro-American and African American canons with freshly rewarding explanations. His praise for African American women writers from Phillis Wheatley to Toni Morrison is balanced, cutting through glib politeness to fundamental issues of dignity and survival. His complementary essays on classic males like James Baldwin and Langston Hughes meticulously tie up loose ends. The quality of his synthetic knowledge, fusing at once comparative biography and literary movements, is impeccable. And the style is consummately clear. First appear his discussions on literary canons as well as on blackness and on humane principles beyond canons; then follow his carefully measured inquiries into the literary forms and metaphors of survival in African American history; subsequently, his broad praisesong for black women writers makes for a nice complement to his wonderful finale on Langston Hughes.

Scholars yet to come, I think, will certainly honor Dick Barksdale. What he gave to the graduate students at Illinois and elsewhere was the opportunity to study with one of the most talented and disciplined exemplars of African American literary history. And any critical theory in America that does not teach us greater respect for this history—and the great literature on which it is based—does not deserve the right to survive. The permanent implication of Barksdale's work is not that the contemporary theory of semiotics and cultural Freudianism (deconstruction) should revert to the literary history of his own obviously earlier time; it is, on the contrary, that even contemporary theorists as modern and postmodern writers are not detached from the kind of academic bigotry evinced by the Victorians.

How does Barksdale, as did Langston Hughes, hear the voice of the future? He writes, "I recommend that as we build our literary canon for the tomorrows that lie ahead in the next century, we remain ever mindful of the need to utilize the politics of survival. This is something to be found in the text of our racial history that ahistorical theorists like a Derrida, a Gramsci, or a Lacan would not begin to understand."[21] His scholarly praisesong compels us back to the spiritual victories within and beyond American history.

NOTES

1. *Life and Times of Frederick Douglass* (1881; New York: Collier, 1962), 414.

2. Now it is apparent that I was personally privileged to hear him at the height of his success. It was my first CLA.

3. Richard K. Barksdale, "In Search of the Unbroken Circle: Black Nurturing in Selected Novels of Toni Morrison." Unless otherwise specified, all works cited are available in the subsequent text. The single exception is the material regarding Langston Hughes, which comes from Barksdale's complete work, *Langston Hughes: The Poet and His Critics* (Chicago: American Library Association, 1977).

4. Barksdale, "White Triangles, Black Circles."

5. Ibid.

6. Barksdale, "Unbroken Circle."

7. Barksdale, "Thomas Arnold's Attitude Toward Race."

8. Ibid.

9. Ibid.

10. Ibid.

11. See "Margaret Danner and the African Connection" and "Margaret Walker: Folk Orature and Historical Prophecy."

12. "Black America and the Mask of Comedy"; "Black Autobiography and the Comic Vision."

13. Barksdale, *"Huckleberry Finn."*

14. Barksdale, *Langston Hughes;* "Comic Relief in the Poetry of Langston Hughes"; "Langston Hughes and Martin Luther King, Jr.—The Poet, the Preacher, and the Dream"; "Langston Hughes and James Baldwin: Some Observations on a Literary Relationship"; "Miscegenation on Broadway: Hughes's *Mulatto* and Edward Sheldon's *The Nigger;* "Langston Hughes and the Blues He Could Not Lose"; "Humanistic Techniques Employed by Hughes in His Poetry."

15. Barksdale, "Comic Relief."

16. Barksdale, *Langston Hughes.*

17. *Nation* 122 (October 1926): 692–94

18. Barksdale, *Langston Hughes*

19. Barksdale, "Hughes and King."

20. "Urban Crisis and the Black Poetic Avant-Garde" (1969); "Humanistic Protest in Recent Black American Poetry" (1973).

21. Barksdale, "Critical Theory and Problems of Canonicity in African-American Literature."

PART 1

Literary Canons
and Blackness

Thomas Arnold's Attitude toward Race

The purpose of this paper is to supplement certain information contained in Mr. Frederic Faverty's very fine study of the ethnological aspects of Matthew Arnold's literary criticism and biblical comment.[1] Mr. Faverty's conclusion that Thomas Arnold, Matthew's father, greatly influenced the racial theories of his famous son is doubtless fully justified.[2] Such a conclusion does suggest, however, a need for fuller clarification of Thomas Arnold's own racial theories. As Strachey has indicated, Dr. Arnold expressed himself forthrightly on many of the problems of his day;[3] and, although he wrote no essay on racial theory *per se*, his comments on the subject are sufficiently numerous to warrant analysis and study. The evidence presented by Mr. Faverty seems to substantiate the view that Matthew Arnold's racial theories were complementary to those held and endorsed by his eminent father. Both apparently believed that separate racial types existed and that these types, over a period of time, developed certain distinctive traits which predetermined, to some extent, their historical development. Mr. Faverty does cite a solitary instance of disagreement between father and son regarding the relative merits of the "Teutons and the Celts"; but, as he indicates, it was more a "friendly family dispute" than a profound philosophical difference.[4] The conclusion therefore seems to be tenable that both the father and son believed in the principle of racial differences. Analysis will reveal, however, that the sources of the elder Arnold's theory of racial differences subtly differentiated his view of race from that held by the majority of his contemporaries.

The first point to be made about Thomas Arnold's racial theories is that they were rooted in his study of history and are thus almost more historical than ethnological. Many of his opinions regarding the races of man were developed during the course of his historical studies. For instance, his comments on the Germanic races, obviously "Teutomaniac" in tone, had a distinctly historical framework, many of them being found in the *Introductory Lectures on Modern History* which Arnold delivered at Oxford in 1841–42. On one occasion he stated that an analysis of historical trends in modern Europe led him to conclude that the Germanic peoples were to be "the regenerating element in modern Europe"; for they had "the soundest laws, the least violent passions, and the fairest domestic and civil virtues."[5] On another occasion, he asserted that the newly risen Prussian government was "the most advancing ever known."[6] In a sense, these comments represent historical conclusions, rather than positive racial theories.

Many of the elder Arnold's opinions on race can be traced to his study and interpretation of Aristotle, the philosopher-historian, who was in many respects the mentor for both Thomas and Matthew Arnold and undoubtedly exercised the greatest influence on this phase of Thomas Arnold's thought.[7] It was Arnold's belief that in the *Politics,* a highly specific study of Mediterranean commonwealths and city states, Aristotle had suggested that racial differences involved differences in conduct, behavior, and religion, rather than differences in appearance. The passage upon which Arnold based such a conclusion was one in which Aristotle implied that racial differences, involving differences in conduct and moral outlook, were a potent source for revolutions. Jowett's translation of this passage is as follows: "Another cause of revolution is difference of races which do not at once acquire a common spirit; for a state is not the growth of a day, any more than it grows out of a multitude brought together by accident. Hence the reception of strangers ... has generally produced revolution."[8] Arnold interpreted Aristotle to mean by racial differences not the broad ethnic differences that today divide the Caucasian from the Mongolian or the Caucasian from the Negro, but the differences in conduct, religious and moral outlook which in Aristotle's day divided Athenian from Spartan or Theban from Corinthian. The Aristotelian distinction therefore implied in Arnold's opinion a distinction between homogeneity of conduct and opinion and heterogeneity of conduct and opinion. No political community could withstand too much of the latter without the risk of revolution.[9]

That this was Arnold's conception of Aristotle's theory of race is indicated by his statement that "a man's race in ancient time was marked by the peculiar worship of his family...."[10] In further clarification of this point, he wrote:

Citizenship was derived from race; but distinctions of race were not of that odious and fantastic character which they have borne in modern times; they implied real differences often of the most important kind, religious and moral. Particular races worshipped particular Gods, and in a particular

manner. But different Gods had different attributes, and the moral image
thus presented to the continual contemplation and veneration of the people
could not but produce some effect on the national character. . . . Again,
particular races had particular customs which affected the relations of domestic life and public [*sic*]. Amongst some polygamy was allowed, amongst others
forbidden; some held infanticide to be an atrocious crime, others in certain
cases ordained it by law.[11]

Arnold's careful explanation of his interpretation of Aristotle's theory of
race not only implies a belief on his part that ethnological theories could
not be divorced from historical facts but suggests two further conclusions
about his own ethnic beliefs. First, it is apparent that he believed that moral
belief and religious practice were the only determinants of race which were
justifiable historically. Secondly, he believed that in modern times "distinctions
of race" had acquired an "odious and fantastic character." Although this
observation, taken out of historical context, does not constitute a flat
rejection of the racial theories widely endorsed by his own generation, the
elder Arnold's disapproval of nineteenth-century racial discrimination is
clear and unmistakable. He appears to be saying implicitly that dissimilarity
of physical appearance never should have become one of the primary
criteria of racial differentiation—that such a development was quite
unhistorical in the light of the genesis of racial differences in Graeco-
Roman culture. In other words, Arnold did not deny the existence of
historically determined racial differences, but he believed that the callous
discrimination resulting therefrom was both "odious and fantastic."

It is also apparent that Arnold, having endorsed the Aristotelian belief
that race was originally determined by uniformity of conduct, could not
fully endorse the Herder theory, so widely held during his own period.
Herder, one of the great Prussian philosopher-historians, laid the ground-
work for many of the racial theories of the nineteenth century in his *Ideas
on the Philosophy of History,* published in four volumes between 1784 and
1791. His emphasis in this important work was on the diversification of
human nature. There existed among all peoples, the Prussian historian
believed, multiple differences; and, each racial group, in reaction to a
particular physical environment, developed its own body of inherited
psychological characteristics. Thus, with the passing of time, racial differences crystallized, and the historical experiences of each race gradually
came to be considered to be a consequence of certain definable inherent
racial traits. Herder also believed that in modern society there existed
proof that racial differences tended to merge with national differences, thus
causing each nationally identifiable race to develop a body of clearly
discernible national idiosyncrasies. In this way, the German philosopher
arrived at his theory of cultural nationalism.[12] The Herder theory further

suggested the possibility of evaluating each nationally identifiable race on the basis of its contribution to history. Thus, in the nineteenth century it became fashionable to use history as a source for the comparative evalua- tion of ethnic groups, and Herder's theory of cultural nationalism furnished a philosophical framework for the patterns of racial discrimination that developed during the century. Men came to believe that those races which had been historically unproductive could be quite justifiably subjugated by those races whose superiority presumably had been confirmed by their historical achievements. Thus it was that Christian white men condoned the eighteenth-century enslavement of non-Christian black men, for enslavement was the historical destiny of a people who could show the world little tangible evidence of cultural and industrial development. Thus it was, too, that the concept of *der ubermensch* developed to puff the racial arrogance of the Nordic peoples and doom the race-conscious nationalities of Europe to an extended period of intermittent nationalistic wars.

Although it is not to be argued that the Aristotelian equation of conduct and racial identity endorsed by Arnold would have eliminated racial discrimination, it is altogether plausible that such a point of view never would have fostered the inhuman racial exploitation which grew out of nineteenth-century imperialism. Thomas Arnold, viewing the panorama of imperialistic expansion around him, clearly saw that a racial theory equating racial and economic opportunism had destroyed the American Indian, subjugated the East Indian, and enslaved the African black man. In this sense, modern racial distinctions were clearly "odious and fantastic."

Thomas Arnold's adherence to the Aristotelian theory of race inevitably led him to conclude that no race could be considered inherently and permanently superior to any other race. This liberal concept is given full explication in his essay on Irish Catholic Emancipation.[13] Arnold based his belief on the proven historical conclusion that the superiority enjoyed by any one race was destined to be temporary, accidental, and conditional. In other words, no race was destined to enjoy the fruits of permanent superiority, as the Herder theory of cultural nationalism seemed to guarantee. For a Christian not to believe in the basic equality of all races was in Arnold's words one of the "most humiliating instances of human folly."[14] He stated further: " . . . they who believe in the common origin of all mankind must conclude that all important moral differences between one race and another, may be gradually removed as they have been created; and that as unfavor- able circumstances made them differ, so a happier system and better institutions may in time restore their original equality."[15] Just as controlling power in societies fluctuated and shifted from class to class, so in world politics controlling power fluctuated and shifted from race to race.[16] Arnold found proof of the validity of this historico-social generalization in the pages of history. For instance, the Gaul, flouted as a barbarian by the proud Roman, eventually saw his erstwhile superior humbled and defeated; and the Jew, builder of the spiritual bulwark of Western civilization, lost both his homeland and the rich heritage of his hero-kings—David, Saul, and Solomon. In the course of history, then, all of the races of the world were destined to enjoy a period of occasional ascendancy only to be leveled into insignificance by the on-sweep of historical events. For, if time were the great practical leveler, Christianity was the great spiritual leveler which would establish "a happier system and better institutions" and eventually restore the "original equality" of the races of mankind.

Arnold believed, therefore, that all races were spiritually and ethically equal, but during each period of history some one race or races enjoyed a temporary superiority. This temporary superiority resulted in inequalities which, however temporary, never were eradicated easily. In some instances, the temporary advantages enjoyed by one race of people were traceable to the advantageous geographical location of that people. It was thus that Arnold explained the reasons for the position of dominance held by his own England during the nineteenth century.[17] And he made the ominous and very accurate prophecy: "Woe be to that generation that is living in England when the coal mines are exhausted and the national debt not paid off."[18] In other instances, certain races enjoyed a temporary advantage or dominion over other races because of an adherence to values which encouraged and endorsed military conquest and expansion. The Spartans, for example, placed emphasis on values which assured them great military success but rendered them "unfit" for the dominion which they enjoyed over other Grecian peoples.[19] Their system of iron discipline which motivated their successful military conquests became, in time of peace, an influential factor in the preservation of institutions and strongly militated against the wise improvement of their institutions. As a consequence, they eventually fell from power; for, wrote Arnold, "Conquest, being the greatest of all possible changes, can only be conducted by those who know how to change wisely; a conqueror who is the slave of existing institutions is no better than a contradiction."[20] The distinctive feature of Arnold's thought in this context is his strong belief that the values adhered to by the Spartans were historically conditioned, not psychologically inherited. The institutions of Sparta were framed solely to ensure success in time of war and therefore could never ensure success in time of peace.[21]

Arnold further believed that racial differences, however temporary and historically accidental, were always a formidable barrier to any social, cultural, and political union among people of different races.[22] He found a practical illustration of his theory in the status held by the Negro freedman in the America of the 1830s. Arnold wrote:

...whenever differences of blood and race are so strong as even after the lapse of ages to constitute a real distinction, as in the case of white men and Negroes, there the perfect amalgamation of the political body becomes exceedingly difficult, if not utterly hopeless; and the daily increasing Negro population of the United States, a population excluded by a feeling of natural diversity from an enjoyment of the rights of citizenship, is perhaps one of the most alarming points in the future prospects of that great and growing people.[23]

Admittedly, Arnold's theory of "natural diversity" reflects the influence of the Herder theory of inherited psychological differences among races. Doubtless, in the 1830s, there were many other English liberals who, although in favor of the abolition of slavery, felt compelled to believe that a "natural diversity" existed between white man and Negro. This fact undoubtedly motivated the back-to-Africa movement which, under the sponsorship of certain liberal groups, resulted in the founding of Liberia in the 1840s. Today we know that the "natural diversity" between the American white man and the American Negro was, in fact, a "natural diversity" existing between slaveholder and slave, between master and servant. Therefore, it was a socially, and hence a historically, conditioned diversity, reflecting differences in moral and spiritual values and in the patterns of conduct by which these values were expressed. Historically, the Negro slave in America was an alien transferred from a tribal African background to become the minion of America's drive for economic power. Thus, the natural diversity which certainly existed was rooted more in differences of cultural background than in differences of appearance and hence reflected the Aristotelian theory of racial differentiation. Arnold's failure to recognize this fact is significant in any appraisal of his racial theories.

Despite this limitation, Thomas Arnold was considerably in advance of his times in his liberal attitude toward racial status among the world's peoples. It is unfortunate that his early death prevented his making a more definitive study of the historical background of the racial conflicts that vexed his century. Today, as forward-looking thinkers plan for a wholesome internationalism which will decrease further the importance of racial distinctions, it is comforting to note that a Greek philosopher of the fourth century B.C. and an energetic nineteenth-century schoolmaster-historian collaborated on a theory which, if understood and applied, quite conceivably could reduce the tensions that exist today among the peoples of the world.

NOTES

This essay first appeared in *Phylon* 18 (1957): 174–80.

1. Frederic E. Faverty, *Matthew Arnold, the Ethnologist* (Evanston, Ill., 1951). In his book Mr. Faverty offers conclusive evidence that Matthew Arnold, like many of his contemporaries, believed that "certain races and nations are on certain lines pre-eminent and representative." "Equality," *Mixed Essays, Irish Essays and Others* (New York, 1883), p. 48.

2. Faverty, *Matthew Arnold*, p. 167, states that "Dr. Arnold and then Renan exerted the greatest influence on Matthew Arnold's literary criticism based on race."

3. Strachey, *Eminent Victorians* (New York, 1918), pp. 222–23. Strachey accused Dr. Arnold of holding decided opinions upon a large number of topics "which he published in pamphlets, in prefaces, and in magazine articles, with an impressive self-confidence."

4. Faverty, *Matthew Arnold*, p. 117. The "friendly family dispute" occurred when Matthew Arnold wrote his mother as follows in May, 1866: "I do not think papa thought of the Saxon and the Celt mutually needing to be completed by each other; on the contrary, he was full of the sense of the Celt's vices, want of steadiness, and want of plain truthfulness, vices to him particularly offensive, that he utterly abhorred him and thought him of no good at all." G. W. E. Russell, ed., *Letters of Matthew Arnold—1848-1888* (London, 1895), 1: 320. Although the expression of this point of view occurred over twenty years after the elder Arnold's death, it was Matthew Arnold's intention to challenge his father's assertion that the Germanic peoples had "the soundest virtues" in modern Europe. A. P. Stanley, *Life and Correspondence of Thomas Arnold, D.D.* (London, 1845), 2: 377.

5. *Introductory Lectures on Modern History* (Oxford, 1842), pp. 44–46.

6. Stanley, 1: 411, note a.

7. According to Mr. Justice Coleridge, Thomas Arnold "cited the maxims of the Stagyrite as oracles" and was so "imbued with the language and ideas" of Aristotle that these colored all of his thought and conversation. Stanley, 1: 17–18.

8. *Politics*, V, 3 (Jowett's translation).

9. This interpretation is supported by Ernest Barker in his translation of the *Politics* (Oxford, 1948). His version of this passage is as follows: "The last of the incidental occasions of change is dissimilarity of elements in the composition of a state. Heterogeneity of stocks may lead to sedition—at any rate until they have had time to assimilate. A state cannot be constituted from any chance period of time. Most of the states which have admitted persons of another stock, either at the time of their foundation or later, have been troubled by sedition." Barker adds the following note: "Stock only means in Aristotle's use, members of a Greek city. In this sense, the Athenians were of a different stock from the Thebans." Barker, *The Politics*, p. 246.

10. *Thucydides*, 3 (1840): xvi.

11. Ibid.

12. Collingwood, *Idea of History*, pp. 87ff.

13. "The Christian Duty of Conceding the Roman Catholic Claims," *Miscellaneous Works*, pp. 5–78.

14. Ibid., pp. 27–28.

15. Ibid., pp. 33–34.

16. In his essay on "The Social Progress of States" (*Thucydides*, 1: 615–57) Arnold asserted that all societies or nations, in the process of their rise to power, moved through three phases of class control. The first phase Arnold described as the period of the ascendancy of the nobility or aristocracy—a period in which blood and family background were the determinants of political power. Historical examples of this first period were the "Homeric Monarchies" of Graeco-Roman civilization and the "feudal monarchies of modern Europe" (*Thucydides*, I, 622). The second period he defined as one in which the principle of wealth was in the ascendancy—a period in which a propertied middle class held maximum power in a given society (1: 626). Arnold's third and final period in his cycle of human history he termed the period of "the ascendancy of numbers." His was the theory that "the tendency of society is to become more and more liberal, and as the ascendancy of wealth is a more popular principle than the ascendancy of nobility, so it is less popular than the ascendancy of numbers" (1: 636). He also believed that the struggle between "numbers" and "wealth" had never "terminated favorably" (1: 633) and usually precipitated a severe crisis in the history of every nation that had attained that stage in the course of its development (1: 634).

17. Arnold asserted in his *Introductory Lectures on Modern History*, pp. 162–63, that "the whole character of a nation may be influenced by its geology and physical geography."

18. Stanley, 1: 275.

19. *History of Rome*, 1: 493–94.

20. Ibid.

21. Arnold wrote: "The Dorians in Sparta were like an army of occupation in a conquered country. . . . Hence the character of the Spartan institutions was chiefly military, more suited to a beleaguered garrison than to men united for mutual benefit in civil society." *Thucydides*, 1: 642. It is also of interest to note that Aristotle believed that Sparta's institutions were inadequate. Spartan women, because of certain laxities in the laws, lived "in every sort of intemperance and luxury." *Politics* (trans. by Jowett), 2: 9.

22. In a sense, here again Arnold is extending the Aristotelian point of view (*Politics*, V, 3) that differences in racial stocks within a state cause revolutions.

23. *Thucydides*, 1: 634.

History, Slavery, and Thematic Irony
in *Huckleberry Finn*

Those who argue that there is a lot of history in fiction have a more plausible argument than those who argue that there is a lot of fiction in history. When Mark Twain wrote his *Adventures of Huckleberry Finn* in the late 1870s and early 1880s describing a series of Mississippi River–town adventures experienced by a rather ne'er-do-well young man, classified by some as "po' white trash," he set his story in slavery-time Missouri. By virtue of the Missouri Compromise of 1820, that state had joined the Union as a slave state when Maine entered as a free state. Accordingly, any story having Missouri as its setting prior to 1865 had its setting in a slave state. Thus, whatever history there is in Mark Twain's novel about a rebellious teenager is slave-time history. In fact, the society or "sivilisation" that Huck was attempting to escape was a society or "sivilisation" that had slavery at its core. Especially was this true along the rivers of the South, the channels of trade and commerce—the Mississippi, the Waccammaw, the Tennessee, the Tombigbee; for as Langston Hughes once wrote, the black man, whether slave or free, had long known rivers and "his soul had grown deep like the rivers."

One gathers a deeper understanding of the meaning of living in a slave society such as Huck and his peers lived in when one understands that throughout the Americas, from the very beginning, there had always been slavery. This was true of Hispanic America in the sixteenth century, of all of the islands of the Caribbean in the seventeenth century, of the original thirteen British colonies of the North American mainland, and of all of the states united into one nation indivisible by the Constitution of 1787. In fact, in 1787 slavery was so pervasive throughout South Carolina and Virginia that whites were in a distinct minority in those two colonies, and this fact gave the founding fathers some cause for concern. Inevitably, as the nation developed, pushing its frontier ever westward, and as slavery in the southern states became an entrenched way of life, the "peculiar institution" began to have a substantive effect on the mores, manners, and values of all of the new nation. Everywhere one looked in the states below the Mason-Dixon line there was a substantial and growing black presence—a huge laboring and servant class—breeding, pulling, hauling, toting, hoeing, threshing, curing, refining, serving, and, above all, obeying. By the time of the Huck Finn story, there were over four million, kept in forced bondage by the whip and the immense police power of the plantation owner and his or her overseers and drivers. And, as Justice Taney stated in the Dred Scott decision, not one of the four million had any more legal status than an animal, and there was nothing about a black man that a white man was bound to respect.

But there was much more to slavery's story than the impact of the institution on the mores and morals of a fledgling nation. There was the slave himself, herself, or itself—the black man, the black woman, and the black child, chained in perpetual ignorance and bound for his or her natural life to a master or to a house or to a plantation field. The world of that slave was restricted to the land or house where he or she worked and to the dismal quarters where he or she lived. Generally, the slave had no choices about anything that affected his or her personal life, and the world beyond his or her master's house and land was a vast *terra incognita* unless the master decreed otherwise. For whatever knowledge came to the slave came only with the express permission and authorization of the master or mistress. Such a system was bound and designed to generate pain, anguish, frustration, and misery for the slave.

From such a background came Mark Twain's Nigger Jim. It is true that apologists for the southern way of life did present, for propaganda purposes, a wildly erroneous view that completely distorted slavery—a view that depicted a happy and contented slave living in happy innocence and mutual devotion and affection with a wise and tolerant master or mistress. Such pictures of the bucolic bliss of chattel slavery were products of the romantic imagination, however, and were not in evidence in Twain's Missouri nor in any of the towns, cities, or plantations that bordered the Mississippi in Huck's day. All were, like Jim, slaves in such a grievous state of distress that they became runaways whenever opportunity for successful flight presented itself.

So Jim, nurtured by a callous and cruel system, was naively ignorant of a larger world and, as a runaway, moved about fearfully and without direction or plan. That he survived in his confused freedom long enough to meet Huck was more than a minor miracle. In fact, because of the Fugitive Slave Act of 1850, all the powers of government—local, state, and federal—

were ranged against Jim's survival. As a runaway slave, he was the preeminent outsider, the existential rebel—the man to be hunted down and punished by all the forces of law and order. Of course, when the hunted black fugitive and outsider meets the disaffected and poor white outsider— one long kept in childlike ignorance of a larger world by slavery's dictum and the other long victimized by his po' white trash status in a capitalist society—Twain, the storyteller, takes over and begins to weave incidents and events into a suspenseful narrative.

It is obvious that Twain's novel about the chance meeting of two runaways, one black and one white, is under attack today because many Americans, guilt-ridden because of the racial divisions that continue to plague our society, have difficulty coping with the historical fact of slavery. Blacks, as part of their long and tortuous fight for social and legal justice, would like to blot the memory of centuries of enforced servitude off the record of history. And whites, in large measure, take no joy in remembering slave times; they would rather take patriotic pride in America's written promises of justice and equality for all, regardless of creed, race, or previous condition of servitude. Indeed, slavery times provoke bad memories for both racial groups—memories of the chaos wrought by incestuous concubinage and the birth of half-white half-brothers and half-black white half-sisters, memories of a dehumanizing system that reduced grown black men and women to "boys" and "gals" and grown white men and women to groveling hypocrites. Blacks, in particular, would have their children shielded from the ignominious shame of slavery, not only because the memory of slavery exacerbates today's racial problems, but also because their children are racially traumatized by any references to their former inferior status. Thus, they ask that anything that might prove to be racially divisive be banned from all educational programs. Such a ban would include Twain's *Adventures of Huckleberry Finn*, a novel in which the word "nigger," the appelation commonly used for slaves in slavery time, is used 160 times.

There are many arguments which can and have been employed to counter those posed by the anti–*Huckleberry Finn* forces. One, of course, is the oft repeated observation that any race that would ignore its history will be condemned to repeat it. This admonition, if heeded, would prod black Americans to remember slavery, however painful the memory, and urge Jews to recall the Holocaust, however painful the memory. Another countering argument is that patterns of racial discrimination are so deeply interwoven in the fabric of American society that not reading about Huck and Jim would have no effect on lowering racial tensions or removing the sharp racial polarities that exist and will continue to exist in America. The proponents of this position argue that a novel like *Huckleberry Finn* is irrelevant. Whether it is required reading or not, racial segregation in housing will continue to exist in all of the nation's major cities and throughout suburbia. Racial discrimination will still haunt the market-place and employment rosters. Demoralizing statistics about the black family will continue to exist—statistics about the large number of female-headed, single-parent families living below the poverty line, statistics about the large number of young black men in the nation's prisons, and statistics about the large number of teenage pregnancies. The pro-ponents of this position argue that black America's continuing depressed status is the result of a pattern of discrimination against America's most visible minority that began with the nation's founding. In their view, slavery was thus more of a symptom than a root cause of racial prejudice in America.

Some of the more radical supporters of this position even argue that, not only is the reading or nonreading of Twain's novel irrelevant, but that a nation that has an achieving majority and a nonachieving but visible minority to victimize and exploit can thereby enjoy national prosperity and good health. The argument advanced in this context is that having such a minority to victimize inflates the psychological self-esteem of the majority and that this self-esteem is essential for the growth and development of a nation. Supporters of this point of view cite the immense success of both republican and imperial Rome, in which there was always a large lower class of plebeians, slaves, and conquered colonial subjects to be victimized and thus bolster the self-esteem of an achieving upper class. And, in democratic America, the argument continues, a powerful white majority, its motives shielded by carefully articulated verbal guarantees of democracy and freedom and justice, proceeds to exploit, deny, and exclude America's most visible minority. In other words, the argument suggests, if there were no black minority to be victimized and exploited, white America would zealously strive to find a fit substitute in order to keep the nation on the cutting edge of national progress and achievement. Obviously, in an ethical and social scenario of this kind, slavery and Twain's Nigger Jim become not root causes of current racial attitudes but providential symbols of what ought to be.

None of this supersubtle sociological and psychological theorizing, however, can fully alleviate the trauma experienced by a young black teenager when he or she encounters racial discrimination or racial slurs or racial epithets in a racially integrated classroom. Nor can it be expected that the average junior or senior high school English teacher would prepare the black teenager and his or her peers to read a novel like Twain's *Huckleberry Finn* with a full awareness of the far-flung historical and psycho-logical causes and consequences. If a work of fiction demands this much preparation and student-teacher orientation, one may be fully justified in advocating that the work be removed from required reading lists and made an optional reading selection.

Unfortunately, the reasoning behind such a recommendation completely ignores, by implication at least, Twain's literary intention when he undertook to tell Huck's story. As has been suggested above, Jim's source, lineage, and status are quite clear; he was a slave who had, in protest over his condition, run away from his mistress. Similarly, Huck, saddled with an improvident, alcoholic father, was a lad without means and a self-proclaimed outcast who, because of his condition, wished to escape "sivilisation." By bringing black runaway Jim into close association with white runaway Huck, Twain obviously desired to explore the ironic implications of such an association in a "sivilisation" riddled by racial division and prejudice. The irony employed here is similar to that used in Puddin Head Wilson's story in which Twain recounts the comi-tragic consequences of a situation in which a light-skinned "colored" baby is substituted for a white baby. In the Huck story, Twain's ironic conclusion is that two human beings, however different in their backgrounds and "previous condition of servitude," will, if far enough removed from the corrupting influences of "sivilisation," become friends. For Twain, like England's Swift or Rome's Juvenal, believed that the social civilization that man labored so hard to cultivate was, in turn, the great corrupter of man. He believed that from civilization came not only values to preserve and protect but the incentives to divide, control, and inhibit. Twain appears to be asking in his story of Huck and Jim how truly "civilized" is an America which since its beginning has cultivated and nurtured slavery. And he knew, as he observed events in the 1880s, that, although slavery no longer officially existed, blacks were still a big servant and laboring class to be exploited but kept illiterate, disfranchised, and socially and culturally oppressed.

So, given the social and cultural conditions that existed in pre–Civil War America, Twain sought to explore the ironic possibilities of the development of an authentic black-white friendship. Under what circumstances could a slave and a white man develop a friendship in slave-time America? Could it occur within the system or would it have to be a clandestine matter hidden from society at large? Twain, the ironist who doubted that social and/or moral benefits could accrue from a civilization beleaguered by greed and prejudice, concluded that, given the nature of slave-time America, a friendship of that kind could develop only outside the normal areas of civil and social discourse. In fact, Twain appears to suggest, with more than an ironic gleam in his eye, that such a friendship could develop only on a socially isolated raft in the middle of the nation's biggest and longest river and thus as far from the shores ruled by law and order as a man could get in middle America. But Twain the ironist did not stop there. He developed, with careful ironic forethought, an interracial friendship between two outcasts who, under civilization's auspices, were normally inveterate enemies. For, during Twain's lifetime and later, it was an observable fact that poor white trash like the Finns had nothing but hatred and disrespect for blacks. Condemned and reviled as economic and social outcasts by "respectable" society, people like the Finns looked for some inferior group on which to vent their social spleen; and, in America's social hierarchy, the only class or group considered to be lower than the Finns and their kin were black slaves who, after 1865, became the openly reviled black freedmen.

Thus, Twain's novel, by motive and intention, is really an ironic appraisal of the American racial scene circa 1884. Herein possibly lies the difficulty encountered in trying to teach the novel. Irony, as all students of literature know, involves a deliberate misstatement—a misstatement designed to highlight the longtime adverse effects of a grossly immoral act or a blatantly dishonest deed or an inhumane and un-Christian practice. If the ironic statement made by an author in a work of fiction is too subtly wrought, it will not be effectively communicated to the average reader. The continuing controversy about the *Adventures of Huckleberry Finn* suggests that the American reading public, in the main, has never fully understood the author's ironic message. It is also probably true that American society—actually the same "sivilisation" castigated by Huck—will never fully comprehend Twain's irony, because one needs to have considerable ethical distance from the object under ironic analysis to appreciate and understand the irony. In other words, students and teachers who are immersed and involved in America's racial problems will never understand the need to develop a disciplined objectivity about those problems before they can appreciate an ironic solution to them. Indeed, ironic fiction is difficult to teach, especially to young teenagers who usually founder on deliberately oversubtle misstatements.

So, although Jim's roots lie deep in the soil of slavery and American racism and although his is an honest and forthright portrayal of a slave runaway and although young black teenagers are traumatized by reading about the Jims of slavery time, the great difficulty with *The Adventures of Huckleberry Finn* is that it is one of America's best pieces of ironic fiction. To a nation that was and is sharply divided on matters of race, Twain's novel suggests that friendships between black and white can best be forged by the least of us and then only under the worst of circumstances. Undoubtedly, only a reading audience of some maturity and preceptive insight—an audience that can probe for lurking truths under surface facts and figures and events—can grasp the far-reaching implications of the adventures of a white Huck and a black Jim floating down the river of American life. As Francis Bacon once wrote, "Reading maketh the full man"; but not all and sundry in our error-ridden society can sit and sup at fiction's table without occasionally feeling the pain and anguish generated by that error-ridden society.

NOTE

This essay first appeared in the *Mark Twain Journal* 22 (Fall 1984): 17–20. Reprinted by permission of the *Mark Twain Journal*.

Critical Theory and Problems of Canonicity in African American Literature

When I first began the study of literature as an undergraduate English major at a small New England liberal arts college some fifty-five years ago, I had absolutely no misgivings about what we were told to study as English literature. It was "Beowulf to Thomas Hardy," with as much crammed in between these two formidable gateposts as possible. In fact, for the convenience of those dedicated few who ventured to travel on the strange, silent seas of literary study, someone had provided a two-volume text entitled *Beowulf to Thomas Hardy*. Not one of us asked a single question about the canon. For instance, no one asked why there was no American literature included. Nor why there was no twentieth-century or contemporary literature. And, in my case, why there was no literature on or about black Americans, or, as we said then, colored people.

Apparently, no one anywhere else asked any such questions, for when we applied to graduate schools, our transcripts were readily accepted and we were all admitted for further and more exacting study of the literature from "Beowulf to Thomas Hardy." In fact, in graduate school the terms "general" and "special" were used to describe what one as a graduate student should know about English literature. We were told that, generally, one should know everything, literarily speaking, from "Beowulf to Thomas Hardy," and there was something called a "general" oral examination whereby properly designated authorities determined the extent of one's "general" knowledge of literary events and history over the some thirteen centuries spanning English life and history from Beowulf to Thomas Hardy. In addition, one was required to focus on or develop a "special" area of interest; from this area one mined a thesis or dissertation. One poor chap, I recall, chose the year 1859 as his "special" area; some years later when I asked him at an MLA meeting about his special interest in 1859, he stated that he still had a special interest in 1859 but only in the life of Melville, an author in whom he had now developed a special interest. Incidentally, my own "specialty" in that faraway time was the Arnolds— Dr. Thomas Arnold of Rugby and his famous poet-critic-school-supervising son.

Not only did we meekly accept the canon presented to us as fixed and immutable, but we became career generalists and specialists within the fixed parameters of that canon. We also accepted very restricted notions about the meaning and function of literature. Literature, we were informed, had moral, emotional, and spiritual meaning; it was stimulating, inspiring, ennobling; and it was thought that those who loved and studied literature moved on a higher plateau of humanistic concern than lesser folk who merely invented or engineered or, even worse, politicked. Thus, literature had no political meaning or political content; if there were political content, then that was not literature; that was propaganda. So Milton in his magnificent sonnet on the slaughter of the Piedmontese Protestants during the Reformation was not making a political statement; he was making a moral statement. Nor was his cutting censure of Eve as but "second" in *Paradise Lost* a political statement but an observation based on Old Testament law and hence a moral judgment. Similarly, the satirical literature flowing forth from the partisan political imbroglios of the Restoration was, when taught, divested of its political content and presented as good, solid examples of satire, a genre with deep roots, particularly in Roman history and culture. So the satires of Dryden and Pope were good neoclassical imitations of the classical satires of Juvenal and Horace, shorn, of course, of political content.

Fortunately, for most of us who were nurtured on the standard pre– World War II literary canon, change began to come with the war and with the events that followed the war. By the 1950s, there was no longer any safe and reclusive literary ivory tower to hide either pedant or pedagogue from intense scrutiny. A madly erratic Senator McCarthy from Wisconsin found that he could make political capital by charging most professors and college personnel with various kinds of Marxist-related forms of treason and political heresy. Not only did the senator's attack on the academy fuel distrust of the professoriate everywhere, but it had a particularly devastating effect on black professors who were trying to survive under intense segregation pressures at black public institutions in the South. Under these pressures, all literature became political, and all writers of literature and all teachers of literature became politicized. If one became exhilarated by reading or studying or reciting a poem, it was first a political exhilaration, and only later an emotional exhilaration. Indeed, the argument advanced then by many in the white literary establishment that a black literature protesting white America's discrimination against its black minority was not acceptable as literature was, in the 1940s and 1950s, challenged on every front. As you can recall, the successful civil rights protest of the 1960s blew the last vestige of that erroneous idea out of the water. Some folk still read Baldwin's "Everybody's Protest Novel," but everyone, white and black, now agrees with Richard Wright's assessment that all literature is a protest against something and that without a protesting and politicized literature, needed changes will never be recognized, discussed, or successfully implemented.

Thus it was that when Keneth Kinnamon and I, following some of the other anthologists of black literature who emerged in the 1960s, began to assemble what became *Black Writers of America,* we were more on fire with political energy than inspired by literary insight. I had been in Atlanta for one of the most exciting decades of my life; I had seen the South change almost before my eyes; and I, my wife, and my youngest son had been in the long line that snaked its way across the Spelman campus to Sisters Chapel to view a martyred leader's remains on a warm April sabbath day.

So, driven by the political furies of the times, Kinnamon and I forged a black literary canon full of political content. I remember setting aside the poetry of Anne Plato, Claudia Ray, Georgia Douglas Johnson, and Lucy Terry's "Bar's Fight" because I thought it lacked sufficient political content. And I recall fighting to include a unit on the "literature" of the black man in the Civil War because it was an event filled with political protest. And I remember losing the fight to include a unit on the literature of the black man in the struggle to win the West, simply because we had, in the view of our Macmillan editor, run out of word space.

The Barksdale and Kinnamon anthology is now seventeen years old. He and I, and I assume the profit-mongers at Macmillan, are glad that our politicized and protest-filled anthology has served several college and university generations. Obviously, given the history that I have presented, *BWA* represents a far cry from my somewhat humble beginnings as a student of literature. Now for me a literary act is a political act, and I now view even the so-called sacrosanct standard English literature canon as a political arrangement designed to glorify English history and the British Empire. For, as I have pursued my research in British antislavery literature, I have found that not one iota of the volumes of writing produced in that genre has ever been included in the official canon of English literature. Newman's *Apologia* and the dull trivia of the Oxford Movement made the canon but James Montgomery's magnificent 1809 epic on the slave trade did not, nor did any of the poetry included in three volumes of antislavery verse. Apparently, the reason behind the exclusion of antislavery literature is that that literature was, in the final analysis, harmful to empire interests. Newman and his Oxford associates left the empire undisturbed and thus met the major criterion for canonicity.

So as we prepare the way for effective formation or reformation of our African American literary canon, we will have to assess, with astute care, the cultural, sociopolitical, and demographic factors which will affect anything occurring in America as we approach the twenty-first century. For instance, demographers pretty generally assert that, by the year 2025, ethnic minorities will in all probability outnumber the current Caucasian majority, especially in urban America. The question can now be asked, To what extent should our canon be enlarged to reflect broader minority interests? Should there be more literature reflecting the urban Hispanic experience, the literature of the Puerto Rican emigré, the literature of the Native American? And then there is the black literary ferment of the Caribbean (some say that there is a pulsating Caribbean esthetic that leaps racial and cultural boundaries). Should the poetry and folk songs and stories of Jamaica, Trinidad, Barbados, Cuba, and Haiti be included in our canon? Historically, the jazz drumbeat that came out of New Orleans had its birth in the drums of Haiti. To what extent should we renew old cultural linkages? Even as we consider these problems of forming a more encompassing canon, let us be ever mindful that something is developing in the vestiges of the British Empire called Commonwealth literature. Black literary scholars who are graduating from Canadian universities, for instance, are seeking employment in American universities as specialists in Commonwealth literature. How should African Americans cope with this development? Remember what the Beatles did to or with black music!

A major problem in African American literary canon formation, however, is the burgeoning influence of the very fanciful critical theories which have come from France and are currently spreading throughout our major graduate schools. Ours is a profession certainly not immune to faddish change, but the adherents and practitioners of the new critical approaches are increasing in large numbers. Indeed, teachers who have developed skills in these new areas of critical interpretation quickly attract advisees, and their growing power and influence in any given English or comparative literature or modern foreign language department have interesting and provocative political consequences. They not only have become the major dissertation directors, but they have a very strong voice in search and hiring decisions. Inevitably, an alert doctoral candidate quickly sees future publishing and employment leverage in associating with the critical-theory power clique in any given graduate department. As a consequence, a large number of graduate students have written and are writing dissertations in the new critical theory mode, and a large number of "theory-grounded" articles are appearing in the professional journals. Indeed, one wonders whether *PMLA* has not become completely enamored of the dense and jargon-ridden style and format practiced by the critical theorist.

In other words, there is a certain amount of professional success associated with the practitioners of the new critical theory. For instance, members of one major Big Eight English department, after a long and frustrating search for a chair, announced with great pride that they had secured a chair who not only had superb administrative skills but was a Lacanian specialist as well.

So critical theorists have built power bases of influence in many departments of literature, not only in the literary bastions of the East and the West coasts, but throughout the departments of the Big Eight and Big Ten universities. Where the universities have publishing presses, critical theorists also usually exercise some influence on publishing decisions, either as press readers or members of press boards. Inevitably, wherever there are minority students or students specializing in minority literature, these students have been affected by the intradepartmental political maneuvering over the status of critical theorists in the departments. Usually, these students become mini-critical theorists.

What is the basis of the appeal of the French-based theories of textual criticism to the American literary academy? As we all know, over the centuries nations the world over have found French products alluring and attractive. French perfumes are irresistible; French couturiers dominate the clothing styles of the West; and the world's best wines come from French vineyards. The French themselves have even declared that, at some point during their hundred-year conflict with England, the English stopped eating their food with their hands and learned to use French-made knives, forks, and spoons. Also the Western world well knows that out of France's revolutionary turmoil of the late eighteenth century came the democratic ideas that are still basic in Western democracies. But nothing imported from France has caused as much concern as Derrida's critical notions of poststructural textual analysis and Paul de Man's ideas about textual deconstruction.

What has always been puzzling is the enthusiasm with which our somewhat conservative literary academics imported these new approaches to textual exegesis. One writer, Frank Lentricchia, in a work entitled *After the New Criticism,* argued in the early seventies that the erosion of the authority of the New Criticism left "a theoretical vacuum" which was quickly filled with European critical theory. Even then, critics like Frank Lauter who were unhappy with the New Criticism's emphasis on ignoring history and personal experience were just as unhappy with the new critical theory's emphasis on an ivory towerish sense of intellectual mystification. Indeed, the continental critical theories seemed to deemphasize totally literature's needed concern for man's social and political welfare. At this point, some of the critical theorists began to discuss with each other the merits and deficiencies of the imported critical theories. One, Frederic Jameson, a neo-Marxist at Duke University, published in 1981 a work entitled *The Political Unconscious* in which he contended that the theories of Derrida, Lacan, and Ricoeur could be used for textual interpretations that would unmask capitalistic contradictions in our postindustrial society. Jameson's work, like most of the works intended to illuminate a neo-Marxist approach to the effective use of the new theories, is not easy reading. Nor is Lentricchia's 1983 response, *Criticism and Social Change,* in which he argues against the social isolation engendered by textual deconstruction and encourages the use of theories advanced by Gramsci and Foucault for promoting individual empowerment.

Arguments between neo-Marxists and non-Marxists about the proper interpretation and employment of critical theory techniques and practices continue to this day. These arguments are long and jargonistic and written in the dense and opaque style that only the truly dedicated critical theorist can understand. In the meantime, notwithstanding conflicts about approaches and interpretations, the use of continental critical theory finds even more defenders, practitioners, and fund raisers than many other humanistic enterprises on the campuses of large research institutions. For instance, in the early 1980s when I was an associate graduate dean at the University of Illinois at Urbana-Champaign, an associate vice chancellor for research told me that the only humanistic organization on campus worth funding was the Unit on Criticism and Interpretive Theory.

So, as we contemplate expanding and broadening our African American literary canon in preparation for an exciting new century, what recognition will we, or must we, give to continental critical theory? My recommendation is that, as we broaden our canon, we ignore deconstruction, poststructural textual exegesis, and continental hermeneutics. African American literature cannot effectively survive critical approaches that stress authorial depersonalization and the essential unimportance of racial history, racial community, and racial traditions. For instance, when I offer a course next spring in "Hurston, Hughes, and the Folk Vernacular," at the outset I shall explain to my students that I will welcome astutely formulated textual criticism of the works of the two authors, but don't travel all the way to Paris's Left Bank for an elucidating theory; just take an imaginative trip to Eatonville, Florida, or New York's Harlem, using either Hemenway's book on Zora or Rampersad's book on Langston. Or use me, the teacher, to elucidate and expatiate and clarify, for I believe not in avoiding history but in elucidating history. Admittedly, I am that old-fashioned kind of historical critic who still stresses the three M's—the man, the moment, the milieu—in approaching a literary work; and, when we get to the text, I stress more M's—matter, manner, mode, meaning. As a graduate student once told me after we finished with an author, "Professor Barksdale, we emmed all over that man!"

But it is easy to state here that we can cavalierly ignore the critical theorists as we build our literary canon for the years that await our scholars in the next century. Actually, it is possible that the pressure on the canon builders will be too great to muster total resistance to the critical theorists. In departments in which they wield power, they will shut black literature programs off and cancel your course or courses. For instance, I am being somewhat naively hopeful that my next semester's seminar will materialize; there is always a chance that the requisite number of students will be advised away and guided into another course or seminar. In fact, I strongly suspect that that is how the University of Illinois's very vibrant program in African American literature withered away to nothing in less than three years. After a record production of eighteen black doctorates in African American literature between 1973 and 1986, there are now no black graduate courses in the timetable and no black candidates in the pipeline.

So, I recommend that as we build our literary canon for the tomorrows that lie ahead in the next century, we remain ever mindful of the need to utilize the politics of survival. This is something to be found in the text of our racial history that ahistorical theorists like a Derrida, a Gramsci, or a Lacan would not begin to understand. And let us not be casual about the struggle that we might have to face as we attempt to compromise an accommodation with a brother or sister who had to accept training as a critical theorist in order to win his or her degree but who still wants to teach African American literature. As a young black man a few days ago commented on TV on the still-ruinous aftereffects of Hurricane Hugo in rural black coastal South Carolina: "Dis heah ral seius. Dis shit *ral* seius!" Translated into academic language, he means, for blacks, "Life ain't no crystal stair," but I prefer his version. It has a realistic ring to it.

NOTE

This lecture was delivered to the Langston Hughes Society in 1989.

PART 2

The Humanities
beyond Literary Canons

Humanistic Protest in Recent
Black Poetry

The tradition of protest against his social, political, and moral condition runs deep in the black man's literature in America. It is not present in the poetry of Phillis Wheatley and Jupiter Hammon, but it is found in Olaudah Equiano's *Narrative of His Life* in 1789. It is found under the facetious poetic grin of George Moses Horton who, while drafting innocuous love songs for University of North Carolina undergraduates, could also bitterly complain:

> Alas! and am I born for this
> To wear this slavish chain?
> Deprived of all created bliss
> Through hardship, toil and pain!

It is found in the work of other antebellum black poets like James Whitfield, Frances Watkins Harper, and Elymas Rogers. One even finds strains of social protest in some of the poetry and prose of that apostle of interracial goodwill, Paul Laurence Dunbar; for, underneath the sometimes mawkish sentimentality, there is the tight anger of "We Wear the Mask"—

> We sing, but oh the clay is vile
> Beneath our feet, and long the mile;
> But let the world dream otherwise,
> We wear the mask.

Certainly, protest is found throughout the innumerable cantos and versatile rhymes of Albery Whitman who, as a contemporary of Dunbar, produced a long poem of protest which is something of a black literary first: *Rape of Florida* is the first protest poem of epic length written in Spenserian stanzaic form about the twin tragedies of the Indian and the black man, using Longfellow's *Hiawatha* as a literary model.

Elements of social and moral protest are also everywhere in the black man's folk literature—in his spirituals, his folk tales, his work songs, his prison moans, his blues. One even finds some protest over the black man's social and economic condition in some of the heroic bad man songs. In these the hero is usually so big and bad and heroically self-sufficient that there is nothing in his path to protest about—like "Stackerlee" who "fought da debbil toe to toe / Den blowed him down wid his forty-fo." But one does find strong social protest in "Po Laz'us," a song about a youngish bad man who, with a steel-blue "shooter" in each hand, stole the payroll from a levee work camp, and then was "blowed down 'tween two mountins" by a host of "depitties." The emphasis in this work song, still shouted out by railroad gangs and convict-lease crews, is not on Laz'us' brief moment of heroism but on Laz'us' sister who could not go to her brother's funeral because "she had no shoes, Lawd, Lawd, she had no shoes."

In the twentieth century, the black man's literary protest has deepened and broadened and, in some instances, become quite humanistic in tone. This latter development has taken place even as the black man's social and economic problems have multiplied and intensified in the sprawling urban ghettoes and the militant tone of his literary protest has become more strident and hostile. Two instances of protest with a humanistic emphasis are found in the two poems that marked a new era in black poetic expression—Margaret Walker's "For My People" and Melvin Tolson's "Dark Symphony." Both poems vigorously protest the black man's social, political, and economic lot and both have a verbal brilliance that is still poetically captivating. What is interesting is the note of humanistic concern that emerges in each poem. "For My People," first published by Miss Walker in 1937 and then selected as the title poem for her prize-winning 1942 volume, sounds the hope that black people, although "distressed and disturbed and deceived and devoured," will help "to fashion a world that will hold all / the people all the faces all the adams and eves. . . . " Similarly, Tolson's "Dark Symphony," winner of the National Poetry Prize in 1940, closes with the humanistic assertion that, as black people advance through and across their own special racial barricades, they will join and advance with "the Peoples of the World." Admittedly, each poem was written during a period in which worldwide pain, sorrow, and affliction were tangibly evident, and few could isolate the black man's dilemma from humanity's dilemma during the Depression years or during the war years. Nevertheless, it is of some interest to note how racial protest in each poem shifts to a concern for the "Peoples of the World"—for "all the adams and eves."

Beyond these two examples there are few, if any, strong expressions of humanistic protest in black poetry during the decade of the 1940s. As the decade drew to a close, the star of Gwendolyn Brooks had fully risen, but her poetry in *Street in Bronzeville* and *Annie Allen* was devoted to small, carefully cerebrated, terse portraits of the black urban poor. The very existence of the characters she presents is both proof and cause for racial protest, but Miss Brooks handles all with a well-disciplined aesthetic detachment and "apoplectic ice." At this point, there is no rhetorical involvement with causes, racial or otherwise. Indeed, there is no need, for each character, so neatly and precisely presented, is a racial protest in itself and a symbol of some sharply etched human dilemma. This fitted in very well with the literary mood of the late 1940s. Both black and white critics had begun to look askance at the idea of literature as a vehicle for protest; and, after the publication of James Baldwin's essay, "Everybody's Protest Novel," in the *Partisan Review* in 1949, the critical discussion about protest in black literature assumed some focus as a dialogue between two groups of black writers. On one side were Baldwin and many articulate literary academicians who believed that black writers should be more concerned with artistic craftsmanship and universal themes and less concerned with specific protest over the black man's lot. On the opposing side were Richard Wright, Chester Himes, and other literary figures who believed that all great literature was written to protest some aspect of the human condition and that black writers need not be any exception. A man, they argued, had to write out of his experience; for, as Arthur Miller wrote, "the fish is in the water and the water is in the fish"; if a man is hungry and rejected and angry, he will write a poem or a novel about hunger, rejection, and anger.

Fortunately, events of the 1950s—the emergence of Malcolm X and the creed of black separatism and new directions in the fight for integration under the inspiring leadership and moral idealism of Martin Luther King, Jr.—solved the problem about whether the black creative writer could turn his literary ploughshare into a sword of protest. The events of the time—the marches, the speeches, the deaths, the confrontations with police dogs and spouting firehoses—left him no choice. By 1960 the dialogue of the 1940s about protest was as anachronistic as the ancient Platonic *caveat* that too much protest from men of literature might topple the state. Under these favoring circumstances, the black man's creative energies became explicitly involved with the fight for minority civil rights, and black poets developed a rhetoric of protest and racial confrontation which was relevant for the times. Much of the protest reflects the anger of the frustrated revolutionary or the racial chauvinism of the black separatist, but in some poets there is the note of humanistic protest found in Tolson and Margaret Walker a generation earlier. Gwendolyn Brooks's "Riders to the Blood-Red Wrath," for instance, ends with the racially self-confident assertion that the American black man's long, bloody, and "continuing" Calvary gives him unique insights about man's inhumanity to man. Her black Everyman speaks:

> But my detention and my massive stain,
> And my distortion and my Calvary
> I grind into a little lorgnette
> Most slyly: to read man's inhumanity.
> And I remark my Matter is not all.
> Man's chopped in China, in India indented.
> From Israel what's Arab is resented.

Miss Brooks's spokesman then concludes that black America will "Star, and esteem all that which is of woman / Human and hardly human." Indeed, the world will be revolutionized for love by black America, for out of the black man's struggle will come the renewal of "Democracy and Christianity."

In the poetry of those young black writers who have emerged within the past five years, the note of humanistic protest is not as strongly and as clearly stated as one finds in "Riders to the Blood-Red Wrath." There are reasons for this. Gwendolyn Brooks's poem expresses the Christian idealism of Martin Luther King, Jr., and her enthusiastic endorsement of his "contretemps-for-love." But in April 1968 this great and noble leader was cut down by an assassin's bullet to join an ever-lengthening list of assassination victims in a death-riddled decade. Indeed, it is something of a minor miracle that one finds in the poetry of Sonia Sanchez, Nikki Giovanni, or Don Lee any expression of humanistic concern whatsoever. For as the decade of the searing sixties ended, the world of the young black poet provided nothing for self-exultation, unmasked laughter, or unfettered joy. It was the kind of world that Etheridge Knight writes about from his Indiana prison cell in his poem "On Universalism":

> I see no single thread
> That binds me one to all;
> Why even common dead
> Men took the single fall.
>
> No universal laws
> Of human misery
> Create a common cause
> Or common history
> That ease black people's pains
> Nor break black people's chains.

Nevertheless, in some of the poetry of recent young black writers there is a broad humanistic concern that breaks through the cloud-cover of confrontation rhetoric to pinpoint the evils of the times, to subject these to trenchant poetical analysis, and to pronounce their desperate remedies for mankind's moral and spiritual salvation.

The worldwide plague of drug addiction is one area of humanistic concern for the young black poet. In the suburbs and in legislative councils the official term is drug abuse, but to Sonia Sanchez and the black community it is the "wite death." If not checked, it will destroy all of the "brothas and sistuhs" everywhere. This is the subject of Sonia Sanchez's "Blk Chant":

> we programmed fo death
> die/en
> > each day the man
> > > boy
> plans our death
> > > with short bread
> for short sighted minds
> with junk to paralyze our
> blk limbs

Especially does Sonia Sanchez believe that the "wite death" will destroy love. She writes:

> i wud not be yo woman
> & see u disappear
> > each day
> befo my eyes
> > and know yo
> reappearance
> > to be
> > > a one
> > > > nite stand.
> no man
> > blk
> > lovers   cannot live
> in wite powder that removes
> them from they blk selves
> > > cannot ride
> majestic wite horses
> > > in a machine age.

The real tragedy for Miss Sanchez is the entrapment of the "young brothas and sistuhs" who look "so cool" in their "wite highs" on every "blk st in wite amurica"; she pleads with them to "c'mon down from yo white highs an live." The alternative is the death of all the young warriors, the death of love, and the death of change and revolution.

The fight against the "wite death" is a desperate "got-to-be" if urban civilization, white and black, is to survive. Occasionally, America's young black poets also express their "ought-to-be's," and here their humanism or their belief in building a better world is obvious. First, one must or ought to begin "the real work" of building families that are strong and stable; "let us begin ... now," says Sonia Sanchez, "while our / children still / remember us and loooove." More important is the need to change the system that enslaves and imprisons and ultimately destroys. What is needed to accomplish this kind of revolutionary change is not violence, anger, or rage; what is needed are political astuteness and moral power. Only through being astute and making the right moral decisions can men, writes Sonia Sanchez, achieve the discipline, "learnen," love and power "to destroy the Beast / who inslaves us." And if love is to be expressed "in communal ways" and if there is to be a real moral revolution, black people will have to take the lead in seeing to it that "no blk person starves or is killed on a 'saturday nite corner.' "

Finally, it is Don L. Lee—the carping, cynical ironist and master of the satirical thrust—who most explicitly exhorts the beautiful people of the world to retrieve "the unimpossibility" by rescuing the world from woe, deceit, and inhumanity and from the "unpeople" who created that world. So, in his final poem in *Don't Cry, Scream,* Lee says to the "beautiful people":

> come
> brothers / fathers / sisters / mothers / sons / daughters
>
>   * * *
>
> walk on. smile a little
> yeah, that's it beautiful people
> move on in ...
> to return
> this earth into the hands of human beings.

In *We Walk the Way of the New World* (1970) the need for change and a pattern of humanistic protest to achieve that change are discussed in the Preface. Lee writes:

> We need innovators and producers of positive change. The older generation's resistance to change is natural; so how do we change without alienating them? How can we reduce if not completely eliminate all the negativism, pettiness and cliquishness that exist and are so damaging? ... How can we create a common consciousness, based on a proven humanism—as we stop trying to prove our humanism to those who are inhuman?

Accordingly, readers of his "New World Poems" in this volume are charged to "change" and "create a climate for change." In the title poem of the volume, Lee closes with a description of his apocalyptical vision of a world in which "our dreams are realities" and all the "ought-to-be's" have been satisfied. In such a world there will be no "dangercourse" to run; men will walk "in cleanliness"

down state st / or Fifth Ave.
& wicked apartment buildings shake
as their windows announce our presence
as we jump into the interior
& cut the day's evil away.

In the new world that Don Lee envisions, "realpeople" and the beautiful people become "the owners of the New World," but they

will run it as unowners
for
we will live in it too
& will want to be remembered
as   realpeople.

Many critics and students of poetry find the poetry of our new young black poets abrasive in tone, offensive in style, and too full of anger and hate. But like other black poets in other times, these new black poets are merely being responsive to the conditions under which they have had to live and write. In order to cope with the world's massive disorders and calamities, they developed a rhetoric of racial confrontation and used that rhetoric in a righteously angry "speak-out" against a dishonest and immoral Establishment. In the process, some poets have paused to reflect on this Establishment, and a few have dared to protest for change and renewal in this Establishment. These few are part of a long tradition in black poetry, for the roots of the tradition of protest run deep in the black man's history. In this sense, the circle from George Moses Horton to Don L. Lee is unbroken. Each black poet has attempted, through his own special pattern of protest, to express a black humanism that would speak to the inhumanity of his times.

NOTE

This essay first appeared in *Modern Black Poets,* ed. Donald R. Gibson (Englewood Cliffs, N.J.: Prentice Hall, 1973), 157–64. Reprinted by permission of Prentice Hall, a division of Simon and Schuster, Englewood Cliffs, N.J.

Ethical Invisibility and
the New Humanism

The passing decades since 1937 have indeed taken their toll. First there was a great World War which raged for five years. Many Bowdoin men were engulfed in its flames, and the youth of the world died like flies on almost every continent and on almost every ocean and on almost every island of the world. With the devastating atomic holocaust of Hiroshima and Nagasaki in 1945, the guns of war were finally silenced, but the world was left frozen with fear and distrust. Those of us in graduate school in the late years of the fatuous forties felt the fear of atomic annihilation and, remembering the Nazi swastika's horrifying *hexentanz* and the piled corpses in the concentration camps, some of us almost longed for a return to the early 1930s. It is true that those had been years of economic tension, but there was no bomb in these years and coffee was a nickel a cup and the world was too poor to wage massive war. Moreover, then, some of us were mere college freshmen full of great expectations and those absurd hopes that bloom in the garden of *naïveté*.

The mood and tensions of the late forties continued into the fearful fifties. In America the voice of McCarthy was loud in the land, intimidating the intellectual establishment and leaving many a politician castrated of both his belief and commitment. But there was something else in the air—a new note of futility and philosophic despair. In 1953, for instance, Richard Wright, creator of Bigger Thomas and Uncle Tom's children and *Black Boy*, published a novel entitled *The Outsider*. Its unknown hero, Cross Damon, was something new in black fiction. Actually, Damon is a nonperson who, through a series of fortuitous incidents, has been able to divest himself of his identity. As a nonperson and outsider there is no control, outer or inner, on his behavior, and so he murders, lies, and deceives with impunity. As a nonperson he can never be guilty or held up to society for judgment;

as a nonperson he has no sense of ethical responsibility. Indeed, as far as the law is concerned, he is invisible. How did Wright conceive of such a character? Certainly, he had encountered no such black person during his own experiences in Jackson, Mississippi; Memphis, Tennessee; Chicago, or New York City. For in all of these places the law had always been too much with the Bigger Thomases and the rest of Uncle Tom's children. Thus, Cross Damon did not come directly out of the black man's American experience. Like Wright's other male characters, he is an angry man; but he enjoys an ethical invisibility not enjoyed by Big Boy or Bigger Thomas.

The answer to the question about the source of Cross Damon is found in Wright's intellectual itinerary after he departed the United States in 1947. Joining an expanding colony of expatriate black Americans in Paris, Wright quickly became associated with Jean-Paul Sartre, Simone de Beauvoir, and other French intellectuals who represented a *nouvelle vague* in French intellectual philosophy. In many an animated conversation in many a Parisian sidewalk cafe, Richard Wright learned about the kind of atheistic existentialism then popular in Europe and how the American black man, cut off from the benefits of law and society for so long, was actually the prototype of the existential man this new philosophy conceived him to be. By the 1950s Albert Camus had already indicated in his novels—in *The Stranger* and in *The Plague*—that man's birth on this planet is an unfortunate accident and his death a fortuitous release from a life of absurd obedience to meaningless codes, laws, and traditions. His *Myth of Sisyphus* has also demonstrated the absurdity of a concept of heroic effort stressing traditions of quest, challenge, and achievement. A man's performance in the light of these codes and traditions had long been the basis by which a man was measured and by which he himself could evaluate his own civic worth and humanity. Only in so doing was he able to emerge with a definable identity and with a sense of ethical responsibility. But Sartre, Camus, and others argued that living or existing on the basis of these assumptions was not enough. In a war-weary world filled with the fear of atomic annihilation, such an existence robbed a man of the essence of his individuality. Society dictated his responses and set the terms under which those responses could be made. So the existential philosophers of postwar Europe fashioned a theory whereby man would be enabled to extricate himself from a fixed pattern of social and historical determinism and find an existence which would permit him to fulfill his essential individuality. Out of such a philosophical and intellectual context came Wright's Cross Damon, a black existential man, shorn of his social, political, civil, and legal identity and possessed only of his anger. Whereas Bigger Thomas, the native son of 1940, was guilty of all criminal charges and, along with the guilt-ridden society that produced him, held morally responsible, Cross Damon, the existential man of 1953, was morally invisible and ironically guiltless in his small guilt-ridden world.

Wright's Cross Damon immediately brings to mind Ellison's Invisible Man and Camus's Meurseult, both outsiders estranged from their respective cultures; but one also recalls the tortured antihero of Kafka's *The Trial.* This last novel, first published in 1925, after Kafka's death in 1924, presents a world of chaotic absurdity in which the hero, Joseph K., is charged with a crime but is never advised of the nature of the charge nor given a chance to defend himself. Kafka's world is one of bewildering bureaucratic complexity—one in which even the law is cloaked in a kind of institutional invisibility. Like Camus's "stranger," Meurseult, Joseph K. is the unheroic victim of a world of meaningless and absurd traditions, and both novels suggest that no one can be held morally or legally accountable or responsible in such a world.

The odyssey undertaken by Ellison's hero in *Invisible Man,* published in 1952, also suggests that a man trying to achieve racial and social justice can become the victim of the absurdities of that very society he seeks to reform. The only answer is to return to the womb of innocence—to fall out of the world of space and time as Ellison's antihero did—and hope ultimately to regain one's identity and ethical visibility and the courage needed for rebirth into a world of pain and affliction. For all of these characters, then—Joseph K., Cross Damon, Meurseult, and Ellison's nonhero—there are two ways to cope with a chaotically absurd world: withdraw or commit suicide. Certainly, the message of these writers seems to be that having a recognizable identity in such a world is in and of itself absurd; and having or assuming moral responsibility is a massive *non sequitur.*

I have discussed these literary works in order to suggest that by the mid-1950s, there appeared to be developing throughout America and the Western world the belief that man had become so alienated from his environment and his culture that few had the psychological strength and moral certitude necessary for attempting a harmonious adjustment to that culture. Many thought the attempt in itself to be absurd. As the "searing sixties" arrived and the "fearful fifties" ended, there was not doubt that there was widespread disaffection on almost every count, particularly among the youth of America and the Western world. And as this terrible decade rolled on, many adults cloaked themselves in an ethical invisibility, locking their windows and their doors so that they could not hear the agonizing screams of a Kitty Genovese as she lay dying on one of New York's crime-filled streets. Others fled to the street of dreams where they could get high or get low on hallucinating drugs and be blissfully invisible and unaware of it all. It was at this time, too, that we turned on our heroes—those who were laboring with that old-time Sisyphean energy to reclaim something from the teeming chaos of life—and in rapid order they were all shot down: John and Robert Kennedy, Martin Luther King, Jr., Malcolm X. The only Sisyphean hero left in America by the end of the decade was John Wayne—not the real John Wayne of Orange County, California—but the one who starred in *Tall in the Saddle* and swayed heroically from the hips when he walked.

By the end of the decade of the "searing sixties" we also began to see more evidence of ethical invisibility, both personal and institutional. Who really did kill John Kennedy? Lee Harvey Oswald? Or Jack Ruby, the man who killed Oswald? And who killed Jack Ruby? Who put the gun and the cash into the hands of James Earl Ray? Did Sirhan Sirhan really act alone? And there was one passionate question ringing throughout the land. Will all of those who are ethically invisible but morally responsible please come forth? Will the real killers please stand up—the sponsors, the consenters, the political godfathers who behind the web of their carefully maintained invisibility gave the nod that death should and would be done.

Institutional invisibility was even worse during this decade, for this was the time of military escalation in Vietnam. The battlefield deaths multiplied; the prisoners of war rotting in North Vietnam prison colonies multiplied; the denials, threats, and accusations in Washington multiplied; grief-stricken homes, stripped of their young men, multiplied. But throughout all of the branches and bureaus and committees and echelons of government and amid the entangled cobwebs of secrecy, was there anyone visibly responsible? Again the question could be heard—will the real Vietnam godfather please stand up and receive the kiss of homage from the damned, the hopeless, the crippled, the widowed, and the orphaned.

Probably the best example of institutional and ethical invisibility occurred following the police shootout of a Chicago Black Panther headquarters early one morning not too long ago. The headquarters was riddled with bullets and two Panthers were killed. A grand jury pinpointed the raiding police as morally responsible for the deaths of the two Panthers and indicted Edward Hanrahan, Cook County District Attorney, for withholding evidence and impeding justice. Who is really responsible for these deaths? Hanrahan, who has just been re-indorsed by his admiring public in the recent Illinois primary? Mayor Richard Daley? J. Edgar Hoover? The Panthers themselves? Or Hanrahan's supporters and endorsers?

But enough of this jeremiad of trouble and woe. The overwhelming question, as we face 1976 and the two hundredth anniversary of the Republic, is How can America be reclaimed—how can it be renewed? How can we throw off the mantle of ethical invisibility and, at the same time, unpollute the atmosphere and the environment, and, as one black poet wrote, "clean out the world for virtue and love"? How can we make America green again, to use Reich's image in his *The Greening of America?* Can we, as he suggests, hide in a "nowness" ethic, eschewing history and assuaging ourselves with what he calls the "truth serum of marijuana"? Will Consciousness III—his level of consciousness provided by the youth of the country— really drive alienation from the land, restore a sense of community, offset the power of the Corporate State, and humanize the law so that it speaks for the individual rather than for the state?

My answer is that America will not be renewed by youthful energy, candor, and vigor alone. Certainly, marijuana with its false sense of euphoria will not help. If it is a truth serum, its truth will not make one free but will neutralize him, imprisoning him and locking him in the twilight that exists between order and disorder. Certainly, too, staring in hypnotic satisfaction at one's navel in Zen-like contemplation will not help. What is needed is the kind of spiritual and moral revolution which can only come through a renewal and reinvigoration of our basic institutions. Even though the American society of the 1970s is far more complex than it was in 1776, or 1787, we must salvage the best from those articles of agreement upon which the nation was founded, supplying the added wisdom garnered from two hundred years of experience.

We now know, for instance, that there is no need to equivocate or compromise about according the black American equal status, holding him to be, not three-fifths of a man, but five-fifths of a man. And no matter which way the school bus goes—up, down, by, or around, or whether it just stays broke-down—every black and every other kind of American is five-fifths of a man in all of his legal, moral, economic, and political dimensions. Moreover, we have learned grim lessons about what industrialization and advanced technology can do to impair, pollute, and sap the environment, and we need more enforceable regulations to keep the kind of environment necessary for man's continued survival on this planet. Nor can we any longer cloak property in its former sanctity and mystique, remembering that, in the final analysis, people are more important than property.

Bound by these understandings we can then seek the aid of our institutions of higher learning in furthering a revolution that will provide a new humanism as an effective counter to the ethical invisibility that has so long dominated our behavior over the last twenty-five years. Hard-pressed as they are, our colleges and universities—particularly those free of political ties—must furnish the politicians, social engineers, humanists, truth-speakers, prophets, visionaries, scientists, statesmen, weirdos, eccentrics, and gurus who can go forth to combat the massive *anomie* and disenchantment that afflicts the land. There can be no new humanism to provide the social, spiritual, and moral renewal I am talking about without the effective participation of our institutions of higher learning.

Specifically, then, I am asking for a new humanism that will restore our institutions and make them both visible and viable. We are also asking for a new humanism that will revive a healthy individualism in what has become a crowded, urbanized, "togetherish" society. I am not asking for the return of the hero or persons of magnificent stature and godlike mien. One can reasonably expect that the time for heroes of this scope is past and that no one will walk the earth with that kind of rapture again. There will be no more Lears—old and redolent with sin and eloquent misadventure—to pin themselves on a whirling wheel of fire—no more Hamlets, groping through the sin and darkness of Elsinore and yet poetizing about the awesome beauty of man, "the paragon of animals." The time for heroes is past but we can reclaim man as individual, give him back his visibility, pull him out of hiding. Our colleges can produce the men and women of spiritual insight and moral probity who will help the individual serve the commonwealth and help the commonwealth serve the individual. When this begins to happen, we will begin to understand the mood of quiet understanding reflected in Browning's lines:

> Oh, we're sunk enough here, God knows
> But not quite so sunk that moments,
> Sure tho seldom are denied us
> When the spirit's true endowments
> Stand out plainly from its false ones.

I and my colleagues of the Class of 1937, covered as we are with the dust of our thirty-five-year pilgrimage through a weary land, ask, Does America, as it approaches its two hundredth anniversary, have its undiscovered problems "yet"? If so, will the real surgeons stand up, put aside their cloaks of invisibility and come forth to perform the social surgery needed to heal the body politic. Tennyson's Ulysses said, "Tis not too late to seek a newer world." I say it is not too late to render the invisible visible—to drain man of his fear and insecurity and give him back his dignity, if not his innocence.

NOTE

This lecture was given at Bowdoin College in 1974.

The Humanities: The Eye of the Needle
in the Black Experience

As I went about preparing to write about "The Humanities: The Eye of the Needle in the Black Experience," I uncovered, amid the dusty clutter of my study at home, two papers which I had previously written on the humanities within the last decade. The first bears the awesome and rather intimidating multisyllabic title "Ethical Invisibility and the New Humanism." The title suggests that I was trying to impress an audience with something approaching heavy erudition, but one or two points are clearly elucidated therein. First, I stated the opinion that there had developed, since World War II, a point of view that declared the Western world to be an absurdity—an absurdity of such dimensions that it could scarcely be tolerated—and writers like Kafka, Sartre, Camus, Heller, Wright, and Ellison had documented the insane absurdity of life in the Euro-West. Secondly, I observed that the most threatening absurdity facing the West was the way individual guilt was hidden in committees, bureaus, corporations, and institutions and that we needed therefore the rebirth of a humanism that would restore the accountable individual. My comment today on the last point is that our problem about the disappearance of the accountable individual has deepened with the development of the computer. Soon it may be that our society will be ordered and controlled, not by identifiable people, but by the completely anonymous computer chip.

My second paper bore the rather intriguing title "The Present Dilemma of the Humanities: A Close Encounter of the Third Kind," and one can readily infer from the title that at the time the paper was written I had seen a certain movie and was somewhat spaced out on spacey ideas. In this paper I again made two points. First, I stated what all of us know—that funding humanities research and projects has long been and will probably remain low on the totem pole of national priorities and that we are living in a postindustrial, high-tech society which is pragmatic to the bone and therefore not always able to cope with the threat of nuclear annihilation or with any other high-tech disaster. In this context, the Bhopal, India, tragedy comes to mind. My second point was that, in a world that is ever threatened by man's cupidity and lust for profits, the humanities, properly valued and properly stressed, become our only viable weapon against hysteria, bewilderment, and depression. But to strengthen the humanities so that they can furnish this kind of bulwark against defeatism, those who are custodians of the humanities—the humanists themselves—have to remove themselves from their small islands of an overly precious specialism—stop counting verbs and explicating imagery in incomprehensibly convoluted syntax—and join the real world. And I added that, if the humanist did not come out of his or her closet of hyperspecialization, then that is where he or she will be when the world totters on to nuclear disaster.

When Christ says in Matthew 19:23, "it is easier for a camel to go through the eye of a needle than for a rich man to enter into the kingdom of God," the implication is that one has to be uniquely qualified and especially prepared to enter into God's kingdom. In fact, in Matthew 19:26, Christ states that passage into the kingdom of heaven is a quintessential experience without human parallel and one that can be achieved only through God's help. So the emphasis is on a purity and clarity of focus and a concentration devoid of any worldly concern or distraction. Certainly, if one is burdened down with worldly goods or material acquisitions or is in any way encumbered, the focus and concentration needed will be lost, and one will never either glimpse the Kingdom or enjoy the deep transformation wrought by the experience.

And so it is with the black man's experience throughout the diaspora. I do not say that to encounter it is comparable to entering the kingdom of God, but I do say that for those who are alien to the culture and value systems of the Black Diaspora, a clear and untrammeled focusing will help; and, if you really want to apprehend and comprehend it fully, first understand the humanities in the black experience—understand the moral values that have deep roots in tribal cultures, understand the force of ancient rituals, rites, customs, and traditions and how these were mutated by the centuries of slavery and by the later generations of quasi-freedom after slavery. And, if one understands how, through song, dance, gesture, speech, movement, and laughter, the blacks of the diaspora express these values, then one has the key to the black experience and can comprehend it with understanding and with unalloyed pleasure—comprehend it, as it were, through the eye of a needle.

In 1984, this can be easily said at a predominantly black educational institution. It could not have been so easily said sixty years ago, in 1924, and not even thought about by "talented tenthers" one hundred years ago, in 1884. For the message twenty years after emancipation was, let us strive to forget everything associated with the monumental disgrace of slavery. And all blacks strove—those who had been slaves and those who had not—all strove to evade the stigma of blackness which in turn was associated with the degradation and dishonor of slavery, and all sought to flee the impact of derogatory epithets and stereotypes which were so widely employed by whites in their interactions with blacks. The message then was for all blacks to prepare themselves for some kind of integration and acceptance into the majority culture as soon as possible. So, if you recall, a long campaign began to unkink our hair, lighten our skin color, talk a little better, stay a little cleaner; and we tried not to laugh too loud and not dress too loud and just not to be "too black." And as you will also recall, the effort to escape blackness was concentrated most heavily for many years at black institutions of learning. As Booker T. Washington's *Up from Slavery* suggests, these schools stressed a somewhat rigid and puritanical white mid-Victorian value system; the idea was to mold a "colored" intelligentsia whose members, in their intense preoccupation with white value systems, would retain no memory whatsoever of slavery or of the traditions rooted in the black experience throughout the diaspora.

Inevitably, there were problems with such a program of indoctrination. For how do you divest yourself of your past and not be condemned to repeat it? How do you dispose of rich folkloric racial memories and traditions? How can you hear the jazz drumbeat and not remember other drums talking to tribal ancestors long ago and far away. How could you consult a numbers dream book or a palmist or a spiritualist and not think of Obeah or Vodun? Especially did the problem become very complex after World War I during the 1920s. As you recall, the uptown section of New York's Manhattan Island known as Harlem became colored America's favorite piece of real estate. Blacks who were then, by their own choice, called coloreds, came into Harlem from everywhere—from the Carolinas, Virginia, Georgia, Florida—from all of the islands of the Caribbean, from California, from Tennessee and Kentucky. But the numbers were not the problem; the life-style exhibited by the newcomers was the problem. They laughed too loud; they strutted up and down Harlem's tree-lined streets with bold abandon and with a rhythmic walk that was out of this world. They held loud rent parties far into the night at which they served pigs feet, whiskey, beer, and gin, rice and blackeyed peas, hog maws, corn bread, chitterlings, rice and gravy, potato salad, and whatever else you could pay for. They played jazz the way it had never been played before, and all of the jazz greats—Ellington, Johnny Hodges, Fletcher Henderson, John P. Johnson, Noble Sissle, and Eubie Blake—lived there. And, of course, they danced madly at cabarets like LeRoy's and in ballrooms like the Savoy, Roseland, and the Rhinelander. They had long parades and on Saturday nights sometimes knives flashed and bleeding folk crowded into overworked emergency wards. And those who had money sniffed coke and smoked gage which they bought from the reefer man that Cab Calloway sang about. Whites drifted up from downtown seeking sin, sex, and syncopation, and at least one—Carl Van Vechten—went back downtown to write about what he had seen and heard. He called his book *Nigger Heaven*.

The black life-style depicted in *Nigger Heaven* in 1926 and later in Claude McKay's *Home to Harlem* in 1928 was, of course, exaggerated, but novels like these did suggest that Harlem was not filled with what was deemed to be a "New Negro." For when, in 1925, Alain Locke announced the birth of a "New Negro" at *Opportunity Magazine's* famous awards banquet, he meant a person of culture, good breeding, and refined artistic and esthetic sensibilities who disdained a murky, shameful past and looked boldly toward a future bright with performance and achievement. Indeed, an avant-garde white world eagerly awaited this "New Negro," for the culturally elite of the white majority was prepared to open doors of opportunity to all "New Negroes" who could write, paint, or sculpt. Relatively new publishing houses like Viking and Knopf and older houses like Harper's were ready to read, review, and publish their stories, novels, or articles. And many arbiters of culture like James Weldon Johnson and Walter White predicted that longstanding racial barriers would fall, once the New Negro fully emerged to be seen, heard, published, and read.

But, even as Alain Locke extolled his new discovery, some who were called representative New Negroes had their doubts. Langston Hughes, for instance, liked what he saw about the life-style of the "Old Negro"—his parties, his parades, his piano-playing blues men, his juke joints—and he participated eagerly in happenings of the day and night and wrote poems about a Harlem which for him was Jazzonia:

> Droning a drowsy syncopated tune
> Rocking back and forth to a mellow croon
> I heard a Negro play.

In fact, Hughes thought that the best subject that a black poet could write about was the very black life-style that seemed to be so offensive to advocates of the "New Negro." So in 1926 the poet, with great clarity, stated his position in an article published in the *Nation*. The title of the article is "The Negro Artist and the Racial Mountain." In it, Hughes stated his belief that every black writer should be free to celebrate his ethnicity in his or her own way, without dictation from anyone. He also promised to celebrate and extol the black life-style, particularly the life-style of the lower black classes.

If the *cognoscenti* did not approve, they could literally go to hell. Those who remember Langston Hughes know that he never broke his promise, and in all of his writings in fiction, poetry, and drama he celebrated the average black man's style and championed his causes. I might add that other writers of the Harlem Renaissance joined Langston Hughes in his stand—the bohemian Bruce Nugent, the intense Wallace Thurman, the flamboyant Zora Neal Hurston, the talented Louise Thompson.

The person who was truly perturbed by it all was William Edward Burghardt Du Bois, editor of *The Crisis* and by every measure a great intellectual in black American life. Du Bois knew about the black life-style and in the chapter on the "Sorrow Songs" in *Souls of Black Folk* (1903) he wrote poetically and with great feeling of one aspect of the black man's artistic response to his experience in the new world. And in his 1924 work, *The Gift of Black Folk,* he wrote that black people had left an indelible "imprint" on America because they exhibited "a certain spiritual joyousness; a sensuous tropical love of life; . . . a slow and dreamful conception of the universe; a drawling and slurring of speech, an intense sensitiveness to spiritual values. . . . " But Van Vechten's *Nigger Heaven,* with its exaggerated and highly naturalistic depiction of Harlem's vice and decadence, so alienated Du Bois that he called a conference in late 1926 to reiterate his opposition to fiction and any of the other expressive arts which celebrated the more sensational aspects of the black life-style and did not propagandize the black man's worthiness for integration. For that, in Du Bois's opinion, was the one objective—to have white America accept Afro-America without discrimination, without segregation, without racial housing convenants, and without lynching. Nor did he want any celebration of the way black folk danced or the way they sang the blues or played jazz. Indeed, he wanted to suppress all of the black man's vast folkloric heritage that he had brought with him out of slavery—all of the secular tunes, all of the stories, all of the tales. These, he thought, were deterrents to integration and, if unduly publicized, would promote further separatism from, and not assimilation into, the majority culture.

What were the consequences of Du Bois's taking this position? The search for an answer to this question takes us into the inner chambers of the NAACP in the late 1920s. As you know, Du Bois had been editor of the *Crisis* since its founding in 1910; and, as the saying goes, he ran a tight ship. From the beginning, he insisted and persisted in defying the NAACP board on many occasions with regard to *Crisis* editorial policy and considered himself really not accountable to anyone in the organization. Some say that he would occasionally listen to Joel Spingarn or to James Weldon Johson after the latter joined the staff in 1916, but the *Crisis* remained firmly under Du Bois's control. Under his guidance it became an organ of strong racial protest and a publication that celebrated Negro intellectual, social, and political achievement. No deviation from this editorial stance was intended when, during World War I, Jessie Fauset, a Cornell Phi Beta Kappa and litterateur, joined the *Crisis* staff as literary editor. Literary reviews would be published and some of the new poetry would either be noted or published, but the overall objective remained—to promote racial uplift and provide social and political data to support and justify racial progress. In other words, Du Bois never intended for the *Crisis* to promote black *belles lettres* or celebrate black art and culture. After Carl Van Vechten's *Nigger Heaven* was published in 1926, Du Bois's position hardened against the celebration of Negro art and the life-style of Harlem's residents. So, after 1926, the *Crisis* held no more award-giving banquets to celebrate Negro art and Negro artists. And Du Bois argued for his position so forcefully that Jessie Fauset resigned her literary editorship after some bitter exchanges with the strong-minded editor, thus terminating a friendship of twenty years. After her departure, Du Bois turned his full, unfettered fury against those members of the Harlem Renaissance writers group whom he called "the debauched tenth"—McKay, Hurston, Nugent, Thurman, and Hughes—and he wrote caustic and searing reviews of their work. His message was crystal clear: Don't celebrate the black life-style with its jazz and blues and laughter and dancing feet and poverty. Instead, plead the black man's economic and social and political worth, and write, paint, and sculpt only to achieve racial integration.

We now know that time has proven Du Bois wrong. Gradually we have come to accept the black man's rich cultural past in all of its varied dimensions—his music of every kind, whether bawdy, bluesy, spiritual, or jazzy—his tall tales of "mules and men" and John the Conqueror. We now recognize his gift for rhythmic dance, his love of color, and his love of exhibition both on the stage and on the athletic field or basketball court. All of this becomes the black humanistic tradition which our predominantly black institutions are obligated to nurture, celebrate, and safeguard. For the artistic and cultural history of the Black Diaspora reflects the moral values and beliefs that are part of our racial heritage. This was the message of the formulators of the concept of Negritude—Senghor, Damas, and Cesaire—in the 1940s and 1950s. And this was the message of the Black Arts advocates of the 1960s. This was the message of Paule Marshall's *Praise Song for the Widow,* a novel in which a respectable and affluent black widow from prestigious North White Plains, New York, reconnects with her African past by participating in the "beg pardon" ritual dance on the island of Carriacou in the Caribbean. And this is the message of Carolyn Rodgers's beautifully wrought poem "It is Deep," in which she describes her mother as a "sturdy black bridge," thus invoking memories of other black mothers who, "girdled in their religion," kept climbing, although life was "no crystal stair." And in this context, we remember the mother of Olaudah Equiano and how, at the age of nine, he was kidnapped from her loving arms. We remember the mother of Phillis Wheatley and how in her Senegalese homeland she broke bread every morning with her face to the rising sun. For black mothering is different, distinctive, and unique—something out of a rich cultural past—a past that preceded the diaspora and the dispersal of the black man throughout the Western Hemisphere.

Can the predominantly black educational institution accept the challenge to be the primary custodian of the black humanities? The answer is yes. Beethoven's sonatas will continue to be played and Voltaire will continue to be read, but students will also read about Billy Bolden, New Orleans's first jazz trumpeter, and about legends of the Anse and the tales of the griot. If the black institution fulfills this trust, we can then remain close to the eye of the needle as far as the black experience is concerned.

NOTE

This lecture was given at the Atlanta University Center in 1984.

PART 3

Literary Forms of Historical Survival

Metaphors of Black American
Literary History

Urban Crisis and the
Black Poetic Avant-Garde

As inevitably as orchids, blood-red in their soaring beauty, spring forth to blossom in the jungle swamp, a new black poetry has burst forth in the Negro ghetto. Essentially this is a phenomenon of America's searing sixties, although the flatulent fifties and even the fatuous forties gave some hints that a new esthetic in poetry was about to be born. All that was needed was the catalyst of racial turmoil, burning cities, screaming sirens, searing poverty amid complacent affluence, and the poets began to speak and write. And they are young—too young to be included in Rosey Pool's 1962 anthology. Some are in Robert Hayden's 1967 anthology, *Kaleidoscope*—like David Henderson, who was born in 1943 and first made the poetic scene with his published poetry in *Umbra* in 1963. Others are even younger and have never been anthologized, like Don Lee of Chicago or Etheridge Knight of Detroit, both of whom are being published by the highly contemporary Broadside Press located right in the middle of Detroit's "riot turf." These poets are a generation away from Gwendolyn Brooks, two generations away from Langston Hughes; their aesthetic "Daddy" is the new LeRoi Jones—not the one who received his M.A. in philosophy from Columbia but the one who received his jail sentence in Newark.

Theirs is not a poetry for comfort-loving academicians or gentle intellectuals with bourgeois graces. They announce that theirs is a poetry by and for and of black people. Writes Don Lee:

> Bravery is that
> little black man
> over there
> surrounded by people
> he's talking—
> truth

> they say
> he's
> a
> poet.

This kind of poet wanders through the ghetto's crowded streets, threading his way through the human litter and the fragmented men and women who hang out on the desperate corners of existence, and his, as Ted Joans writes, is a "Voice in the Crowd":

> If you should see
> a man
> walking down a crowded street
> talking aloud
> to himself, don't run
> in the opposite direction
> but run toward him
> for he is a poet!
>
> You have nothing to fear
> from the poet but the truth.

One might venture to ask what kind of poetry can come out of a ghetto. There are many descriptive adjectives that can be used to answer such a query, but the first and best is the word "revolutionary." Like the poetry of John Donne or Percy Bysshe Shelley, the poetry of the black avant-garde makes a sharp, clean break with the past. There are no literary prognosticators who can explain or predict developing patterns and trends. As a matter of fact, these poets, like so many other poets in the past, will have no truck with academicians and literary prognosticators. They are eloquently antiestablishment and anti–power structure and they vilify academicians who, according to one poet, have minds that have been raped by *Reader's Digest,* European history and promises. Similarly, they are also antireligion and anticleric and heap scorn on the Negro preachers driving Volkswagens and explicating the Judeo-Christian truths which, somehow, still have left the black man entrapped in his ghetto. For these young poets, no traditional institution of Western civilization needs to be preserved or venerated or protected or enshrined or respected. Western history for them is a curse and the American here-and-now an abomination. Like other revolutionaries, they are groping for some coherent and disciplined approach to an understanding of the particular aspects of their human condition. Indeed, they are black Tom Paines of poetry, seething with angry denunciations of the *status quo,* and will probably be, just like the white Tom Paine, buried deep in the slag of human history by that very *status quo.* Rejecting Western history, they will probably never encounter the paradox hidden in that history that both revolutions and revolutionaries tend to devour each other and that all sweet and great revolutionary causes are somehow sicklied o'er with the pale cast of an inexplicable, pernicious, and often self-defeating masochism.

But stating that these young black poets are antihistory does not really define their "thing." Their "thing" is protest—strident, articulate, arrogant, bitter, caustic protest. And they present their protest in language that has no verbal fat. Their poems will never wither away because of too much literary cholesterol. Like John Donne, the young black poet achieves a direct confrontation with emotional experience but there is no tortured, Donnesque verbalization of that experience. Theirs is always the direct statement denuded of qualifying niceties to appease a squeamish bourgeoisie. For instance, Calvin Hernton writes in "Street Scene":

> I met my dream
> Walking down the street—
>
> *Hello, Dream!*
>
> Dream spoke back—
> "Go to hell, sonofabitch!"

And of course, sex, about which so many other poets like Whitman and Rossetti have danced stately verbal pirouettes, is reduced to explicit four-letter words, and the word "mother" is ghettoized into something more than a disyllable meaning female progenitor. For some inexplicable reason, it becomes a hard-nosed polysyllabic and somewhat incestuous adjective, full of sound and fury and signifying nothing but the postured and somewhat theatrical flippancy of the young poet who would protest too much. Be that as it may, sex is handled at times with an elegant verbal condensation. Ree Dragonette writes, for instance:

> I was God
> In her tongue and fingers
> I broke like glass.

Or a young poet like Joe Johnson writes as Andrew Marvell wrote of his coy mistress. The difference is that ghetto citizen Joe Johnson's mistress is not only not coy but she's white. Their interracial sexual encounter, however, is full of a Marvellian hostility and bitter amorous strife:

> . . . We'll relieve the hostile
> Eons;
> Breathe, Lashing the frigid
> Nonrhythmic opaqueness. Your
> ignorance of Alaga syrup, fat back,
> Johnny Ace's pain;

> I'll give the synthetic kiss
> And wait for the white tear.
> Hold time baby; I'll give it to you
> 'Cause a staid spade is not a
> shade—the tear is cold.
> I'll give you the kiss
> 'Cause a razor stings and lye burns
> And Booker T can't speak and
> Malcolm's hard and sharp:
> Hold time, baby, it's coming.

But there is more to be said about the black poetic avant-garde than that theirs is a poetry of protest or that they describe emotional experience with an explicit directness. Allen Ginsberg and the beat poets of the fifties achieved this much. Ron Karenga, the West Coast apostle of black cultural nationalism, argues that the poetry of the black avant-garde has a specific and identifiable ideological thrust. It is a poetry dedicated to the achievement of radical social change and hence is "functioning, collective and committed." In this ideological context the poet can never be an alienated or isolated individualist communing with himself within the sacred walls of his own emotional privacy. Rather he speaks for and to and with a black audience. An example of the collective poetic statement might be Ted Joans's "Think Twice and Be Nice":

> All God's spades got shades
>   and some of God's Spades
> (you'll never know which one)
> has got long-sharp protective
>   blades   So I shall repeat
> (though he may be raggidy or neat)
> All God's spades got shades.

In another sense, James Emmanuel seems to be saying in his "The Negro" that ironically the black man has always been denied a unique individuality:

> Never saw him.
> Never can.
> Hypothetical
> Haunting man;
>
> Eyes a-saucer
> Yessis boss-sir
> Dice a-clicking
> Razor flicking.
>
> The-ness froze him
> In a dance

A-ness never
Had a chance.

There is even some hint in Karenga's esthetic of commitment that the blues with its emphasis on the eloquent but passive suffering of an isolated individual cannot fit into the cultural context of the black avant-garde. Somehow the almost romantic *cri-de-coeur* of the blues singer highlighting the plight of an individual is too self-pitying to effect social change. Rather than the lament of a lost love or a song of sorrow about the psychological impact of a rainy Monday, Karenga would prefer Don L. Lee's "Bloodsmiles":

> I remember the time
> when I could smile
> smiles of ignorance ...
> now—smiles do not come
> as easily as
> they are
> supposed to.
> My smiles are
> now fixed
> and
> come slowly
> like the gradual
> movement of tomatoes
> in a near empty
> ketchup bottle
> about to be
> eaten.

Both Karenga and Lee would argue that "Bloodsmiles" speaks for all black people entrapped in poverty-stricken ghettoes. The blues singer talks about losing his woman; Don Lee talks about losing his soul.

There are, however, two important omissions in Karenga's exposition of the black avant-garde esthetic. The first is the risk involved in any art exclusively dedicated to effecting social change. Sometimes, the net result may be poetry that is not art but an angry diatribe against the *status quo*, like LeRoi Jones's lines about "wrassling cops into alleys, taking their weapons, leaving them dead with tongues pulled out and sent to Ireland," or Don Lee's "The Black Christ," which is full of corrosive bitterness, biting irony, and black hatred of the establishment:

> without a doubt
> rome did the whi
> te thing when it
> killed
>> christ

it has been proven
that j.c. was non-white
in the darkest
way possible

                    . . .

all the negro
preachers are driving
volkswagens & back
in night high school
                    taking black speech
                    & black history
off one god
can't get hooked on another elijah

This passage, however, is not nearly as explosive and full of a stridently rhetorical black anger as Joseph Bevan Bush's "Nittygritty":

We all gonna start thinking
In terms of total protection
And preparing ourselves for the
Third World; realizing that
We are "struggling with depraved
Eagles" who, having a horrible
    history
Of mass murder and inflicting pain,
Will stop at nothing to destroy us.
All this is to say: throat-
Cutting time is drawing nigh and
We all gonna be ready.

These lines are full of violent revolutionary zeal; the program for social change is clear and unmistakable; but the question arises, is this poetry or mere revolutionary rhetoric?

A focal question to be asked and, I hope, given at least a partial answer, in an attempt to evaluate the black poetic avant-garde, is, How angry can a man be and remain a poet or an artist? With these young men and young women there is total engagement, total commitment, total involvement and immersion in their "thing"—social revolution. Esthetic distance is impossible and unforgivable; a cool, disciplined detachment which would free the poetic imagination to play with viable esthetic alternatives to satisfy the poet's soul is unheard of. If the black poet should ever try such a white play, he would promptly be accused, in the words of Etheredge Knight, of pandering his individual experience to the white world and hence working in the foundry where his chains are forged. In other words, the black avant-garde poet does not have the freedom to choose, select, and reject themes, and this lack of freedom of the imagination to seize upon any truth and make it plain is a serious defect in the artistic health of the movement. In other words, the black poetic avant-garde needs the wise counsel of Gwendolyn Brooks who, when asked "Should black writers direct their work toward black audiences?," replied, "No. They should concern themselves with TRUTH. Truth should be put upon paper. That phrase 'direct their work' suggests a secret contempt for the intelligence of the black audience." And she might have added that if the black artist is forced to function within a limited and prescribed cultural context, his esthetic reach will never exceed his grasp. To talk with the tall angels of his fancy, he must first be freed of his anger.

One final word about this young poet who has come forth from the rubble and decay of the ghetto; he is a sort of existential man. There is not in his poetry any discernible metaphysical "otherness"—no grand referent with which all things cohere and to which all things refer. There are no viable institutions—no religion, no history. As LeRoi Jones states at the end of "A Poem for Democrats":

> Distress
> Europe has passed, we are alone.
> Europe frail woman dead, we are
> alone.

In this world of direct existential confrontation with blackness, the black poet can talk with himself or seek a black identity with a black audience, it is true. And moving in such a world, he avoids the Kafkaesque patterns of absurdity of a man completely devoid of faith. But will he ever write a poem about snow and how someone does something with snow to make robins and roses come and how the earth secretly softens and keeps poems and seeds warm for "us who sleep in one another's arms"? I doubt it. And therein lies the pity of it all. He will never sing of spring or birdsongs or love. The poet of the black avant-garde, I am afraid, will continue to move in a world of charred beams and splintered glass and roasted rats where men die outraged and indecently "shouting impieties and betrayal." For him there will never be any searing apocalyptic vision—only the cobweb of creative insecurity and the dance of death on some "paddy's" extremities.

NOTE

Reprinted with permission from *Black American Literature Forum* 3, no. 2 (Summer 1969): 40–44.

White Triangles,
Black Circles

World-wide dusk
Of dear dark faces,
Driven before an alien wind,
Scattered like seed
From far-off places
Growing in soil
That's strange and thin.

Hybrid plants
In another's garden,
Flowers
In a land
That's not your own,
Cut by the shears
Of the white-faced gardeners—
Tell them to leave you alone!

These lines, written by Langston Hughes and published in *Opportunity Magazine* in 1930, reflect the poet's use of the alien-exile theme, as Arthur Davis has pointed out in his essay on Hughes in *From the Dark Tower* (1974). But the poem "Black Seed" says something more. The poem shows that by 1930 when Hughes was twenty-eight years old he had already become sensitized to what we now learnedly refer to as "the Black Diaspora"—that long and massive and forced dispersal of black people from their native Africa to the Americas, and to the islands of the Atlantic and the Caribbean—a vast forced migration that went on for four centuries to feed Europe's greed and develop and exploit the richnesses of the new land in the West. During the centuries-long trauma which bled many African tribes of their people power and left them powerless to resist the later imperialistic rape of Africa of the nineteenth and twentieth centuries, "Black Seed[s]," to use Langston Hughes's most appropriate phrase, were scattered from the Rio de la Plata—Argentina's "River of Silver"—all the way up into Canada and along the inhospitable shores of Nova Scotia. Undoubtedly, what went on was Europe's most successful venture in sustained capitalistic exploitation and ruthless profiteering. Millions of black bodies were kidnapped and then moved to the barracoons that dotted the western coasts of Africa. Then, evil-smelling slave ships made millions of trips to deposit their cargo in Jamaica, in Brazil, in Guadeloupe, in Newport, Rhode Island, and in Charleston, South Carolina. Once emptied of human cargo, these ships were then loaded with the produce of slave labor—silver and gold from Hispanic America, sugar and spices from the Caribbean, cotton and tobacco and rice and indigo from the American Southland, and thus the pattern for the great trade triangle was formed. For ships that carried the kidnapped in chains for forced labor in the Americas and returned to Europe and England with their holds full of the product of forced labor could then return to Africa with the bullets, guns, and cloth and rum used in the trade for more kidnapped black labor.

But our convention theme—"Le Circuit Triangulaire"—implies far more about triangles than the trade triangle built by European capitalism. Not only does the theme suggest a magnificent paradox—a forced blending of two unlike principles, circularity and triangularity—the kind of blending of unlikes that fascinated Donne and Herbert and the seventeenth-century English metaphysicals, but the theme suggests that in the process of building a "circuit triangulaire," black people and their seed were caught up in and enmeshed in triangles—triangles not of their own making—triangles that inhibited and suppressed and compressed and fragmented them. For instance, in *The Big Sea,* Langston Hughes describes how he shipped out to Africa as a merchant seaman after that somewhat catastrophic year at Columbia and how, as he approached the green-clad hills of Africa, he exulted: "My Africa, Motherland of the Negro peoples! And me a Negro!" Then, almost immediately he became aware that, long before his time, human triangles had been formed to shape and predetermine his life and destiny. For the Africans he met told him that he couldn't be a Negro with that kind of hair and that kind of skin. For this reason, the poet states quite flatly in *The Big Sea,* "Unfortunately I am not black." Behind his assertion is the fact that on his father's side there was some triangulation involving a Jewish slave-dealer of Kentucky and a distiller of Scottish extraction. And on his mother's side there was triangulation involving a white great-grandfather, a Virginia planter named Captain Ralph Quarles, and a great-grandmother who in turn was the product of the union between a Cherokee woman and a French merchant. So Langston Hughes, on a personal basis, knew how black seed had been blown in many directions by alien winds, and he knew how past human triangles promoted by lust and greed had made his return to Africa not the homecoming he had envisioned.

At this point, let us pause briefly to explore the oppositional concepts of triangularity and circularity and hopefully gain a fuller understanding of their cultural and historical meanings as far as black people are concerned. First, let us look at the triangle. In geometric terms, it is a sort of three-legged monster, full of sharp angles and jagged corners. About it there is no symmetry, and, with the exception of the equilateral triangle, very little or no harmonious equivalency. Usually one leg is unequal, or one angle is unequal. Indeed, one may hypothecate that the one singular property of the triangle is that somewhere within its jagged confines there is some element that is unequal. Indeed, triangularity suggests inequality. But, moving away from plane geometry implications, triangularity suggests something else. A triangular figure like the medieval archer's bow suggests a killing power and strength. One of the basic principles of artillery gunnery is the principle of triangulation; the artillery piece, the target, and the forward observer form a triangle, and, I might add that the principle of inequality still pertains; in this case it is the target, particularly after the target has been zeroed in, which process is in and of itself a form of triangulation. Moreover, in architectural terms, buildings which use the principle of the triangle have great strength and endurance. The Egyptian sphinx is just such an example. And I do not doubt that an element of triangulation is behind the tremendous force that propels a swept-wing jet fighter through the upper air at speeds faster than sound. So triangularity connotes inequality, a killing thrust and power, and a time-resistant endurability.

In this sense, the black man, throughout the centuries, has been harassed and almost destroyed by white triangulation—a triangulation that has been ruthlessly enduring and compact with smothering inequities. And here the reference is not only to the triangulations involved in the fearsome rape and shameful begetting of mulattoes, mustees, zambos, and mustifinos when captains and overseers and bosses made "their retching rampage among the luminous Black pudding," to use Gwen Brooks's phrase. Triangulation here also refers to movement and harried flight, trying to get from "can't to can" and ending up in "won't and want." Study, if you will, the triangulated movements of Martin Delaney, moving from Charlestown, Virginia, to Chambersburg, Pennsylvania, to Pittsburgh, to New York, to Chicago, to Canada, to Philadelphia, and then that long hypotenuse leap to the Niger valley—restlessly in search of a home and peace of mind. A brilliant man by any standard, Martin Delaney lived a life that was cut up into sharp angles of movement—angles of movement so typical of the free black in antebellum America. And the patterns of angular flight and movement did not end with the Civil War. In a desperate search for a living, blacks in the post-Reconstruction years of 1879–80 fled first to Kansas under the leadership of a self-styled black Moses named Pap Singleton, and once in Kansas where the climate was cold and white folks hostile they made little desperate triangles of movement from this place to that place to that other place, striving to get "anyplace but here," to use the title given the book by Bontemps and Conroy. And there is no history book about twentieth-century America that does not recount the black man's angles of flight from South to North and from city to city during the great migrations of World War I and the equally fevered migrations from South to West during World War II. Some of us sing, "God bless the child that has his own," but there is also another song, God bless the child who in the zigzag angularities of life knows when to zig and when to zag.

If the black man as a free man has led a life full of sharp angles, how much more bedeviled by sharp angles of movement and changes was the black man in slavery. Living at the whim of the master and fully in his power, the slave was the victim of a triangle that pitted his master and all of society against him. He was the target against whom every law and every gun pointed. Elizabeth Keckley's *Behind the Scenes, or Thirty Years a Slave and Four in the White House* is a book that is full of her triangulations as a slave. In it

> the reader senses the hopeless monotony of a slave's existence—the floggings, the tensions, the conflicts, the endless concern for the trivial proprieties and insipid amenities of the master-slave relationship. One also senses how quickly a slave's life could suffer radical alteration at a master's whim or some change in family fortunes. It was thus that as a young woman, Mrs. Keckley (then plain "Lizzie") was moved out of a warm family relationship in Virginia to a rather complicated situation in St. Louis, Missouri. Of particular interest was her stay in Hillsboro, North Carolina, for here she not only suffered a brutal and forcible rape, which was the usual lot of the female slave, but something else even more sinister in the catalogue of slavery's evils. For several months, a young Christian minister flogged her every Saturday because he thought it his Christian duty to induce in her a demeanor more fitting for a slave.[1]

For this reason, those who, like Fred Douglass and Henry Garnett, angled their way to a sort of freedom were giants for their time and age. So were the "maroons," or "cimarróns," as the Spanish called them—those clusters of fugitive slaves, who in the seventeenth and eighteenth centuries in Brazil, Guadeloupe, Saint Domingue, and Jamaica banded together in large guerrilla groups and waged sustained warfare against plantation owners. One such cimarron leader on Guadeloupe in the seventeenth century was Francisque Fabulé. A tall and able military leader, he was never defeated. In the end, French colonialists signed a treaty with him, granting him his freedom, a thousand pounds of tobacco, an official hug, and a ceremonial sword.

But Francisque Fabulé was a notable exception on Guadeloupe. In the late eighteenth century a slave woman named Solitude, so realistically portrayed in a novel entitled *A Woman Called Solitude* by André Schwarz-Bart, did not fare so well. Conceived on a slave ship as the result of a union between an unknown seaman and a young black woman named Bayangumay during the so-called *pariade,* Solitude was born, so the record states, about 1772 on the du Parc plantation in the commune of Carbet de Capesterre on the island of Guadeloupe.[2] Initially, because of her light skin, the young slave girl was named Rosalie and moved to the big house to be given a genteel rearing befitting her *métis* coloring. But, somehow, her life was full of sharp angles and jagged corners, despite the fact that she was a beautiful *métisse.* Somehow, she became known as a zombie, a sort of deluded sleepwalker, at times immobile and silent, at other times filled with shrieking laughter. When, in 1795, the French Revolution came to the island, Solitude's life angled off first into comedy and then into tragedy. After the confusion and turmoil of revolution left plantations burned and slaves scattered, she joined a group of runaways and with them enjoyed a few months of happiness living deep in a rain forest; here she conceived a child with a gentle man from Mozambique known as Maimouni—a man who, shortly after arriving in Guadeloupe, had escaped into the depths of the rain forest. Then, after a short anguished flight from pursuing soldiers, Maimouni died; and there was so much death and killing that a saying went around among the blacks: "The white man is like God; whatever you do, he kills you." And the record reads that the woman called Solitude, aged thirty, was executed on 20 November 1802, one day after her child was delivered. A M. Vigneaux, a notary who was among the fashionable persons attending her execution, wrote that, as she marched to her death guarded by four horsemen of the empire, she looked like a pathetic old woman with her gaunt and bony figure clothed in a tattered Creole nightgown and her gray hair matted with sweat over her forehead. Although it is also written that, as she approached the guillotine, she burst out laughing, her story is one of a woman hopelessly enmeshed in jagged triangles, from her birth to her death.

In this sense, then, triangulation implies inequity, power ruthlessly exercised, and persons hopelessly victimized. Racial triangles endure with all of their jagged pain and hurt for generations, driving a man like Langston Hughes to write, first, a poem called "Cross" about a man who was "neither white nor black," and then another poem entitled "Mulatto," and then a play called *Mulatto,* and then a short story, "Father to Son," about the same subject, and finally a musical entitled *Barrier* about the same subject. It may safely be conjectured that these five approaches to the mulatto theme in four different genres reflected the poet's painful absorption in one of the triangles bred of slavery. Other writers from William Wells Brown and Harriet Beecher Stowe down to Nella Larsen, Jessie Fauset, and William Faulkner have also explored the tragedy and pain of those who are "neither white nor black," but only Hughes had the versatility and the apparent psychological need to treat the subject five times in four different ways.

If the triangle symbolizes painful inequities and jagged points of power, the circle is on the other hand all symmetry and harmony. It connotes a beginning and a return—a voyage that does not abandon one among strangers but a voyage that returns one to the warmth and love of his or her homeland. Geometrically speaking, circles irradiate the principle of equality; they can be cut up into matching halves and quarters, and all circles, big and small, have circumferences that span the same number of degrees. And any point on that circumference is equidistant from the center. Indeed, a circle can give the appearance of some kind of equality even to a triangle, for it is written that if a circle is drawn so as to intersect the angles of a triangle or what geometricians call the vertices, perpendicular lines drawn from the three sides of the triangle will then meet in the center of the circle. So circles can give a glimmer of coherence and order even to the triangle. In art, the circle betokens beauty and fulfillment, and circular rounded forms suggest the fecund and the fruitful. As the sun and the moon and the stars circle the earth which itself moves on something of a circular orbit, one almost senses that circularity is the rule of the Universe itself—wheels within wheels within wheels, to paraphrase Ezekiel. For do not the seasons recur in some kind of predictable circular fashion—the renewal of spring always following the blight and death of winter? Do not the great birds of the air follow the seasons in their departures and their returns? So the circle implies a returning, a rebirth, and a renewal. Admittedly, the circle begat the wheel which in turn begat a medieval instrument of torture and the wheel has in turn spawned the speed that kills, but circularity still implies symmetry, harmony, a felicitous returning, a second coming and a second going. In such a world, one can have a Ulysses venturing forth for ten years and then returning to Ithaca and his beloved Penelope.

For black people engulfed in slavery, of course, there was never any felicitous returning. They knew nothing about the renewals and the rebirths implied by the principle of circularity. At least, they did not know it as something of this earth, and it may be conjectured that the appeal of the

Great Awakening to the slave in the American eighteenth century is that it gave him a sense of a world and a place where there could be a returning and a rejoining. So they could sing their hope that the circle would be unbroken and they could sing when friends and relatives were being sold and separated:

> Goodbye, Goodbye
> If I nevah, nevah see you any mo.
> Goodbye, Goodbye
> I will meet you on the other side of the sho.

In other words, they spoke of a returning and a rejoining that was not of this world. All yearned to return to their homes and villages and tribal sanctuaries, and all yearned to find the saltwater on which the slave ships had plowed their way, but it was an empty dream quickly dissipated amid the sweat, the floggings, and the relentless torture of slavery.

But you can't flog away the dreams of all the dreamers and the songs of all the singers. During centuries of enslavement, black people kept on singing and their songs held the memory of Africa and, as art forms, retained a certain kind of circularity. Through music there was a kind of returning to a lost homeland. When they worked in the fields, they sang; when they worked on the water, they sang; when they worked in the "big house," they sang; and when they worked on the docks, they sang. Indeed, their songs had a certain circular pattern about them, for they usually involved a call and a response. One singer would shout: "Early one mo'ning!" And another singer would answer, "Early one mo'ning!" And white folks who heard these songs for the first time—folks like Fanny Kemble and those who went to work in Port Royal and on the Sea Islands early in the Civil War—said that they were strange and wild and disturbing songs, simply because they reflected an African and not a European harmonic system. It was a music of bluesy thirds and flatted fifths, interspersed with whoops and hollas. It was a music that circled back to Africa—a music of polyrhythmic intensity—a music that made people dance—a music that was a cathartic for the pain and misery of slavery.

As we know, there were many over the centuries who fought the system and some who, through luck, courage, and fortuitous circumstances, actually broke out of the encompassing triangle of master, overseer, and "pateroller." One such was Olauda Equiano, who was kidnapped and enslaved from Iboland at the age of ten. Initially, he was the helpless and powerless victim of enthralling triangles. Sold in Barbados. Sold in Virginia. A few years of freedom at sea during the conflict between the British and the French. And then sold again in the United States. Fortunately, he was able to buy his freedom from this last period of enslavement and flee to

England. Here he became involved with Granville Sharpe and others in the effort to establish a colony for black freedmen in Sierra Leone, and here he began to dream of a return to his African homeland. When he was placed in charge of provisioning the ships with food and cargo, he seemed assured of a chance to see his beloved Africa once more. But difficulties developed; when Equiano exposed some instances of theft and double-dealing with ships' stores, he was dismissed from his position. How dare a black man bring such charges! Undaunted by this reversal in a life filled with reversals, he then applied to be appointed a bishop for the new colony. This application was turned down also. So Equiano never completed the circle and never returned to Africa. His disappointment was great, but he found some alleviation in the fact that he had worked hard to help to get the Sierra Leone project underway. He was also compensated both psychologically and financially by the immense success of his 1789 account of his life and travels. The book went through nine editions after his death in 1797.

There were other blacks, however, who were a little more successful in their efforts to fight the system and return to Africa. One such was Thomas Peters, who had been a slave in Wilmington, North Carolina, until he and his wife, Sally, escaped to British lines during the Revolutionary War. Peters joined the British forces and rose to the rank of sergeant in a British army unit known as the Black Pioneers. Inevitably, Cornwallis's defeat at Yorktown put Thomas Peters and the three thousand other Black Pioneers in severe jeopardy, for one of the provisions of the 1783 Paris Peace Treaty was that all slaves and other property would be returned to their rightful owners. The British, however, craftily evaded a showdown with American slave-owners by announcing that anyone with proper papers of identification and ownership could make his or her claim on a given day in New York City. Since few such claims could be conveniently made, thousands of ex-slaves were loaded on ships and deposited in either Bermuda or in St. John, New Brunswick, or in Nova Scotia. Thomas Peters and many others landed in Annapolis, Nova Scotia. There he had to compete for land and goods with thousands of similarly displaced whites, and inevitably the black ex-soldiers and ex-slaves never got the land promised them nor the provisions promised them. Many died of starvation and disease. But Thomas Peters was a fighter who believed that promises should be kept and that some way could be found to get him and the fast-disappearing contingent of Black Pioneers away from the cold and poverty of Nova Scotia. So, motivated by his dream of returning to his African homeland, he, at the age of fifty, went to England to plead his case and that of his fellow ex-soldiers. Leaving Nova Scotia involved some risk for an escaped slave, but Peters took the chance. The result was that authorities heard his plea, agreed on a course of immediate action, and in March 1792 approximately eleven hundred Black Pioneers landed in Sierra Leone. For Peters the circle was completed, even though he died four months after arriving in Africa.

There were many others who converted triangles into circles—Henry Highland Garnet, who, born a slave in Maryland in 1815, returned to Africa in his sixty-sixth year, and died of fever after only a few months in his beloved Africa; John Russwurm and Edward Jones, the black college graduates of 1826, who went to Liberia and to Sierra Leone, respectively; and Alexander Crummell, who labored in Liberia for twenty years. But there is the story of one black man who found fulfillment by moving in a different circular pattern. Born in Spanish Town, Jamaica, in 1795, Richard Hill received his education and training in England, joined the British antislavery movement, and then, in 1834, right after emancipation in Jamaica, returned to that troubled island where he served as head of special magistrates for thirty-eight years and labored to help his brothers and sisters during slavery's grim aftermath.

Today, now that slavery is no more, there are many stories of felicitous returns, renewals, and rebirths. There is no story more fascinating in sheer drama than Alex Haley's rediscovery of his relatives in a distant tribe in Africa's heartland. An equally exciting story is told of the visit of a young American soldier to Dr. Samuel Johnson's house in Gough Square in London. The young man identified himself as the great-great grandson of Francis Barber, Dr. Johnson's manservant to whom the doctor had bequeathed all of his personal property and all of his savings. As all good Johnsonians know, Francis Barber, born a slave in St. Mary Parish, Jamaica, had lived with the learned doctor for thirty-two years, from 1752 until Dr. Johnson's death in 1784. Barber himself died in 1802, and his grandson emigrated to North Carolina sometime in the 1890s. The young man who presented himself at the Johnson house in Gough Square identified himself as the grandson of that Barber. The fact that the American army correctly listed him as a blue-eyed Caucasian had nothing to do with his urge to complete his genealogical circle and find his roots.

In closing, let me say that all that I have said above about the force of imprisoning triangles and liberating circles in the black man's history represents one man's opinion. Presumably, a more gifted and more discerning person or one given more to casuistical argument than I could offer an even more persuasive discourse in favor of imprisoning circles and liberating triangles. Undoubtedly, the wisest course would have been to let the matter stand as stated—"Le Circuit Triangulaire." For it is wholly possible that only with such a phrase can we understand the full complexity of the traumatic history of black people as they served as economic pawns in the four-hundred-year thrust for empire. However, if we let such beautiful statements stand unchallenged and quivering with levels of meaning and paradoxical intensity, what will intellectual pickpockets like myself do? Like Othello, we will have lost our occupation. And such an end would, in and of itself, be a kind of imprisoning triangle.

NOTES

Reprinted from *CLA Journal* 18, no. 1 (June 1975): 165 76. Copyright The College Language Association. Used by permission of The College Language Association. This was the presidential address delivered at the College Language Association's Thirty-fifth Annual Convention, New Orleans, Louisiana, 10 April 1975.

1. Richard K. Barksdale and Keneth Kinnamon, *Black Writers of America* (New York: Macmillan, 1972), p. 306.

2. It was the custom aboard French slave ships to set aside a specified day about a month before the ship was due to reach port. On such a day, the slave women were washed with seawater and drunken sailors freed to wreak sexual havoc. This custom was known as the *pariade*—a time of abuse, rape, and drunken confusion.

Comic Irony

Black America and the
Mask of Comedy

Since his enforced migration to America from the shores of West Africa, beginning in the seventeenth century, the black American, both as slave and freedman, has had to resort to many strategies of offense and defense in order to cope with the manipulative devices and subtle depredations of a powerful white majority. At times he has used the strategy of angry physical confrontation and revolt in an attempt to wrest some vestiges of power out of the hands of the white man. Almost always such an offensive strategy has had the net ultimate result of crystallizing the defensive fears of a somewhat paranoid white majority. Both the Nat Turner revolt of 1831 in Southampton County, Virginia, and the black ghetto riots in America's large cities in the late 1960s inspired a fear of the black presence which hardened racial attitudes and increased racial distrust. In neither instance did a powerless black minority gain power or achieve any radical alteration in its relationship to a powerful white majority. Following Turner's revolt the black remained a slave until emancipated by force of arms in a bloody Civil War thirty years later; following the big urban riots, the majority of America's blacks have remained entrapped in ghetto areas where they continue to suffer various kinds of social, political, and economic discrimination. Black anger still exists and finds some outlet in the activities of activist groups like the Black Panthers and in the literature of racial confrontation of some young black writers like Don L. Lee, Sonia Sanchez, and Nikki Giovanni. Generally, however, today's black leadership is searching for more subtle offensive strategies which will not have the self-destructive fury of the big-city black ghetto riot but rather will achieve some transfer of political or economic power to the black masses.

In the meantime, the black man continues to place his stress on a wide variety of defensive and offensive strategies which the racial encounters of the centuries have taught him are necessary for survival. During the period of his enslavement, his primary defensive strategy was one of accommodation to, and suffering endurance of, the rule of the overseer's whip. During this time he was fortified by the Christian hope that "trouble would not last always" and that earth's pain would be compensated by heaven's joys. Admittedly, there were many who, like Frederick Douglass, Moses Roper, Henry Bibb, Lewis and Milton Clarke, and William Craft, refused to accommodate or endure and escaped to freedom. Others who resisted the cruelties of slavery comprise the nameless thousands who, throughout the centuries, suffered an early death at the hands of slavemaster or slavemistress or overseer. After Emancipation the chief proponent of a formula for accommodation and survival through economic self-help and political uninvolvement was Booker T. Washington. Today it is still debated whether his defensive strategy, broadened somewhat but not substantially changed from the accommodationism of slavery, was effective or necessary. To most blacks it is remembered as a degrading and racially demeaning kind of capitulation to the white power structure, which can be dismissed as Uncle Tomism, a term developed from the dominant attitude expressed by Harriet Beecher Stowe's principal character in *Uncle Tom's Cabin* (1852). Some blacks today, however, view Washington's emphasis on economic self-help as a necessary first step toward black separatism and racial self-sufficiency.

Two other strategies of racial confrontation have had both the survival value of an effective defensive strategy and the psychological inspiration and lift of a good offensive strategy. One, the recent movement led by the Reverend Martin Luther King, Jr., sought through nonviolence and Christian charity to convert the white majority to the cause of racial integration. The moral idealism of the movement broke the back of legal racial segregation in the American South and almost converted the rest of America to the cause of racial charity and understanding. And, although the movement's inspired leader was assassinated in 1968, America as a Christian nation still remembers how close it came to a full implementation of the moral and social truths of Christianity.

The second strategy, having both defensive value and the kind of racial gratification found in a subtle but effective offensive strategy, is the use of comic ridicule. Actually, the black man's use of comic ridicule is as old as the black man's presence in America. During slavery it was an effective means of counterbalancing the self-demeaning accommodationism demanded by the powerful white majority. So there was hidden black laughter in songs and ballads and stories in which the white slaveholder was subtly ridiculed. These songs and ballads and stories were part of a rich, oral folk tradition which the black man had brought with him from

Africa. Not only were there the bestiaries or Brer Rabbit and Buh Bear stories in which Brer Rabbit, symbolizing the powerless slave, always outtricked Buh Bear and the other animals who represented the white power structure; but there were also broadly circulated tales in which the "Marsa" was manipulated or humiliated or ridiculed. One story, "Swapping Dreams," pits a Master Jim Turner against a witty slave named Ike. The Master had had a seemingly disturbing dream about a "Nigger Heaven" in which the streets were strewn with garbage and filled with ragged and dirty blacks who lived in torn-down houses. To this Ike replied that he "sho musta et de same t'ing . . . 'cause Ah dreamed Ah went up ter de white man's paradise." There, he went on, the streets "wuz all ob gol' an silvah" and there were "putty pearly pearly gates" and "lots o' milk an' honey"—but "dey wuzn't uh soul in de whole place." Stories like these in which the black slave donned the mask of comic ridicule effected no broad shifts in the power relationships between master and slave, but they were excellent psychological compensation for the cruel physical and mental harassments of physical enslavement. Thus they provided the spiritual stabilization of a good defensive strategy and the emotional lift of a good offensive strategy.

After Emancipation many of these stories continued to circulate. Indeed, freedom gave the storyteller more opportunity for narrative elaboration and embellishment. The conversion of the many stories about John, the witty slave, into a continuous story about "High John the Conqueror" is a case in point. During slavery times there had circulated many separate stories about John who performed with high comic heroism in ridiculing his master or engaging in hazardous but successful competition with other slaves in order to outwit and ridicule their masters. In "High John the Conqueror," as the story developed in a time of continued folk enrichment during the late nineteenth and early twentieth centuries, the John incidents were linked together and given a beginning, a middle, and an end. At the end, John's master asks John to drown him in a gunny sack in an effort to make some money, and John quietly complies with his master's last request.

In this context some notice should be made of the fact that with freedom and emancipation a creative black literature which had had its beginnings in the eighteenth century began to expand, and a corps of known and identifiable authors emerged. Many of these poetized and fictionalized or editorialized in protest over the black man's lot as a freedman in America; others wrote escapist literature and hence avoided the problems of race. But one author, Charles Chesnutt, drew many of his short story plots from black folk literature ("The Goophered Grapevine" and "The Conjure Woman" are examples), and at least one of his stories— "The Passing of Grandison"—is in the tradition of comic ridicule, so effectively communicated through the black man's folk literature. Chesnutt's account of how Grandison, an apparently loyal slave, carefully plots his escape and effectively ridicules both young and old masters is related with disciplined narrative control and suspense. The net effect of the story is comic in the best sense of the word, for Grandison's departure to freedom provides a full psychological and moral release in a story dominated by slavery's distrust, fear, and suspicion.

In the twentieth century the major black writers have devoted most of their literary energies to works of social and moral protest over the black man's lot in America. Much of Langston Hughes's poetry, all of Richard Wright's fiction, and all of the poetry of contemporary young black poets like Don L. Lee fall into this category. In a sense, their literature is part of the black man's offensive strategy in race relations. A second but related emphasis in twentieth-century black literature has been the glorification and celebration of the black life-style and the affirmation of the beauty of blackness. The novels of Claude McKay—*Home to Harlem, Banjo,* and *Banana Bottom*—celebrate the black life-style and extol the primitive vigor of blackness. This is also true of the Harlem detective fiction of Chester Himes, although his novels provide only swift, panoramic glimpses of black life-styles in the urban ghetto. Behind this emphasis on the beauty of blackness is the growing importance of the concept of *négritude,* a world-unifying creed of blackness first formulated by Senghor of Sénégal, Césaire of Martinique, and Damas of French Guiana in the Paris of the late 1930s. It should also be noted in this context that the concept of *négritude* received considerable reinforcement from the French intellectual establishment, largely through Jean-Paul Sartre's 1948 essay, "Orphée Noir," which served as an introduction to Senghor's anthology of African and West Indian poetry. The principal thrust of Sartre's essay is that the cultural and artistic emphasis on blackness is an excellent defensive strategy for blacks in their continuing struggle with the worldwide white power structure.

Fortunately, these two major emphases in contemporary black literature have not precluded some concurrent developments in a literature of comic ridicule. Admittedly, in a time of continuing racial tumult and confusion, it is difficult for a black writer sensitive to racial problems to muster the disciplined detachment and objectivity demanded by the comic mode. Generally, novelists and dramatists can do this, since a certain amount of objectivity is essential for success in their respective crafts. By the same measure, poets who generally write out of the immediacy of their emotions and private fancies usually do not write with detached objectivity. For this reason, contemporary black writers most noted for their use of comic ridicule of white characters are the two novelists James Baldwin and Ralph Ellison and the playwright Douglas Turner Ward.

Of James Baldwin's several novels—*Go Tell It on the Mountain, Giovanni's Room, Tell Me How Long the Train's Been Gone, Another Country*—at least the last three named present characters who are involved in interracial love affairs. However, only in Ida's characterization in *Another Country* is there comic intensity as she relates to her two white lovers, Vivaldo Moore and Steve Ellis. Actually her relationship with her white lovers is on a somewhat confused love-hate continuum, characteristic of black-white relations in urban America. Vivaldo is kind, understanding, and fully worthy of her love; but white America must pay for the way it took her brother Rufus's soul, talent, and body. So Ida says to white America: "You don't have any experience in paying your dues and it's going to be rough on you, baby, when the deal goes down. There's lots of back dues to be collected, and I know damn well you haven't got a penny saved." But sex looms large in this novel, and Baldwin has his black heroine focus her comic ridicule on white America's sexual inadequacy. On one occasion she speaks to Vivaldo in a tone of unrefined raillery: "Can't none of you white boys help it. Every damn one of your sad-assed white chicks think . . . they don't piss nothing but ginger ale, and if it wasn't for the spooks wouldn't a damn one of you . . . *ever* get laid. That's *right*. You are a fucked-up group of people. You hear me? A fucked-up group of people." And of white sex Ida comments: "I used to watch them wriggle and listen to them grunt, and, God, they were so solemn about it, sweating yellow pigs, and so vain . . . and I wasn't touched at all. . . . Oh yes, I found out all about white people, *that's* what they were like, alone, where only a black girl could see them. . . ." At the end of the novel, Ida, somewhat purged of her comic disdain of the white world, finds true love with Vivaldo. Nevertheless, even though assured of Vivaldo's love and companionship, Baldwin's black heroine retains her broad comic view that the world of white America is "just one big whorehouse" in which everyone must "pay his dues" for services rendered.

The odyssey of the hero in Ralph Ellison's *Invisible Man* mirrors the pain, frustration, and psychological victimization not only of the American black man but the massive failures of twentieth-century man. The great appeal of this novel is that the antiheroic exploits of the central character are supported by incidents and anecdotes that reinforce his sardonic conclusion that life is better spent hiding in womblike seclusion than participating in "the struggle that nought availeth." One of the more interesting incidents that help the hero to arrive at this conclusion is the Trueblood incident which occurs in the second section of the hero's odyssey—the section relating his college experiences with the infamous Dr. Bledsoe. The Trueblood incident stands out because it pits a black man of truth against a white man of wealth in an essentially comic confrontation. The black man is a peasant, living so far back in time and history that he occupies a cabin actually built in slave times. In his circumstances and expectations Trueblood is a century removed from Dr. Bledsoe, the black college president, and two centuries removed from Mr. Norton, the white Yankee college trustee.

As the narrative unfolds, the hero, who is an innocent but emotionally involved observer (actually he is chauffeuring Mr. Norton around the college environs, at Dr. Bledsoe's request), is most unwilling to have the white patron and the black peasant meet. Somehow, he feels that this would be an accident with unfortunate consequences. In a sense, the novelist aids the reader in preparing for the psychological implications of the encounter of patron and peasant. First, we are told that Norton has had a daughter, now deceased, of whom he was inordinately fond and whose premature death left him paralyzed by a grief which was still with him. Early in their ride, Norton somewhat emotionally displays the picture of his deceased daughter to his chauffeur; she is a person of surpassing beauty, and Ellison's hero is quick to understand the college trustee's grief. On this occasion, however, there is a significant omission of any mention of the girl's mother or of Mr. Norton's wife. Second, we are told that Trueblood has been guilty of the ancient but heinous crime of incest with his daughter—the crime that drove Oedipus to scratch out his eyes and Elektra to bemoan her fate. Trueblood even wears the stigmata of his guilt—a festering axe wound on one side of his face, placed there by an angry wife when the horrible deed was discovered.

Although Norton, the white patron, is fully aware of the black peasant's crime, his disturbed chauffeur is unable to dissuade him from introducing himself to Trueblood in order to hear the latter's story. When they shake hands across the centuries of time and circumstance, the comedy begins. The black peasant, whose roots are in an earthy primitive past, relates in naïvely copious detail how in a dream he had done his terrible deed. The white patron listens with an eye-riveted fascination, for he, too, had once had such a dream, which intense Freudian fears forced him to repress; and his stigmata is an infinite regret that sears his soul.

The Trueblood incident, then, in *Invisible Man* is comic because it confronts a black man who has nothing but his truth with a white man who has everything but his truth. The listener who cannot but hear and the speaker who cannot but speak remind one of the confrontation in Coleridge's *Rime of the Ancient Mariner*. There are one or two singular differences, however. First, Trueblood, whose very name indicates that he is, perforce, a truth-speaker, has committed a crime far more heinous in Western culture than slaying an albatross. Second, Mr. Norton, the enraptured listener, is emphatically involved in the story; for driven by ancient desires and longings, he had pondered the deed which Trueblood had accomplished.

The net result of the incident is comic ridicule of a white man's civilization which places a greater emphasis on repression and suppression than on expression and fulfillment. Moreover, the social inversion that places a black man's primitive deed stage-center in the somewhat whitened, antiseptic world of the middle-class black college is also comic—just as comic as Norton's unrestrained and eager participation in the incident and his silent adoration of Trueblood's sexual heroism.

Comic ridicule of white America is much less subtle and indirect in Douglas Turner Ward's two plays, *Day of Absence* and *Happy Ending*. In fact, the dramatic purpose in each play is to ridicule white America's racial mores. *Day of Absence* is a blatantly farcical treatment of a racial event in the small-town, rural South; and *Happy Ending* examines comic ridicule of a white family in a Northern urban setting. In both plays the racial content is purposely exaggerated and overstated; truths are illuminated about black-white relationships, but these are blown up and flashed on a screen much larger than life-size.

The plot of *Day of Absence* may be briefly summarized. On a routinely hot, lazy summer morning in a small town in the American South, it is discovered that all of the "Nigras" have vanished. As a consequence, many essential services—baby care and nursing, garbage disposal, all cleaning chores, maid service everywhere—have been left undone. Soon a situation of crisislike proportions develops in the small town, and a frantic official search begins to locate the hiding place of the "Nigras." In the meantime, it is discovered that even some who passed for white and were actually black all the time had left with the "Nigras." This is most poignantly revealed in the case of Mr. Woodfence who, as the mayor's son-in-law and assistant, has actually been a black man, spying on white folks in high places. The town's most unusual dilemma quickly becomes an exciting news item on national television, and all the nation begins to fear that what has begun in this small town will spread nationwide or at least to all of the small towns of the American Southland. If either happens, a national crisis will assuredly be at hand.

As excitement and neurotic civil tension mount in the small town so adversely affected by a total withdrawal of black menial labor, the mayor of the little community promptly assumes a leadership role in an attempt to redress the situation. In so doing, he quickly becomes a caricature of the loud-mouthed southern politician blown up to farcical levels. At one point he is momentarily comforted by the realization that some "Nigras" might be found in the black wing of the hospital or in the black section of the city jail. Assuredly, these will tell where the others went, for, historically, blacks had always informed on other blacks. But it is quickly discovered that the blacks in the hospital are all in a mystifying coma and that the automatic

cell-block door will not open in the black section of the jail. So both of
these avenues of solution are mysteriously closed. By midday of the "Day
of Absence" the situation has grown desperate. Says the community's major
industrialist:

> Half the day is gone already, Henry. On behalf of the factory owners of this
> town, you've got to bail us out! Seventy-five percent of all production is
> paralyzed. With the Nigra absent, men are waiting for machines to be
> cleaned, floors to be swept, crates lifted, equipment delivered and bathrooms
> deodorized. Why, restrooms and toilets are so filthy until they not only
> cannot be sat in, but it's virtually impossible to get within hailing distance
> because of the stench.

Moreover, a businessman complains that "the absence of handymen, porters,
sweepers, stockmovers, deliverers and miscellaneous dirty-work doers" has
paralyzed the entire marketing process. Then, too, "a plethora of unsanitary
household disasters" looms forth threateningly—things like food poisoning,
"severe indegistitis, chronic diarrhea, advanced diaper chafings"—largely
because of the absence of black cooks and maids. The "Day of Absence"
closes with the harassed community on the verge of a collective nervous
breakdown. Long-established traditions are in danger; the social order of
whites over blacks is about to become meaningless; the prospect of no
more "Nigras" to patronize, resent, insult, or lynch is a shattering prospect
to this community. Then, the next day, as silently as they vanished, the
"Nigras" return; and what had been a "sick" town on the "Day of Absence"
becomes once again a "healthy" community.

After the manner of good and well-plotted farce, *Day of Absence* relates a
highly improbable event; but it is, nevertheless, extremely effective comic
ridicule. Under the pattern of ludicrous episodes, certain racial truths are
forcibly stated about the black man's economic and social status. He works
at the lowest economic scale and lives on the lowest social level. And yet,
the ironic question is implied, why is one so abused by white America
yet so needed by white America? Possibly, Ike, the witty slave in the folktale
"Swapping Dreams," had an explanation if not an answer when he described
how empty of inhabitants was the white man's heaven.

Ward's second play of comic ridicule, *Happy Ending,* has a somewhat
different thrust. The locale is not the small-town South but the urban
North. The principal characters are two sisters who work as maids for a
wealthy white suburban family and the somewhat sophisticated, middle-
class nephew of the sisters. He has been to college and bitterly resents the
fact that both of his aunts work in service. At the beginning of the play's
action both of the aunts are crying uncontrollably because the family for
whom they have been working is about to be dissolved by divorce. This is

too much for the college-bred nephew, who, using considerable revolutionary rhetoric, upbraids his aunts for crying over a subservient maid's position. In his thinking, all of them could well convert this event into the beginning of a long-awaited and long-needed economic, political, and social revolution against white domination over blacks in America. Then an overwhelming truth begins to emerge. The aunts have been stealing all kinds of consumer goodies—shoes, food, clothing—from their employer for years; the ending of their employment means the end of the thievery; and it is for this grievous state of affairs that they weep. When the once scornful nephew hears the truth about the heroic thievery on such a massive scale by the aunts, and begins to understand that whatever material affluence enjoyed by him is attributable to their efforts, he too raises a cry of lamentation and grief. All understand that another maids' position would never afford the spacious opportunity for such in-depth thievery; it takes years of careful planning and a certain kind of employer to reach that kind of maid-mistress relationship. There must be just the right amount of trust, craft, guile, and mutual admiration for a stealing maid to be successful with a gracious and kind employer. The important thing is that the maid who steals must not feel guilty and the mistress or employer must not be suspicious. After such experienced comments on the need and nature of black domestic thievery, word is received by the two aunts that the planned divorce that would have dissolved the family for whom they work is cancelled. Accordingly, they can return to their stealing and what had appeared to be an unmitigated tragedy now has a "happy ending."

Underneath the farcical humor of Ward's play there lies the comic truth that, given the social and economic and political inequities on the American racial scene, the black man in his ghetto has the right to steal to redress the racial balance. Inevitably, the playwright's "truth" is in direct opposition to sacred American "truths" about the sanctity of personal property and the need for honesty in social and economic transactions. But, as Chesnutt's Grandison learned and used as a basis for the action which he eventually took, there are at least two sets of truths—one black and one white. Indeed, in multiracial America, as the phenomenal success of the Italian Mafia proves, there may be many kinds of truths governing social and economic transactions.

As indicated initially in this discussion, the black man's comic ridicule of white America in his literature is an offensive-defensive strategy in race relations that causes no radical alteration in the power relationships between a black minority and a white majority. The black man still remains relatively powerless and the white man relatively powerful. But comic revelation of social sin and immorality provides America's citizenry with the opportunity for the kind of therapeutic laughter that can help to heal the long-festering wound of racism.

NOTE

Black Autobiography and
the Comic Vision

In Vernon Logginss's *The Negro Author,* a work which appeared just as the Harlem Renaissance was beginning to drift into the Depression years, the author observed that "With the exception of his folk songs, the Negro's most valuable contributions to American literature have been in the form of personal memoirs."[1] Today, almost fifty years later, few would argue with such a criticial assessment. Beginning with the earliest published slave narrative—John Saffin's *Adam Negro's Tryall* in 1703—and continuing to this day, black Americans have produced more autobiographical statements than any other American minority. And these have come from a wide spectrum of black America—all the way from distinguished leaders like Douglass, Washington, Du Bois, Daniel Payne, and Benjamin Mays to Icepick Slim, the king of the pimps on Chicago's Southside. Sometimes the titles of these autobiographies are simple and direct, like Richard Wright's *Black Boy* or Babs Gonzales's *I Paid My Dues;* at other times they are both evocative and provocative, like Daniel T. Grant's *When the Melon Is Ripe* or Robert Lee Grant's *The Star Spangled Hustle.* Sometimes, like some of the slave narratives written for abolitionist propaganda purposes between 1830 and 1860, some autobiographies are written with the collaboration and assistance of a second party (particularly true of successful athletes and entertainers who want to take advantage of a large captive audience but do not have the requisite writing skills to exploit such an advantage). Some, like *All God's Dangers* and *The Autobiography of Malcolm X,* are not collaborative works but transmitted directly through a second party. Theodore Rosengarten is listed as the author of *All God's Dangers,* but there is no doubt that the one authentic voice in the work is that of Nate Shaw, or Nate Cobb as he was known in his home in black rural Alabama. Similarly, although Alex Haley transmitted the story of Malcolm X, the authentic voice is that of the Muslim leader himself.

So black autobiography is rich and varied. It represents the collective self-appraisal of a rich variety of Afro-Americans—a challenging melange that cuts across all groups, sects, and classes in black America. Robert Brignano, who published an annotated bibliography of black autobiographies in 1974, estimated that 459 such works had been published since the Civil War.[2] The overwhelming question to be answered, however, is not how many, but why so many? Do we have here a racially indigenous genre for which black Americans have a unique and special capability? Is the urge to tell one's story a racial urge to testify or bear witness—to be spiritually accountable? Or is the autobiographical urge a racial trait with African roots, like blues and jazz and the love of yams?

The obvious answer to all of these questions is no. Benjamin Franklin and Benvenuto Cellini have through their autobiographies supplied abundant evidence that the gift for writing in this genre was not transmitted from Africa nor has it ever been the special literary forte of black Americans only. The inescapable conclusion then is that the roots of the black autobiography syndrome lie deep in a soil fertilized by American racism and watered by the tears of the oppressed. Other literary critics substantiate this general conclusion with more subtle and sophisticated argument. For instance, Sidonie Smith, author of *Where I'm Bound,* a study of patterns of slavery and freedom in black American autobiography, argues that all writing in this category was and is motivated by the black man's or black woman's search for identity.[3] Just as the fugitive slave wrote his story and thereby gained a political and social identity, so a Baldwin, suffering from an identity crisis, began to find and know himself as he wrote *Nobody Knows My Name.* Other critics, noting that blacks in America suffer from a kind of cultural schisophrenia, say that the autobiographical statement is a thera peutic catharsis that heals the black psyche, making cohesive and unitary what Du Bois called "two warring selves in one dark skin."[4] In addition, there is a school of critical thought which asserts that black autobiography is a form of historical writing and the product of a genuinely creative historical imagination.[5] Having been excluded from involvement in the creation of history as history is defined by Western tradition, black people have, through their autobiographies, provided their own histories—stories of their journey from "can't to can" and their flight from oppression to an ever elusive quasi-freedom.

It is difficult to conclude which one of these theories explaining the nature and origin of the black autobiography is *the* explanation. Possibly, all have some degree of critical legitimacy. But one can safely conclude that, because each autobiography records a given persona's encounter with racism, each autobiography directly or indirectly reacts to the violence, anger, confusion, and psychological chaos that accompanies that racism. Chester Himes's *The Quality of Hurt,* for instance, is a book full of anger and the violence that is engendered by the implacably hostile environments that Himes encountered on his journey from "can't to can." And this anger and violence infect all of Himes's relationships, making him paranoid and suspicious about both friend and foe alike. Even his attitude toward his mother is strained and, at times, surly and intractable. For Richard Wright's initial kindnesses in helping him get settled in Paris he is not in any way grateful but, instead, elaborates at some length on the baser and less angelic side of his fellow writer's character and personality. On one occasion, the violence even invades the bedroom, and the hero emerges therefrom with a broken toe, self-inflicted when a poorly directed kick missed the intended victim and smashed against an unyielding piece of sturdy furniture. This last event does bring to an otherwise humorless and darkly somber work a smidgen of humor, especially when we note how maladroitly our broken-toed persona maneuvers in the service of Venus immediately after the self-inflicted fracture.

It should be pointed out in this context that in those autobiographies which recount the persona's ascent to success, anger, woe, and violence are usually muted. There are few of these so-called negative factors, for instance, in Booker T. Washington's *Up from Slavery,* a work obviously modeled on Franklin's success-story *Autobiography.* The violence of a reconstructionist South ever lurks in the background of Washington's story, but this is carefully masked and screened from the reader's view; in the foreground we have Washington, the stalwart Christian, a man of ingenuity, industry, and enterprise—making his journey from "can't to can" not on the backroads of earlier fugitive flights but on the bright highway of personal achievement. And Du Bois in his *Autobiography* travels on a similar high road. Man's inhumanity to man based on color is ever present in this work which Du Bois completed in the final years of his long and distinguished career, but the violence engendered by racism is kept in the background. The patterns of international travel are important in this work; admittedly the traveling is done to serve the ends of racial justice, but oftentimes for the reader of this autobiography, "where" becomes more important than "why."

Over and above these general characteristics, however, there is one additional feature of black autobiography that merits further probing and analysis. This I choose to call the literary device of comic distancing. This occurs when autobiographers who have the gift of comic vision rise above racism's drab and cruel realities and inject a note that lightens the mood of the reader and lifts the tone of the narrative. Needless to say, black autobiographers with this gift are by no means numerous. Very few of the nineteenth-century slave narrators, for instance, demonstrated any evidence of this kind of comic vision. Undoubtedly, the circumstances under which they were forced to survive were so horrendous and dehumanizing that there was no opportunity for comic detachment or comic distancing from the daily routine of pain and suffering which all slaves had to endure. Similarly, the great autobiographers of the Reconstruction and post-Reconstruction periods—Douglass, Payne, Washington, and John Langston—were seriously involved in recounting their achievements in the face of racism's overwhelming odds; hence, they were unable to detach themselves from the flow of events and objectively note the social ironies and subtle comic nuances that make the *comédie humaine* what it is. These were men who, according to the general consensus of history, "had crossed the broad rivers of racial discrimination and climbed the towering peaks of racial prejudice"; so their lives reflected the kind of moral commitment that demanded involvement and precluded detachment. One must admit that Douglass did have a pronounced penchant for heavy irony and sarcasm in his ever-running fight with American racism, but he used the sledge hammer of denunciation and not the scalpel of wit. By and large, then, autobiographers who have demonstrated an ability to employ a comic vision are twentieth-century authors. The three writers who provide the best examples of comic distancing in their autobiographical statements are Langston Hughes, Zora Neale Hurston, and Rosengarten's Nate Cobb in *All God's Dangers*. Before analyzing their autobiographies for evidence of this phenomenon, however, I would like to discuss two minor instances of what I choose to call comic authorial detachment from the pain and woe of racial experience.

The first instance, surprisingly, is found in one of the slave narratives recorded by the WPA Writers Project in the late 1930s and published in Botkin's *Lay My Burden Down*[6] in 1045. The narrator is Ellen Betts, a ninety-year-old ex-slave who, at the time of the interview, resided in Opelousas, Louisiana. In general, her memory of "slave times" was like the "remembrances" of the other old ex-slaves who were interviewed in the WPA Writers Project. Slavery was remembered as a time of cruel "tribulation," sorrow, and woe. Families were broken up and children sold down river from grieving mothers; grown women and men were, for the slightest offenses, strung up and given the customary thirty-nine lashes with a bull whip or with a cat-o'-nine-tails. Despite her painful memories, however, Ellen Betts provides a comic lilt as she recalls her years as a child and a young adult before "surrender come."

> Miss Sidney was Marse's first wife, and he had six boys by her. Then he marry the widow Cornelia, and she give him four boys. With ten children springing

up quick like that and all the colored children coming 'long fast as pig litters, I don't do nothing all my days, but nurse, nurse, nurse. I nurse so many childrens it done went and stunt my growth, and that's why I ain't nothing but bones to this day.... When the colored women has to cut cane all day till midnight come and after, I has to nurse the babies for them and tend the white children, too. Some them babies so fat and big I had to tote the feet while 'nother gal tote the head. I was such a little one, 'bout seven or eight year old. The big folks leave some toddy for colic and crying and such, and I done drink the toddy and let the children have the milk. I don't know no better. Lawdy me, it a wonder I ain't the biggest drunker in this here country, counting all the toddy I done put in my young belly! (pp. 125–26)

There is the same amount of comic detachment as well as the exaggeration that usually accompanies comic distancing in Ellen Betts's account of her adult years as a wet nurse on the Parsons' plantation:

Two years after the war, I git marry and git children of my own and then I turn into a wet nurse. I wet-nursed the white children and black children, like they all the same color. Sometime I have a white one pulling the one side and a black one the other. (p. 126)

It is conceivable that the time that had elapsed since slavery helped Ellen Betts achieve some comic distancing from her experiences as a slave. Nevertheless, in her account of those bitter times, she was able to apprehend certain comic relationships that others, engrossed in pain and misery, were unable to see. She also had a distinct knack for graphic description. In her account of the devastation dealt the Parsons' sugar plantation after a Yankee attack, she said, "Lasses run in the bayou, and blood run in the ditches."

A second example of comic detachment in autobiographical writing resulted from an unusual "happening" at Williams College when Sterling Brown, distinguished literary scholar and Afro-American folklorist, returned to his alma mater in Williamstown, Massachusetts, for his fiftieth anniversary. The speech which he gave on this occasion is full of memories of his four-year stay at the small New England college. It was recorded and is now in print in an anthology.[7] Entitled "A Son's Return: 'Oh, Didn't He Ramble,' " the speech recounts, with wit and wisdom and levity, the major events of Brown's undergraduate years. One might add that the speech was apparently an impromptu piece of autobiographia, and the author rambles, just as the title of the old folksong promised that he would. The tone is established when Sterling Brown, commenting on his long association with Howard University, says: " . . . I was hired, I was fired, I was rehired, I was retired, I was again rehired. If I tell many lies tonight and you get them taped, I may be refired" (p. 3). What is interesting about the speech for my purposes are the comments made by Brown about the racial experiences at Williams. He remarks how he had been told before leaving Washington, D.C., the so-called hub of black upper society in the 1920s, that his stay at Williams was going to be racially traumatic. His fellow undergraduates at the prestigious institution were to be graduates of Andover, Exeter, and Groton; they, the young Washingtonian was told, had never seen and associated with anyone of his racial group, and he had never been associated with a white man of comparable age and standing. So the young Brown traveled from Washington to Williamstown in 1919 with considerable foreboding. When he arrived, however, somewhat to his apparent disappointment, he found that he was treated with "benign neglect." In fact, nothing overtly racial happened; there were no searing racial crises. Says Brown:

> I did not meet with anything blatant. I did not meet with anything flagrant. Carter Marshall was called a "nigger" on Main Street, and he knocked the guy down. And I was right behind him to help on that. I was not a fighter, but I had my race to defend.... One of the big shots in my class from Louisiana would come to us (we wore knickerbockers in those days), and he would say "Look at the little 'knickers' " but you didn't know whether it was *ck* or *gg*. And the last lie I want to tell is that they used to call me Brownie. But how the hell could I object to them calling me Brownie? My name was Brown.... (p. 8)

Sterling Brown then goes on to relate how he converted, for his own less than honorable purposes, an excessive chapel-cutting experience into a minor racial crisis.

> ...you could not cut consecutively, you could not overcut...and I had overcut and consecutively, and Dean Howes said, "Mr. Brown, you have got to go. You have got to be suspended." I knew that as much beating as my fraternity brothers had given me that was nothing to what my father was going to give me. I (then) committed one of the worst deeds of racism in my career. I said to Dean Howes, "You would not do this if I were not a Negro." It was the college law ... I had broken the law. I threw race at him and said he (was) picking on a poor little Negro. And it worked. He was the descendant of abolitionists. This man's grandfather had probably fought at Chickamauga or something, and he nearly cried. He said, "Mr. Brown, do you really feel that?" I said, "Yes, and the other fellows feel it too." From then on I not only consecutively cut, you know, I ain't thought about chapel. (p. 10)

Not only was Sterling Brown's anti-chapel ploy an early example of reverse racism, but it also illustrates some comic distancing from an incident of racial import.

Of the three twentieth-century autobiographers whose works provide further examples of comic distancing or the use of comic vision, Langston Hughes is undoubtedly the most interesting. This very versatile man of letters made his living as a writer and published in every literary genre during his forty-seven-year career. He wrote poetry, drama, fiction, and literary criticism, assembled anthologies, and collaborated on musicals and operas. And he also completed two autobiographies, *The Big Sea*[8] in 1940 and *I Wonder as I Wander*[9] in 1949. In the first he related his travels and experiences up to his twenty-ninth year. In the second, he gave an accounting up to and including his thirty-fifth year. Thus, Hughes, who lived from 1902 to 1967, covered his life in the two autobiographies from his boyhood in Kansas and the Middle West in the early years of the century up through 1937, the year he spent in Spain covering the Spanish Civil War for the *Baltimore Afro-American Newspaper.*

Critics in general and Hughesian specialists in particular have never been happy with either of these autobiographies as sources of information about the poet. They complain that both volumes contain too little about Hughes and too much about others. In fact, Blanche Knopf, when considering the manuscripts for publication, raised a question about the kind of noncoverage Hughes provided about himself in the two autobiographies. Her company finally published *The Big Sea* with some reluctance but rejected *I Wonder as I Wander* when it was offered for consideration in 1949. It was finally published in 1956.

Essentially, the critics were right regarding the dearth of information about Hughes in these two autobiographies. For instance, the circumstances concerning the collapse of Hughes's friendship with Zora Neale Hurston over *Mule Bone,* a play on which the two writers collaborated, are only lightly touched upon in two pages at the end of *The Big Sea.* On the other hand, Robert Hemenway's biography of Zora Neale Hurston devotes an entire chapter, including eleven rather comprehensive footnotes, to the incident.[10] Nor is the *Goodbye Christ* episode, considered by many to be of focal significance in the development of Hughes's literary career in the 1930s, even mentioned in *I Wonder as I Wander.* Apparently, Hughes purposely masked his interior personal world and, instead, devoted full attention to the flotsam of the world in which he moved and had his social being.

Actually, Hughes as autobiographer reflected the same authorial demeanor that he revealed as Hughes the poet. He was not a poet driven and dominated by moods and inner states of feeling. In fact, because he was so personally detached, he became a master of comic vision, and the literary products of his comic vision were five volumes of the Simple stories and the numerous poems describing Harlem's rich gallery of characters.

In other words, Hughes's penchant for detachment improved and enriched his comic vision in the two autobiographies. As a result, *The Big Sea* is filled with wonderful characters who are portrayed with deftness and dramatic finesse. One is Maria, Hughes's English student in Cuernavaca, "a very delicate little woman . . . with a great mass of heavy black hair and very bright but sad eyes" (p. 68); another is Bruce, the one-eyed black chef at Bricktop's restaurant in Paris who was moved to a knife-throwing frenzy when his boss suggested that he be terminated because of his surliness, hostility, and general inefficiency in the culinary arts (p. 183). Of even greater interest are Hughes's portraits of the so-called Harlem literati who were involved with him in the Harlem Renaissance. There was Rudolph Fisher who, although he died prematurely at the peak of his literary career in 1934, was both "a good writer" and "an excellent singer" and was the wittiest among the literati. Then there was Wallace Thurman, the brilliant and mercurial author of *The Blacker the Berry* who drank gin excessively and always threatened "to jump out of windows at people's parties and kill himself" (p. 235). And one cannot forget Hughes's portrait of Zora Neale Hurston. She is described as a pleasant, vivacious young woman who traveled throughout Harlem with an anthropologist's ruler measuring heads for Franz Boas, Columbia University's great anthropologist. Hughes also presented "downtown" literati who were involved in the Renaissance—Van Vechten, Ernestine Evans, Jake Baker (he had the dubious distinction of owning the largest erotic library in New York), Rebecca West, and George Viereck. About all of them Hughes provided some colorful incident or bit of memorabilia. He described the annual birthday party that Van Vechten staged for himself, James Weldon Johnson, and Alfred Knopf, Jr., because their birthdays fell on the same day. Every year there were three cakes, "one red, one white, and one blue—the colors of our flag. They honored a Gentile, a Negro, and a Jew" (p. 254). Hughes adds that "the differences of race did not occur to me until days later when I thought back about the three colors and the three men" (p. 255). Finally, Hughes described a bon voyage party given by Van Vechten in the Prince of Wales suite aboard the Cunarder:

> As the champagne flowed, Nora Holt, the scintillating Negro blonde entertainer de lux from Nevada, sang a ribald ditty called "My Daddy Rocks Me with One Steady Roll." As she ceased, a well-known New York matron cried ecstatically, with tears in her eyes: "My dear! Oh, my dear! How beautifully you sing Negro spirituals!" (p. 254)

So Hughes's autobiographies are crowded with people and incidents molded and formed by his comic vision of life. We see nothing or very little of Hughes per se; he is a detached observer—a disciplined reactor and rarely an actor—almost an invisible man. At one point in *The Big Sea* he observed that he felt his second book of poems, *Fine Clothes to the Jew,* was a better book than his first, *The Weary Blues,* "because it was more impersonal, more about other people than myself" (p. 241). His autobiographies have that same quality of impersonality and objectivity and hence are comic in the best sense of the term.

Zora Neale Hurston's autobiography, *Dust Tracks on a Road*, [11] was published two years after *The Big Sea* appeared. Although it sold well, critics have been as unhappy with the Hurston autobiography as they have been with the Hughes autobiographies. Robert Hemenway, in his epochal study of the life and works of Hurston, says that it is a "discomfiting" work—that it is difficult to determine whether the authentic voice in the auto biography is that of a folksy figure from black Eatonville, Florida, or the voice of the successful writer who graduated from sophisticated Barnard College (p. 283). Another critic, Darwin Turner, claims that *Dust Tracks on a Road* is a "disappointing blend of artful candor and coy reticence" and full of "contradictions and silences."[12] His conclusion appears to be that the autobiography reveals far too little about Zora Neale Hurston. Of course, this duplicates the charge made against the Langston Hughes autobiographies. Instead of being clearly visible, the subject of the autobiography tends at times to be almost invisible.

Hemenway has provided some information that helps to explain why *Dust Tracks on a Road* became a "discomfiting" disappointment. First, Hurston herself did not want to write it—because she found it difficult to reveal "her inner self." To a large degree, the book proves that Hurston's statement was a self-fulfilling prophecy. Secondly, her Lippincott editor demanded an extensive revision of the first manuscript draft and demanded, as well, deletion of all matters relating either to international politics or to American race relations.[13] The result was a work in which the author cautiously avoided any subjects bearing on integration, discrimination, or colonialism. In other words, Lippincott's very conservative editorial policy left Hurston alternately floating on a cloud of down-home folksiness or hidden in a fog of personal anonymity.

Fortunately, something of critical value is retrievable from this rather parlous state of affairs. For, even if *Dust Tracks on a Road* does have a low critical rating as a useful and functional autobiography, it does provide several excellent examples of how the comic vision can enliven autobiographical writing. In this sense, Hurston as autobiographer is comparable to Hughes as autobiographer. Hurston's description of her own birth is a good case in point. Although she related an incident fraught with potential tragedy, the story as it develops provides considerable comic alleviation—

> My mother had to make it alone. She was too weak after I rushed out to do anything for herself. . . . She was so weak, she couldn't even reach down to where I was. She had one consolation. She knew I wasn't dead, because I was crying strong. (p. 37)

The "birthing" incident continues with the arrival of a white neighbor who, hearing "me spread my lungs all over Orange County," rushed in, whipped out his trusty "Barlow knife" to cut the navel cord, and then sponged off the newly born Zora. Keeping her comic distance from the event and masking the pain and misery of an untended birth, Hurston concludes the incident with the arrival of Aunt Judy, the midwife:

> She complained that the cord had not been cut just right. . . . She was mighty scared I was going to have a weak back, and that I would have trouble holding my water. . . . I did. (p. 38)

This passage has a tone of intimate folksiness, but it is also comic. As Langston Hughes once wrote:

> Birthin is hard
> And dyin is mean
> So get yourself a
> Little lovin in between.[14]

In reality, "birthing" was hard for Zora Neale Hurston too; but, by gaining some distance from the trauma of the event, she got herself a little autobiographical comedy "in between."

There are two other incidents in *Dust Tracks on a Road* that have comic significance. The first involves Zora's philandering Uncle Jim who, bearing gifts of sugar cane and peanuts, sneaks off to visit his secret love. He is followed by his axe-bearing spouse, Aunt Caroline. When she returns, she is not only carrying the axe, but draped on one shoulder are Uncle Jim's pants, shirt, and coat, and on the other, two sticks of sugar cane. It should be noted that this incident gives the reader little or no information about Zora Neale Hurston except that she apparently enjoyed that good old down-home humor which apparently also appealed to her Lippincott editor. The incident provides no comic masking from trauma, unless marital infidelity can be considered a trauma. One gathers that in Eatonville it was not.

The second incident in the autobiography which I wish to discuss is comic because it describes, with mock-heroic gusto, a fight between Zora and her new step-mother. The fight rages for four pages. Of course, Zora emerges as the victor and, if the reader has no stomach for a fight filled with hair-pulling fury, he or she emerges as the loser. It should also be noted that this mock-heroic extravaganza provides no comic masking from racial trauma, but it does show how vulnerable step-mothers were in Eatonville and how exuberantly Zora Neale Hurston could play the role of "La Belle Sauvage," again to the apparent delight of her Lippincott editor.

As I have noted above, *Dust Tracks on a Road* was purposely purged of matters of racial concern, so it contained little or no intentional comic masking of racial trauma. This was not true of *All God's Dangers.* [15] In this work, Nate Shaw tells the story of his life as a black tenant farmer in east-central Alabama, and racial tension and trauma abound throughout the book. Shaw grew to young manhood in the early years of this century, a time when rural Alabama was a hard and bitter land for the illiterate black tenant farmer. Despite this fact, he was able to achieve some comic distancing from the pain and misery that engulfed him. For instance, a delightful comic scenario develops when a youthful Shaw becomes embroiled in a fight with a neighbor named Luke Millikin. The fight develops when Luke attempts, for some minor reason, to knife Shaw and Shaw responds by smashing him on the head with a rock. The comedy begins when the victim's mother, stricken with grief, summons her lover forth from sleep to assist in avenging what she thinks is her son's foul murder. Her lover, a Mr. Flint, who just happens to be white, responds to the mother's screams for aid. Shaw relates the incident as follows:

> What you reckon that white man done? He grabbed his double barrel breech-loader and runned out there in his drawers, me peepin around the corner of the house lookin at him. . . . Old man Flint standin there, double barrel breech-loader in his hands, didn't have nothin on but his sleepers and them was his drawers, two piece worth. (pp. 44–45)

Fortunately, the incident ends without bloodshed, but it indicates that the potential for bloody violence was ever-present in Nate Shaw's rural Alabama.

Nate Shaw was also able to squeeze some comic relief out of a second incident which had even greater potential racial violence. This occurred when he walked into a country store called Sadler's Store in a town near his farm to buy some shoes for his children. While the clerk was waiting on him, a white man in the store became exasperated when he noted the white woman clerk climbing up and down ladders trying to serve a black customer. The white man, a Mr. Chase, grabbed a shovel and attempted to drive Shaw from the store. When Shaw refused to move, Chase then grabbed a rifle off the store's gun rack and loaded it. Fortunately, he was restrained from using it. In the meantime Shaw noted:

> There was a old colored fellow down at the door at Sadler's Store the whole time this ruckus was goin on inside . . . he beckoned me to run out . . . the old man tickled me . . . heavy built old colored man. And he had on one of these old frock-tail coats and it hit him just below the knee and it was cut back like a bug's wings. And he just stood there and bowed and beckoned for me to run out there. And ev'ry time he'd bow, that ol coat would fly up behind him and when he straightened up it would hit him right back there below the bend in his legs. Tickled me, it tickled me. I thought it was the funniest thing I ever

saw. He was scared for me and wanted me to run out of there. I didn't run
nowhere. I stood just like I'm standin today ... when I know I'm right and I
ain't harmin nobody and nothin, I'll give you trouble if you try to move me.
(pp. 169–70)

This passage proves that Shaw had a discerning eye for the comic, even as
he stood surrounded by "All God's Dangers."

Four conclusions can be drawn from this discussion of black autobiographies and comedy. First, some of black America's best autobiographical
statements contain no comedy. Second, some of those autobiographies
which do contain comedy are mediocre autobiographies. Third, comedy
tends to be an impersonal art. Those writers who are more impersonal tend
to employ comic devices more often. And, fourth, there is no such thing as
a good impersonal autobiography.

NOTES

Reprinted with permission from *Black American Literature Forum* 15, no. 1 (Spring
1981): 12–27.

1. Vernon Loggins, *The Negro Author: His Development in America to 1900* (New
York: Columbia University Press, 1931), p. 4.

2. Russell C. Brignano, *Black Americans in Autobiography* (Durham, N.C.: Duke
University Press, 1974), p. 91.

3. Sidonie Smith, *Where I'm Bound* (Westport, Conn.: Greenwood Press, 1974),
p. ix.

4. Stephen Butterfield, *Black American Autobiography* (Amherst: University of
Massachusetts Press, 1974), p. 94.

5. Albert E. Stone, "Patterns in Recent Black Autobiography," *Phylon* 29 (March
1978): 21.

6. B. A. Botkin, *Lay My Burden Down* (Chicago: University of Chicago Press,
1945). Subsequent references to this book are noted parenthetically in the text.

7. Michael Harper and Robert Stepto, eds., *Chant of Saints* (Urbana: University of Illinois Press, 1979). Subsequent references to this book are noted parenthetically
in the text.

8. Langston Hughes, *The Big Sea* (New York: Alfred Knopf, 1940). Subsequent
references to this book are noted parenthetically in the text.

9. Langston Hughes, *I Wonder as I Wander* (New York: Hill and Wang, 1956).

10. Robert Hemenway, *Zora Neale Hurston* (Urbana: University of Illinois Press,
1977), pp. 136–58.

11. Zora Neale Hurston, *Dust Tracks on a Road* (New York: Lippincott, 1942).
Subsequent references to this book are noted parenthetically in the text.

12. Darwin Turner, *In a Minor Chord* (Carbondale: Southern Illinois University
Press, 1971), p. 91.

13. Hemenway, *Hurston,* p. 288.

14. Langston Hughes, *Selected Poems* (New York: Vintage Books, 1974), p. 264.

15. Theodore Rosengarten, *All God's Dangers* (New York: Knopf, 1974). Subsequent references to this book are noted parenthetically in the text.

Comic Relief in
Langston Hughes's Poetry

In August 1925, in his introduction to Hughes's first book of poetry, *The Weary Blues,* Carl Van Vechten wrote:

> His verses ... are by no means limited to an exclusive mood; he writes caressingly of little black prostitutes ... ; his cabaret songs throb with the true jazz rhythm; his sea pieces ache with a calm, melancholy lyricism. ... Always ... his stanzas are subjective, personal. They are the ... expression of an essentially sensitive and subtly illusive nature, seeking always to break through the veil that obscures ... the ultimate needs of that nature.[1]

This passage is notable for two reasons. First, like most "critical" statements, there is a "veil of verbalism" that occasionally obscures the meaning. Second, there is no mention of Hughes's great skill at writing poetry that is at once socially and emotionally *engagé* yet comically detached and impersonal. Van Vechten undoubtedly failed to comment on Hughes's gift for comic detachment simply because there is little or no evidence of this unique poetic skill in *The Weary Blues.* There are blues poems, like "Blues Fantasy" which begins with "Weary / weary / trouble, pain" and ends with "laughing / hey, hey / laugh a loud / hey, hey." But such abrupt emotional transitions are inherent in the blues statement. One always recovers from the blues. All that is needed is another place or another face. It may be argued that the emotional metamorphosis wrought by the blues suggests the comic, simply because there is movement from sorrow and grief to laughter and relief. But the blues mood is essentially emotional, whereas comedy's laughter is thoughtful.

So Van Vechten was right in 1925. Hughes, the master of the comic mode, had not yet emerged. The poet himself did comment on what he deemed to be a tone of authorial impersonality in his *Fine Clothes to the Jew,* but there is no indication that he considered himself in that volume of poetry to be a writer who had a distinct gift for comic detachment.[2] His poetry of the 1920s and 1930s, then, reflected great personal and emotional involvement in the glitter and glow of the black life-style and in the grim social and political issues that dominated the thirties, but the comic element was lacking from that poetry. Hughes probably first began to be aware of his comic gift when, stepping outside himself, he published his first collection of short stories, *The Ways of White Folks*, in 1934. Possibly as a traveling man who dared to venture all the way from Kilby Prison in the racist heartland of Alabama to Tashkent in the USSR and then to Madrid and Spain's searing civil conflict, he was forced to develop a protective detachment which, in turn, strengthened a natural disposition for the comic.

In any event, by the time he wrote *Shakespeare in Harlem* (1942), he began to cast many of his poems of social and racial protest in the comic mode. This did not please some of his critics. They criticized him for a lack of seriousness. One critic charged that reading *Shakespeare in Harlem* was comparable to seeing and hearing "a cartoon doing a blackface, white-lip number."[3] Another perceived Hughes to be a poet whose work was marred by a "facile superficiality" that emphasized the frivolous and the trivial and ignored the serious.[4] And when the poet issued his selected poems in 1959, another critic condemned the entire volume. In that critic's view what Hughes had considered his best should have really been consigned to a wastebasket.[5]

Conscientious reassessments of Hughes's poetry have proven these critics to be wrong.[6] For instance, in the section of *Shakespeare in Harlem* entitled "Seven Moments of Love—An Un-Sonnet Sequence of the Blues," the poem "Supper Time" presents a male persona who has not only been abandoned by his lover but is completely depression-ridden and bereft of money, food, and fuel:

> I look in the kettle, the kettle is dry.
> Look in the bread box, nothing but a fly.
> Turn on the light and look real good!
> I would make a fire but there ain't no wood.
> Look at that water dripping in the sink.
> Listen at my heartbeats trying to think.
> Listen at my footprints walking on the floor.
> That place where your trunk was, ain't no trunk no more.
> Place where your clothes hung's empty and bare.
> Stay away if you want to, and see if I care!
> If I had a fire I'd make me some tea
> And set down and drink it, myself and me.
> Lawd! I got to find me a woman for the WPA—
> Cause if I don't they'll cut down my pay.[7]

As these lines indicate, the persona's foremost evident need is not to repair his abject physical fortunes but to get another woman to replace his "recently departed." His WPA relief check will continue in its present amount only if he can meet relief requirements with a suitable and acceptable replacement. The poem's title is ironic, because there is nothing for supper at supper time except air sandwiches and wind pudding, but our very pragmatic persona remains undaunted. He is not overwhelmed by his economic improvidence; he will eat and drink and be warm again once a woman is established in his small apartment and his WPA legitimacy has been restored. In such an instance, the persona's dilemma is comic and not tragic and the reader can safely conclude that economic salvation awaits those who can manipulate their personal circumstances and negotiate the system successfully. The reader leaves "Supper Time" fairly well convinced that the persona's fortunes will soon be repaired.

In the same section of *Shakespeare in Harlem,* there is a poem entitled "Sunday" in which comic relief is adroitly blended with a particular brand of Hughesian irony:

> All day Sunday didn't even dress up.
> Here by myself, I do as I please.
> Don't have to go to church.
> Don't have to go nowhere.
> I wish I could tell you how much I *don't* care
> How far you go, nor how long you stay—
> Cause I'm sure enjoying myself today!
> Set on the front porch as long as I please.
> I wouldn't take you back if you come on your knees.
> But this house is mighty quiet!
> They ought to be some noise....
> I'm gonna get up a poker game and invite the boys.
> But the boys is all married! Pshaw!
> Ain't that too bad?
> They ought to be like me setting here—feeling glad! (p. 7)

Obviously, the persona is disturbed about his former loved one's absence, but his instincts for survival are strong and he is determined to put the best face he can on his circumstances. There are, he argues, advantages to being alone: one enjoys full freedom of movement, and, although his "house is mighty quiet," he is "glad" to be able on this particular Sunday to do exactly "as I please." The irony in this poem is comic because the persona is not drowned in defeat but is attempting to find socially and psychologically constructive solutions to his dilemma. Obviously, ironic misgivings abound, but the reader can scarcely doubt that the persona's Sunday, so free of conventional commitments, was not in some measure relaxed and personally gratifying.

In "Declarations," another section of *Shakespeare in Harlem,* the poem "If-ing" has comic connotations of a slightly different kind. The poem relates all of the grandiose things that the persona would do if he only had some money and then concludes:

> But I ain't got a million,
> Fact is, ain't got a dime—
> So just by *if-*ing
> I have a good time! (p. 39)

In this conclusion, Hughes suggests the kind of psychological adjustment that Depression-ridden blacks had to make in order to achieve some measure of self-acceptance. In other words, the poet is here universalizing one aspect of the black experience—the substitution of the fantasy of fulfillment for the reality of emptiness. Here again, we have a survival technique that is psychologically sound, providing, of course, that "by if-ing" a person can have a good time. The solution is comic because it leaves the persona in the rare emotional good health that results from full self-acceptance.

Another example of a comic solution to a rather delicate social problem is found in the poem entitled "50-50" in the "Lenox Avenue" section of *Shakespeare in Harlem.* Unlike the poems considered above which are monologues, "50-50" is a dialogue between a man and a woman. In his dialogue poems, Hughes was able to achieve considerable comic detachment, standing fully apart from the subject under discussion. In this specific instance, the two personae are discussing the often strained relationship between the desire for love and the need for money:

> I'm all alone in this world, she said,
> Ain't got nobody to share my bed,
> Ain't got nobody to hold my hand—
> The truth of the matter's
> I ain't got no man.
>
> Then Big Boy opened his mouth and said,
> Trouble with you's
> You ain't got no head!
> If you had a head and used your mind
> You could have *me* with you
> All the time.
>
> She answered, Babe, what must I do?
>
> He said, Share your bed—
> *And your money, too.* (p. 117)

Some would argue that there is more cynicism than comic relief in the male persona's final suggestion, and yet his something-for-something offer is a practical solution to the female persona's self-denied dilemma. Lovers do share their worldly goods so the idea is socially salubrious and, hence, comic in the best sense of the word. In fact, the best partnerships—be they commercial, legal, or emotional—are sharing partnerships. And the more equitable the sharing, the stronger and more binding the partnership. So, this particular Hughes poetic dialogue contains both comic and ironic innuendos about how enduring partnerships can be formed in an often casual fashion.

Undoubtedly, Hughes's greatest comic creation in poetry is "Alberta K. Johnson/Madam to You." She is formally introduced in the poet's 1949 volume, *One-Way Ticket,* and there is no doubt that Madam Johnson is a poetic spin-off from that wonderful comic creation in prose—Jesse B. Semple, the hero of the Simple stories.[8] Both emerged during the 1940s and are evidence that, after his experiences during the depression-ridden 1930s and the war-torn 1940s, Hughes began to develop a comic vision—a vision that enabled him "to play it cool," to avoid personal and often emotionally eroding commitments and comment on the ever-changing social and political events with some objectivity and comic distancing from the events themselves. After all, during the 1920s and 1930s, as his autobiographies indicate, there were occasions when he was trauma-ridden over a series of apparently insoluble moral, racial, and social dilemmas. The new comic perspective that he developed is probably best explained in the poem "Motto" which was first published in *Montage of a Dream Deferred* in 1951:

> I play it cool
> And dig all jive.
> That's the reason
> I stay alive.
>
> My motto,
> As I live and learn,
>   is:
> *Dig And Be Dug*
> *In Return.* [9]

There is no doubt that Madam Alberta K. Johnson's poetic portrait reflects Hughes's comic technique at its best. Self-reliant and aggressively independent, she represents the resolute black matriarch who, despite ghetto pressures of ever increasing magnitude, revives and survives. During her life, she has been a hair dresser, a barbecue stand proprietor, a cook, and a maid. She also has occasionally mothered neglected orphans who were wards of the state, labored as a maid, cook, and general pack-horse "in

a twelve-room house," and then almost died when "old death" tried to pay
her a visit one night. In fact, Madam Johnson represents the persona of "Still
Here," a Hughes poem written to praise the survival power of black people:

> I've been scarred and battered.
> My hopes the wind done scattered.
> Snow has friz me, sun has baked me.
>   Looks like between 'em
>   They done tried to make me
> Stop laughin', stop lovin', stop livin'—
>   But I don't care!
>   *I'm still here!*[10]

All of the "Madam to You" poems reveal a light comic touch, but two of the
poems reveal considerable mastery of the comic technique. These are
"Madam and the Number Writer" and "Madam and the Phone Bill." The
first poem tells a story well known in the gambling world. Both Madam and
her numbers man play the wrong number—he 6-0-2 and she 7-0-3. The
number that comes out is 3-2-6. At this point Madam Alberta K. Johnson
makes her now famous comment:

> I said, I swear I
> Ain't gonna play no more
> Till I get over
> To the other shore—
>
> Then I can play
> On them golden streets
> Where the number not only
> Comes out—but repeats!

The runner's response is equally provocative:

> The runner said, Madam,
> That's all very well—
> But suppose
> You goes to hell?[11]

The second poem presents a humorous dialogue between Madam and the
long-distance telephone operator about a collect call made from Kansas
City by a former boyfriend named Roscoe. The poem is one of Hughes's
best dramatic monologues. The poet's authorial posture throughout is
consistently objective. He remains a disciplined neutralist—one who never
interferes with the story line:

> You say I O.K.ed
> LONG DISTANCE?
> O.K.ed it when?

My goodness, Central,
That was *then!*

I'm mad and disgusted
With that Negro now.
I don't pay no REVERSED
CHARGES nohow.

You say, I will pay it—
Else you'll take out my phone?
You better let
My phone alone.

I didn't ask him
To telephone me.
Roscoe knows darn well
LONG DISTANCE
Ain't free.

If I ever catch him,
Lawd, have pity!
Calling me up
From Kansas City

Just to say he loves me!
I knowed that was so.
Why didn't he tell me some'n
I don't know?

For instance, what can
Them other girls do
That Alberta K. Johnson
Can't do—*and more, too?*

What's that, Central?
You say you don't care
Nothing about my
Private affair?

Well, even less about your
PHONE BILL does I care!

Un-humm-m!...Yes!
You say I gave my O.K.?
Well, that O.K. you may keep—

But I *sure* ain't gonna pay![12]

The great merit of the poem is that, although it depicts a particular incident, it provides comment on a universal happening. Madam resolutely refuses to accept a charge which she deems to be unfairly levied, and once again the puny individual in society is pitted against the all-powerful corporation. The poem ends with Madam asserting, "I sure ain't gonna pay." Thus the individual triumphs; the corporation suffers a defeat; the result is cheering to the average reader who can only empathize with someone who is harassed by the minions of big business. Once more it is confirmed that big is not necessarily better, and that resolute and self-assertive individualism can triumph in our society. This conclusion is comic because it reaffirms that social justice does exist. That which we all fear—a society completely dominated by large impersonal corporations, boards, and bureaucratic agencies—cannot prevail as long as there are Alberta K. Johnsons to speak up. A venturesome Roscoe sitting in Kansas City is funny; Madam Johnson's successful confrontation with AT&T is comic.

Hughes reaches his peak as a comic poet in his 1961 work *Ask Your Mama.* The tone is different from "Madam to You" and from the earlier attempts at comic irony in *Shakespeare in Harlem.* The comedy in this work does not develop in scenes that emphasize the black life-style. Rather *Ask Your Mama* is a long protest poem, and the comedy is embedded in the irony which a wisely observant Hughes found at the heart of the black man's reaction to American racism. This comic wisdom of black folk permits them to survive as they adjust and readjust to American racial patterns. Music has always helped, but laughter has long been purgative and therapeutic. For instance, there is the dream of a comic reversal in race relations—a dream that has haunted the imaginative black man ever since he began his "John the Conquerer" tales in slavery times. In the "Cultural Exchange" section of *Ask Your Mama* Hughes writes:

> Dreaming that the Negroes of the south have taken over . . .
> Martin Luther King is governor of Georgia . . .
> Wealthy Negroes have White servants,
> White sharecroppers work the Black plantations,
> And colored children have White mammies . . .
> *Culture,* they say, *is a two-way street:*
> Hand me my mint julep, mammy. Make haste![13]

Such a deliberate misstatement is ironic; but it is an irony enriched by Hughes's comic vision. The poet's lament for those "Dear, dear darling old White mammies / Sometimes even buried with our family" (p. 9) sheds little or no light on the black man's social and moral problems and provides no solutions for victims of American racism. But the game of make-believe works; the reader's mood lightens, and he knows that, however dismal the scene, there's always the sound of a laughter that is truly a healing balm for the fatigued and the worn.

Hughes also provides some laughter when, in the section entitled "Ride, Red, Ride," he writes about a "subversive" Santa Claus:

Santa Claus, forgive me,
But your gift books are subversive,
Your dolls are interracial.
You'll be called by Eastland.[14]
When they ask you if you know me,
Don't take the fifth amendment. (p. 14)

Even toyland is touched by American racism, and the forces of bigotry are not above investigating society's most favored mythic symbol of mirth and good cheer. There is another passage beginning "Santa Claus, forgive me" in the "Ode to Dinah" section of the poem, but there the mood is dead serious:[15]

Santa Claus, forgive me,
But babies born in shadows
In the shadow of the welfare
If born premature
Bring welfare checks much sooner
Yet no presents down the chimney. (pp. 28–29)

This long poem of social protest also has some lines which provide excellent background commentary that is both comic and informative. For instance, at the beginning of the section entitled "Horn of Plenty," the poet talks about the great money-makers in the world of black entertainment and big-time professional athletics and mentions "gospel singers who pant to pack / golden crosses to a Cadillac" (p. 42). In another section, describing the favorite urban haunts and hangouts in the black belts of Kansas City, San Francisco, Chicago, and Oakland, the poet writes:

On the corner picking splinters
Out of the midnight sky
In the quarter of the Negroes
As Leola passes by
The men can only murmur
My!. . . My! My! (p. 63)

Unfortunately, the tragic events of the 1960s blunted Hughes's penchant for comic observation. *The Panther and the Lash,* published posthumously in 1967, is a somber volume of poetry. Its tone reflected the times. One guesses that Hughes knew that the black man's gift for laughter still existed, but in that decade of war, riot, assassination, and bloodshed, the laughter was necessarily muted. There were too many bombed children and roasted ghetto rats and slain heroes. And one even doubts that Hughes, had he lived on into the 1970s, would have recovered his "cool" comic detachment. Martin Luther King's death, the bloody charade in Viet Nam, Watergate and its acrimonious aftermath—all of these events may well have sealed the poet in a tomb of gloom and forever blighted his comic vision. And, if he had had the opportunity to search the scene for comic relief, what would he have found? There probably would have been nothing to be comic about. The Alberta K. Johnsons, so valiantly vibrant a generation earlier, would have been either dead or huddled with geriatric fear behind paper doors in a crime-ridden corner of a crime-ridden city. So Hughes and his gift for cool comedy belonged to a time when there was room for laughter in the sprawling black urban enclaves.

NOTES

Reprinted with permission from *Black American Literature Forum* 15, no. 3 (Fall 1981): 108–11.

1. *The Weary Blues* (New York: Knopf, 1926), p. ii.

2. *The Big Sea* (New York: Knopf, 1940), p. 241.

3. Owen Dodson, "Review of *Shakespeare in Harlem*," *Phylon* (Third Quarter 1942): 337–38.

4. Alain Locke, "Annual Review of Negro Literature, 1949," *Phylon* (First Quarter 1950): 5–12.

5. James Baldwin, "Review of Selected Poems," *New York Times Book Review*, 29 March 1959, p. 6.

6. See R. K. Barksdale, *Langston Hughes: The Poet and His Critics* (Chicago: American Library Association, 1977), and Onwuchekwa Jemie, *Langston Hughes: An Introduction to His Poetry* (New York: Columbia University Press, 1976).

7. *Shakespeare in Harlem* (New York: Knopf, 1942), p. 4. Subsequent references are from this edition and are noted parenthetically in the text.

8. See Barksdale, pp. 85–86.

9. *Selected Poems* (New York: Knopf, 1959), p. 234.

10. Ibid., p. 123.

11. *One-Way Ticket* (New York: Knopf, 1949), p. 12.

12. Ibid., pp. 13–15.

13. *Ask Your Mama* (New York: Knopf, 1961), pp. 8–9. Subsequent references are from this edition and are noted parenthetically in the text.

14. Eastland was a U.S. Senator from Mississippi during the 1950s. A bitter foe of Negro progress, he participated in congressional investigations designed to limit black freedom.

15. Several themes are repeated and reintroduced at random throughout the poem. For a discussion of how the poet introduces and utilizes a pattern of thematic discontinuity modeled on bebop jazz models, see Barksdale, pp. 112–13.

PART 4

Praisesong for Black Women Writers

Diction and Style in Selected Poems of Phillis Wheatley

Before one can engage in an effective discussion of the diction and style employed by Phillis Wheatley in her slim volume of poetry published in London in 1773, one must make certain that Wheatley and her poetry are placed in proper historical perspective. First, it is well to remember that she wrote her poetry in Boston which, in the 1760s and 1770s, was at best an English colonial outpost, not quite as distant geographically from London as Sidney, Australia, or Bombay, India; yet, nevertheless, not only a city embroiled in revolt against the Mother Country, but a city which from its inception was far removed from London in terms of its culture, mores, and life-style. For Boston was founded by seventeenth-century English Puritans who, after Cromwell's decline and fall in the 1650s, became a hated and despised sect throughout England in general and in London in particular. Whereas London, thanks to the cathartic of Restoration hedonism, was by Queen Anne's day purged of Puritan gloom, eighteenth-century Boston continued to be a rigidly puritanical city, obsessed with ostentatious piety and terrified of witches, ghosts, goblins, and sins of the flesh.

Inevitably, a city with a pronounced puritan bias did not provide an environment favorable to the cultivation of literature and the arts. Phillis Wheatley's Boston had no theater, no elegant literary salons like those of Madame de Stael in Paris, no Samuel Johnson meeting with his fellow writers in an atmosphere of clubbable conviviality. Instead, Doctors of Divinity and grim religionists prowled Boston's cobblestone streets and alleys, and even those prayerful Bostonians who owned African slaves sought to cultivate their souls even as they exacted physical toil and labor. Somehow they reasoned that a slave whose soul had been saved was, ergo, a better slave, and both the master and his slaves could hover under the huge umbrella of Christian charity and love, masters on their side and slaves on theirs. And Harvard, the Bay Colony's premier institution of higher learning, of which it was justifiably proud, stressed not the study of the literary arts but the study of theology and the classics—the classics purged, of course, of their immoral and heretical trappings. The students studied and read Horace and Virgil and Cicero, but not Ovid, Juvenal, and Lucretius. When they wrote, they did not write epics, lyrics, or fiction; they wrote laboriously wrought moral treatises.

Given the cultural atmosphere of Boston and its surroundings, the literary achievement of Phillis Wheatley is remarkable. But it is even more remarkable that in her poetry one finds mirrored the literary practices and style of the writers of London's elegant Augustan Age—writers who were so far removed culturally and geographically from Boston. Somehow, despite the confused alarums of war and despite the Bay Colony's long-established antipathy for the secular arts, the diction found in Phillis Wheatley's poems and the style with which she crafted those poems came from England. Indeed, a careful study of her poetry suggests that, in trying "to snatch a grace beyond the reach of art" and in trying to present "what oft was thought but ne'er so well expressed," Phillis Wheatley walked in the footsteps of the great Augustan poet Alexander Pope. Ironically, the latter's life in London and in Twickenham had been, as he indicated, "one long disease," and hers in faraway Boston, forty years later, an agonizingly short disease; but both courted the same muse in their fashion, the elegant Augustan with intellectual arrogance and a wit as sharp as a serpent's tooth, the humble black girl with gracious shyness and humility.

The great model for eighteenth-century diction and style was Pope's *Homer,* and it was from the diligent study of this work that Phillis Wheatley quickly mastered the style and poetic diction so fashionable in Augustan England. Margaretta Odell, a collateral descendant of Mrs. Wheatley, Phillis's mistress, and the author of the 1835 *Memoir* of the poet's life and career, stated that, in addition to a "decided taste for the stories of Heathen Mythology," "Pope's Homer seems to have been a great favorite" with Phillis.[1] There is no evidence that the young poet was able to broaden her knowledge about eighteenth-century poetic diction and style; as far as we know, she did not have an opportunity to read Pope's *Essay on Criticism* or the essays on the poetic art by Vida, Boileau, or Horace. And there is no evidence that she was acquainted with Johnson's *Lives of the Poets,* which contained that author's fine essay extolling Pope's *Homer.* Nevertheless, Phillis Wheatley's poems reveal a practical mastery of all of the major features of eighteenth-century poetic diction and style. The poets and critics of that period stressed, first, that poets should use "select words, phrases and other 'ornaments' "—a practice which, according to one critic, received "splendid emphasis and exemplification in Pope's translation of Homer."[2] Or as Johnson stated in his *Lives of the Poets,* proper poetic diction demands "a system of words at once refined from the grossness of domestic use, and free from the harshness of terms appropriated to different arts."[3] In Johnson's opinion, language was "the dress of thought" and "splendid ideas lose their magnificence if they are conveyed in low and vulgar words."[4] Inevitably, the stress of the Augustan Age on a poetical language that was refined, selective, and ornamental led to the kind of stylistic excess that Romantics like Wordsworth and Coleridge decried at the end of the eighteenth century—a diction and style that resulted in poetic phrases like "the lowly kind ruminating in the contiguous shade." Or there was excessive periphrasis; birds were never birds but "the feathery tribe," and summer's insects were "the wandering nation of a summer's day" or frogs "the loquacious race."

Fortunately, Phillis Wheatley's poetry is not filled with worst-case scenarios of excessively bad eighteenth-century poetic diction and style. One finds extensive use of personifications and abstractions but these are, after Pope's manner, fittingly used. Latinisms occur infrequently and there are no archaisms at all. There is considerable periphrasis, particularly in the two mini-epics, "Niobe in Her Distress for her Children Slain by Apollo" and "Goliath of Gath." Similarly, noun-adjective inversions, a favorite eighteenth-century stylistic device, occur with some frequency. And, finally, one might add that Phillis Wheatley's poetic language is not ostentatiously decorative nor overly ornamental nor aggressively intellectual. This may be attributable in part to the nature of her poetic subject matter; more than half of her slender volume of poems is comprised of elegies written to assuage the grief of the fathers, mothers, husbands, and wives of recently deceased loved ones. But the nature of Wheatley's own personality may be an important factor in this regard. Odell in her 1835 *Memoir* stresses that she was noted for her "meekness of spirit" and that she was "gentle-tempered" and altogether free of "literary vanity."[5] Indeed, one of her elegiac poems begins with the following invocation:

> Indulgent Muse, my groveling mind inspire
> And fill my bosom with celestial fire.[6]

Few, if any, of the more prestigious poets of the Augustan Age would admit to having a "groveling mind."

Probably the most noticeable eighteenth-century feature of Wheatley's poetry was her use of the heroic or decasyllabic couplet. The following lines from "On Imagination" demonstrate the facility and ease with which the poet rendered the famous rhyme:

From Helicon's refulgent heights attend,
Ye sacred choir, and my attempts befriend:
To tell her glories with a faithful tongue,
Ye blooming graces, triumph in my song.
Now here, now there, the roving Fancy flies,
Till some loved object strikes her wandering eyes,
Whose silken fetters all the senses bind,
And soft captivity involves the mind.[7]

On rare occasions there is a bad couplet rhyme, as in "wrote" and "thought" and "skill" and "reveal," both of which occur in the mini-epic "Niobe in Her Distress." And in the same poem one questions the rhyme between "spouse" and "brows." These are exceptions, however; in most of her poetry the couplets seem to have been composed with skill and ease. A dedicated Pope specialist would very likely charge that her couplets are not as smoothly wrought as those of the chief poet of the Augustan Age. However, she does on occasion match the master and "snatch a grace beyond the reach of art," as in the well-wrought onomatopoetic lines from "To Maecenas."

When gentler strains demand thy graceful song,
The lengthening line moved languishing along.

Similarly distinctive is the drama-packed couplet in "Niobe in Her Distress":

Soon as the arrow left the deadly wound
His issuing entrails smoked upon the ground.

This last couplet suggests that the poet who sought to comfort so many who had suffered the death of close ones was by no means squeamish about describing the specifics of dying.

As has been suggested above, Phillis Wheatley in some of her poetry made extensive use of personifications and abstractions. In "On Imagination," for instance, there is reference to "the frowns of Winter" and to "Fancy's raptured eyes." In other poems there are references to "Death's domain," to "Virtue, the Auspicious Queen," and to "Celestial Chastity." And in the poem "Thoughts on the Works of Providence," "Power, Wisdom and Goodness shine"; "Wisdom rules"; Night wears a "sable veil"; and Reason speaks to "her great companion, Immortal love." In no instance, however, are these personifications and abstractions obtrusive or distracting.

Another mark of eighteenth-century poetic diction—the use of Latinisms— is found only rarely in Phillis Wheatley's poetry. This is surprising because there is evidence that the poet was well-schooled in Latin and in the literature of Rome. There are many references to Virgil or to Maro or to the Mantuan, and "Niobe in Her Distress" is based on the sixth book of Ovid's *Metamorphosis*. Nevertheless, there are few Latinisms. In the mini-epic "Goliath and Gath," the young David stands with "Goliath's head *depending* from his hand" [italics are mine]; and, in another section of the same poem, "ideas range / Licentious and unbounded o'er the plains." The poet also uses the word "profound" as a substantive, as in the phrase "from his profound / Old Chaos heard." In another poem, the poet writes of "sublunary scenes" and in yet another "unerring Wisdom guides / With eye propitious." One may justifiably conclude that Latinisms are few in Wheatley's poetry because of her obvious preference in many instances for a plainly wrought monosyllabic style. In the following couplet from "To Maecenas" there are two dissyllables with the rest of the couplet devoted to monosyllables:

> But here I sit, and mourn a grovelling mind
> That fain would mount, and ride upon the wind.

Similarly, in a poem entitled "To a Lady, On the Death of Her Husband," there is the couplet:

> From the cold shell of his great soul arise
> And look beyond, thou native of the skies.

Probably, the poet's most famous monosyllabic lines are:

> Should you, my lord, while you peruse my song,
> Wonder from whence my love of Freedom sprung
> Whence flows these wishes for the common good,
> By feeling hearts alone best understood,
> I, young in life, by seeming cruel fate
> Was snatch'd from Afric's fancied happy seat.

Of the forty-six words in this passage, thirty-three are monosyllables, twelve are disyllables, and one word is a polysyllable. As Phillis doubtless knew, it is difficult to be both Latinic and monsyllabic at the same time and in the same place.

Although Wheatley, unlike her eighteenth-century counterparts, did not use a highly Latinic vocabulary in her poetry, she followed her peers closely in her extensive use of periphrasis and noun-adjective inversions. Of all the eighteenth-century forms of poetic diction, periphrasis was the most stylistically idiosyncratic. The object, of course, was to avoid the vulgar and the mundane language of ordinary pedestrian discourse and use what was thought to be the language of esthetic elevation and intellectual cultivation. After all, neither Homer nor Virgil had resorted to the use of literal language, and the neoclassical writers sought to emulate their distinguished predecessors. To Homer, the Mediterranean was always "the wine-dark sea," and to Virgil, death was always Charon, the dreaded boatman on the River Styx. Phillis Wheatley was no exception. The ocean at dawn becomes "the orient main." In the same poem, "Thoughts on the Works of

Providence," the "sons of vegetation rise / And spread their leafy banners to the skies." Flowers become "the flow'ry race," and "the dreaming lover" sighs to his "kind fair." Death is "the deep impervious shade" that brings "never-waking sleep." In "Goliath of Gath," David, the shepherd boy, keeps "the fleecy care." When Apollo in "Niobe in Her Distress" approaches Niobe's children to avenge Niobe's insult to his mother, Latona, his arrows become "the feathered vengeance quivering in his hands." And, as with her eighteenth-century fellow poets, birds are never birds but "feathered warblers" soaring through the "cloud-girt regions" on "seraphic pinions."

Similarly, Phillis Wheatley's poetry contains many examples of noun-adjective inversions. Many of these are found in the mini-epic "Niobe in Her Distress." The poem's spirited invocation reads:

> Apollo's wrath the dreadfull spring
> Of ills innumerous, tuneful goddess sing.

Niobe, of royal race, boasts of "charms unnumbered." Indeed, she is "Beyond description beautiful." When the vengeful Apollo sends the arrow of death toward Sypylus, Niobe's first-born, the boy hears "the language of fate portentous whistling through the air." Sometimes, the inversion is dictated by a needed rhyme:

> To cultivate in ev'ry noble mind
> Habitual grace and sentiments refined.

Finally, in "Goliath of Gath," Goliath wears a "coat of mail" to grace his "form terrific."

What is interesting about Phillis Wheatley's use of periphrasis and noun-adjective inversions is that they are generally lacking in her elegiac poetry. One may quite plausibly conclude that in these poems the poet sought to deliver a message of consolation in language that was plain and direct and shorn of ornamental poetic devices. As has been indicated above, these elegy poems are free of Latinisms and compact with simply wrought monosyllabic lines that sought to assuage grief and not be poetically decorative. A good example of a poetic statement of this kind are these lines from "To a Gentleman and Lady"—a poem that presents its message in language that is direct and meaningful:

> The glowing stars and silver queen of light
> At last must perish in the gloom of night;
> Resign they friends to that Almighty hand
> Which gave them life and bow to his command.

Inevitably, in any final consideration of Phillis Wheatley's poetic diction and style, one is tempted to speculate about what might have happened had she not returned to Boston in 1773 and remained in London instead. Suppose that she had become a Londoner and friend of great literary figures like Hannah More, Cowper, Goldsmith, Gray, and the African writers Ignatius Sancho and Olaudah Equiano. Would she have followed Gray and Collins and other pre-Romantics of the day and been influenced to develop a less ornate style—a style as direct and unadorned as that found in some of her elegies? This, of course, we will never know. For all that we have is a slim volume of poems written by an adolescent slave girl, who was kidnapped at an early age from her African homeland, transported in chains across the Atlantic to an alien land, and kept in slavery's bonds in accordance with the laws of that alien land; but she was an adolescent who had the spiritual resilience to overcome her status as a slave and sing her song in gloom-ridden Boston town. Phillis Wheatley's literary output was small but it speaks volumes for the indomitable will and intelligence of the "ventrous Afric."

NOTES

This paper was presented at The Phillis Wheatley Conference, Illinois State University, Bloomington, in 1984.

1. Margaretta Odell, *Memoir and Poems of Phillis Wheatley* (Boston: Light and Horton, 1835), p. 20.
2. Thomas Quayle, *Poetic Diction: A Study of Eighteenth-Century Verse* (London: Methuen, 1924), p. 14.
3. Samuel Johnson, *Lives of the Poets*, ed. G. B. Hill (1905), 1:420.
4. Johnson, *The Rambler*, no. 158.
5. Odell, *Memoir*, pp. 15–16.
6. Wheatley, "To a Lady," in *Memoir*, p. 83.
7. Wheatley, "On Imagination," in *Memoir*, p. 77.

Margaret Danner and the African Connection

Several years ago, Dionne Warwick, one of black America's top vocalists, combined with a gifted young composer named Burt Bacharach to entertain music lovers with several songs that were rhythmically bouncy and jazzily innovative. One of the tunes produced by this musically creative duo was "Do You Know the Way to San Jose?" It was a musical question phrased with vocal elegance by Dionne's consummate artistry. Today we have another question posed by another black artist in another medium. She, too, is gifted and innovative and, in every respect for her time and her medium, just as consummate in her artistry as Dionne Warwick. The question that she asks, however, is different in import and significance from Dionne's question. Somehow the question so elegantly phrased by Margaret Esse Danner in the beautiful edition of her poems, *The Down of a Thistle,* is laced with history and the clash of empire. It's a question that smells of smoky slave barracoons and the stench of slave ships wallowing in the middle passage. It's a question that echoes and reechoes across oceans and continents, bounding and ricocheting off the walls of the blood-spattered centuries. It's a question that provokes bitter memories of black children torn from the tortured embrace of black mothers. It's a question that is noted in the forced removal of fifteen million Africans throughout a period of travail that lasted 450 years. It's a question that suggests shattered tribal rituals and a weary pilgrimage amid unending hardship, toil, and the flesh-cutting whip-lash. Margaret Esse Danner's question, posed with poetic aplomb, is "How far is it from Beale Street to Benin City?" Or to put it another way, "What is the cultural distance between the black hands that molded a Senufo Firespitter mask and the black hands that painted the Jeff Donaldson wall in Chicago?"

So Margaret Danner's poetry is concerned with the artistic implications of the African continuum, just as Herskovits was, at an earlier time, interested in the anthropological implications of the same historical phenomenon. But, as many of you can recall, when Herskovits first posed the question, black America's collective objective was integration into the mainstream of American life, and there was much skepticism about the legitimacy and validity of the concept of an African continuum. Back in those days, as some of you also remember, we were all athirst for new wine from new bottles or what we thought was new wine in new bottles. Many of us found the bottles, if you recall, but never even sipped the wine. Or, if we did, we sang with the blues singer—

> Movin on down the line
> Where the wine don' tase
> Like turpentine

And remember, too, what black poets wrote about Africa at an earlier time in this century. Remember Langston Hughes, who later became a fervent Third-Worlder, writing:

> So long,
> So far away
> Is Africa.
> Not even memories alive
> Save those that history books create,
> Save those that songs
> Beat back into the blood—
>
> . . .
>
> So long
> So far away
> Is Africa

In the poetry of Margaret Esse Danner (b. 1910) there are no questions nor doubts about a broad cultural highway from black America to black Africa, and her firm belief irradiates her work. This is explicitly stated in her poem "Africa, Drifting Through Me Sings":

> Africa: I turn
>   to meet this vast land of bittersweet.
> Africa; whose creviced walls
>   cradle myriad waterfalls.
> Africa; where black men stride
>   toward freedom's ever inching tide.
> Africa; the paradox
>   do I pry Pandora's box
> Africa: I read these things
>   her blood drifting through me, sings.

But the mark of a first-rate poet is not so much what is said but how it is said, and Margaret Danner writes of Africa with a verbal brilliance that is both bedazzling and enlightening. Indeed, in reading her work, one is reminded of Pope's lines written so many years ago—

> True wit is Nature to advantage dress't
> What oft was thought but ne'er so well express'd.

The principal advantage enjoyed by Margaret Danner is her superb gift for imagery. Nothing is plain or direct. Her ideas are articulated with the careful cerebration found in the poetry of Gwendolyn Brooks, but the image and the careful word configurations dominate. And, through the plethora of images, the reader emerges with a crystal-clear view of an immense, shining cultural highway leading from Beale Street down through the stressful centuries back to Benin. For instance, even the world's most precious metal, gold, takes on a heightened cultural and esthetic significance when the African connection is imagistically explored:

> Gold is the shade Esperanto. Gold is the paragon.
> The time of the sun at noon, at setting
> Is gold. Gold the first tinge of dawn.
>   . . .
> And gold is the color that poets all use:
> Golden lights, golden days are never cliché.
> Gold is coined without tricks or excuse.
> And few turn a hand toward a rainbow tint.
> Few of ebony, flesh, or tan tone stray.
> Few dare daub a sunset or hazard a hint
> Of the urge to sonnet to one. So the bold
> Indigo witchery and tangerine haze
> Which heightened our African ancestor's gaze
> Has remained
> And the sunset today, like a beacon blaze
> Is a vision of glittering gold.

What is truly golden lies in the "Indigo witchery and tangerine haze" which heightened "our African ancestor's gaze." Those who remember this need never "daub a sunset" or write a sonnet to a sunset. And it is thus that a racial memory becomes a symbol of the gold that men in the Western world have fought, bled, and died for.

Margaret Danner's poetically expressed fascination with African *objets d'art* also helps to build a cultural highway through a forest of folk memories. The poem "The Lady Executive Looks at a Mangbetu Palm Wine Jug" provides a good example. First, the poet praises the curvilinear "femininity" of the molded jug. Indeed, although it stands "full flared" and is pregnant with history, its maternal destiny has never been fulfilled. The poet writes:

> But though it seems to stand full flared,
> It has long been denied. Its role upset.
> This womb is neither warm nor wet.
> This African jug is dry.
>
> Look, see, there are no flowers here,
> No plunging stems or roots
> From which the living buds can shoot.

The author concludes that the Mangbetu palm wine jug is to be admired for its feminine beauty and charm, even though it houses an "emptiness, a glassed-in space." The poem further implies that, although the palm wine jug now bears nothing, things that are born will grow and then die; the palm wine jug is a thing of art that will live forever. Thus, we have the Danner version of the ancient proverb, *Ars longa, vita brevis*. Or should we more accurately say, *Ars Africana longa, vita brevis*?

Undoubtedly, Margaret Danner demonstrates her greatest poetic gift in presenting images of color in describing African *objets d'art*. Her favorite color is tangerine, although words like "indigo," "ebony," "bronze," and "gold" often appear. In a short poem entitled "Beale Street . . . Reaffirmed," for instance, she describes how a young black artist, in imitation of black artists of the distant past, carves in tangerine, on the black tarpaper roof of a Mississippi boulevard shack, "the long neck and back of a Mangbetu lady." But her most colorful "tangerine" poem is "Etta Moten's Attic." Not only is the color everywhere, touching all of Ms. Moten's splendid collection, but the poet, using a plethora of participles, makes the color an active agent of beauty. When one views the incomparable collection of Moten's African *objets d'art*, it is as if a huge "paintpot" of Gauguin's "incomparable tangerine" is "splashing," "spilling," "dripping," "splotching," "tipping," "dyeing," "quickening and charming" everything in view. The poem reads:

> It was as if Gauguin
> had upset a huge paintpot
> of his incomparable tangerine,
>
> splashing wherever my startled eyes ran
> here, there and at my very hand on
> masks and carvings and paintings not seen
>
> here before; spilling straight as a stripe
> spun geometrically in a Ndebele rug
> flung over an ebony chair,

or dripping round as a band on type
of bun the Watusi warriors
make of their pompadoured hair,

splashing high as a sunbird or fly moving
over a frieze of mahogany trees,
or splotching out from low underneath as a root,

shimmering bright as a ladybug, grooving
a green bed of moss, sparkling as a beetle,
a bee, shockingly dotting the snoot

of an ape or the nape of its neck or as clue
to its navel, stamping a Zulu's intriguing mask,

tipping the lips of a chief of Ashanti's who
was carved to his stool so he'd sit
there forever and never fear a slipping

of rule or command, dyeing the skirt
(all askew) that wouldn't stay put on the
Pygmy in spite of his real leather belt,

quickening and charming till we felt the bloom
of veldt and jungle flow through the room.

Ms. Danner's poetic concern for Africa goes beyond her colorful imagistic description of African art and sculpture. She is also concerned with historical events and the monumental ironies and gaping inequities that powered those events. A good example of such a racial statement is a poem entitled "And Through the Caribbean Sea." Because of its emphasis on the "kaleidoscopic" nature of the world of the Black Diaspora, the poem is somewhat reminiscent of Langston Hughes's poem "Black Seed." But passivity runs through the Hughes poem; the black people of his diaspora have been "driven before an alien wind" and "scattered like seed." They are "Hybrid plants in another's garden," and there is no mention of a vigorous and life-sustaining African connection. In the Danner poem, on the other hand, there is swirling movement and a strong suggestion that, wherever the black man traveled, he kept his African connection.

We, like shades that were first conjured up
by an African witch-doctor's ire,
(Indigo for the drum and the smoke of night,

tangerine for the dancing smudged fire)
have been forced to exist in a huge kaleidoscope world.
We've been shifting with time and shifting
    through space,

at each whimsical turn of the hands that have thrown

the kaleidoscope, until any pattern or place
or shade is our own.

The indigo shifted from its drumlike vein
toward the blue of the sky that the Goths attained.
The tangerine became the orange of the tango, again

The red of the Susy Q., and each time the turning
invaded one pattern, a new one was formed
and in forming each pattern we traded

Until, who questions whether we'd be prone to yearn
for a Louis Quinze frame, a voodoo fire,
Rococo, Baroque, an African mask or a Gothic
      spire
or any style of any age or any place of name.

In other words, black people have been in kaleidoscopic movement for so long that the black presence has been culturally felt and traded off almost everywhere.

Finally, in a poem entitled "To the Bronze Masque," Miss Danner asks the silent mask whom she nicknamed "Miss Benin Bronze"

What happened in Benin?
What welled the hate, gore, pillaging?
Were you, Bronze lady, the substantial lure?
Was to own you, their Nemesis?
Was this why the thirty streets halo'd for
their high, wide, length became the bier of
      their creators?

Naturally, the bronze mask can provide no answer about the destruction of Africa's great city of splendor and gold. Possibly, it is not necessary for a poem to provide such an answer. The important thing, Ms. Danner would say, is to see the connection—the African connection.

Margaret Walker: Folk Orature
and Historical Prophecy

Like Robert Hayden and Melvin Tolson, Margaret Walker has written poetry in the shadow of the academy. In fact, both of her advanced degrees from the University of Iowa—the master's degree in 1940 and the Ph.D. in 1966—were granted because of her achievements in creative writing. Her first volume of poems, *For My People,* which in 1942 won the Yale Series of Younger Poets Award, helped her to gain the master's degree; and the prize-winning novel *Jubilee* fulfilled the central requirement for her doctorate. But Margaret Walker's poetry is quite different from the poetry written by Hayden or by Tolson. For instance, many of Hayden's poems are full of intellectual subtleties and elusive symbols that often baffle and bewilder the reader. Similarly, Tolson's verse, particularly his *Harlem Gallery,* is often intellectually complex and obscure in meaning. On the other hand, Margaret Walker's poetry is clear and lucid throughout, with sharply etched images and symbols presented in well-formed ballads and sonnets. It is now clear in retrospect that Hayden and Tolson were influenced by the academy poets of the 1930s and 1940s—Ciardi, Tate, Lowell, Wilbur, Auden, Dickey—poets who developed their craft within the bosom of the academy. Their poetry, as a consequence, has an academic gloss, suggesting richly endowed libraries in the sophisticated suburbs of learning. Only rarely do these poets seem to be sensitized to problems and dilemmas confounding an unintellectualized, urbanized, racially pluralistic America—a concern which, as will be noted further in this essay, dominated Margaret Walker's poetry.

In other words, although she too spent all of her days in academia, she was never as a writer held captive by the academy. Indeed, an analysis of her poetry will reveal that in subject, tone, and esthetic texture, her poetry is remarkably free of intellectual pretense and stylized posturing. Instead, one finds the roots of the black experience in language that is simple, passionate, and direct. If one asks how Margaret Walker as a writer remained in the academy but not of the academy, the answer undoubtedly can be found in the circumstances governing her family life and background.

In the first place, Margaret Walker was the daughter of a preacher man, and not just an ordinary preacher man. Her father, Sigismond Walker, was a native of Jamaica who, in 1908, four years before Claude McKay's arrival, came to America to study at Tuskegee. Unlike the poet McKay, however, Sigismond Walker persevered academically, gained a degree at Atlanta's Gammon Theological Institute, and then joined that small band of educated black Methodist ministers who ventured forth to preach the Word in the pre–World War I South. So Margaret Walker grew up in a household ruled by the power of the word, for undoubtedly few have a greater gift for articulate word power than an educated Jamaican trained to preach the doctrine of salvation in the black South. Indeed, personal survival in the Walker household undoubtedly demanded word power and well-honed verbal skills. The poet admits that in a home filled with song and singing inspired by her musician mother, she struggled successfully to survive without the gift of song; but survival without the mastery of words and language was impossible. So by the age of twelve, Margaret Walker was writing poetry and sharpening her communication skills; and, when, at the age of seventeen, she transferred from New Orleans's Gilbert Academy to Northwestern, she took her well-honed verbal skills with her. As she noted in *How I Wrote Jubilee,* she quickly discovered at Northwestern that she did not know how to convert the rich orature of her talking, word-filled New Orleans household into a novel, but she was fully convinced that she had carried the power of the word with her to Evanston.

Not only was there a preaching father in the Walker household, but there was a talking maternal grandmother—a grandmother full of tales of "befo' dah wah" and "duin da time afta da wah." So there were stories to be listened to and placed in the vault of memory. And there was also New Orleans with its rich background of folk mythology, its music, its red beans and rice and jambalaya, its assortment of racial experiences to be remembered and recalled through the power of the word.

So Margaret Walker as a poet and as a writer was not dependent on the academy for her subject matter, for her style, nor for her authorial posture. Indeed, the rhetorical power of the poem "For My People"—the verbal arpeggios, the cascading adjectives, the rhythmic repetitions—has its roots in the "preacher-man" rhetoric of the black South. Similarly, Vyry's eloquent prayer in *Jubilee* came from the black man's past and from the deep folk memories of a trouble-driven people.

The poet would also be the first to admit that her "down-home" grounding in the principles of the Judeo-Christian religion, black-style, protected her against the frivolous intellectualism of the academy. She had no need to join movements and bow to trends and identify with esoteric cults. Her religion also stood her in good stead when, in 1935, she graduated from Northwestern and joined other writers in Chicago's rather radical WPA Writers Project—writers like Nelson Algren, Richard Wright, Studs Terkel, Willard Motley, James Farrell, and Jack Conroy. In 1935, Chicago lay by the shore of Lake Michigan like a beached whale, panting its way through the Depression, and the world and Chicago were ripe for social and political revolution. Racism, gangsterism, corruption, and political radicalism were everywhere. But Margaret Walker kept her home-grown faith through it all, calling not for violent revolution but for "a new earth" that would "hold all the people, all the faces, all the adams and eves. . . . "

The poet's career started out with a bang. In 1937, when, at the age of twenty-two, she published her first volume of poems, called *For My People,* she became the youngest black writer ever to have published a volume of poetry in this century. Langston Hughes had published "The Negro Speaks of Rivers" at the age of nineteen, but his first volume of poems was not published until 1926 when he was twenty-four.[1] Moreover, when the volume won a poetry prize in 1942, Margaret Walker became the first black woman in American literary history to be so honored in a prestigious national competition. But these achievements are not what is notable or significant about *For My People.* The title poem is itself a singular and unique literary achievement. First, it is magnificently wrought oral poetry. It must be read aloud; and, in reading it aloud, one must be able to breathe and pause, pause and breathe, preacher-style. One must be able to sense the ebb and flow of the intonations. One must be able to hear the words sing, when the poet spins off parallel clusters like

> . . . the gone years and the now years and the maybe years
> washing ironing cooking scrubbing sewing mending hoeing
> plowing digging planting pruning patching dragging along.

This is the kind of verbal music found in a well-delivered down-home folk sermon, and, as such, the poem achieves what James Weldon Johnson attempted to do in *God's Trombones*—fuse the written word with the spoken word. In this sense, the reader is imaginatively set free to explore what Shelley called the beautiful "unheard melody" of a genuine poetic experience. The passage is also significant in its emphasis on repetitive "work" words describing the age-old labors of black people. The activities are as old as slavery—slavery in the "big house" or slavery in the fields. Adding "ing" to these monosyllabic work verbs suggests the dreary monotony of black labor in slave times and in free times. Without the "ing," they remain command words—enforcing words, backed up by a white enforcing power structure.

And behind the command has always lurked the whip or the gun or the overseer or the captain or the boss or Mr. Charlie or Miss Ann. Indeed, black laborers, long held captive by Western capitalism, were forced to work without zeal or zest—just "dragging along." Somehow, they remained outside the system of profit and gain; no profits accrued to them for their labor; thus, they dragged along, "never gaining never reaping never knowing and never understanding." In just these few lines, Margaret Walker performs a premier poetic function: she presents a succinct historical summary of how the black man slipped into an economic and social quagmire when, first as a slave and then as a quasi-free man, he was forced to cope with the monster of European capitalistic enterprise.

Not only does *For My People* have word power, but it is a poem filled with subtle juxtapositions of thought and idea. When the scene shifts from the rural South to the urban North—to "thronging 47th Street in Chicago and Lenox Avenue in New York"—the poet describes her people as "lost disinherited dispossessed and happy people." At another point, they are depicted as "walking blindly spreading joy." This Donnesque yoking of opposites linking happiness with dispossession and blind purposelessness with joy reveals the depth of Margaret Walker's understanding of the complexities of the black experience. In fact, the poet here is writing about the source of the black man's blues, for out of his troubled past and turbulent present came the black man's song—a music and a song that guarantee that happiness and joy will somehow always be found lurking behind the squalor of the ghetto or behind the misery of the quarters or in some sharecropper's windowless cabin in the flood-drenched lowlands. For whenever there is trouble, a Bessie Smith or a Ma Rainey or a Bill Broonzy or a B. B. King or someone with the gift of song will step forward to sing it away. In fact, the song gets better when one is real lowdown and disinherited and even suicidal:

> Goin' down to the railroad
> Put my head on de track
> Goin' down to the railroad
> Put my head on the track
> When No. 3 come rollin in
> Gonna pull ma big head back.

So, although misery and woe are ever-present in the black community, suicides remain low. If things get too bad, there is always tomorrow; so one sings, "Hurry sundown, see what tomorrow bring / May bring rain / May bring any ol' thing." As the poet indicates, joy and misery are always juxtaposed in the black experience.

Margaret Walker also states that blacks die too soon, the victims of "consumption and anemia and lynching." Each word in this triad of death has its own history in the black experience. Consumption (or the more clinical but less poetical word, tuberculosis) became a famous word in the white experience when it became "the white death" that ravaged the industrial nations during and after the Industrial Revolution. No capitalistic society was spared; and, since it was highly contagious, it quickly spread from white millhands and miners to all levels of Western capitalistic society. Famous poets and artists—Keats, Dunbar, Dumas's Camille, Rosetti's Elizabeth Siddal—died of consumption. Indeed, for some the dying cough became a very romantic way to depart this troubled earth. For those, however, who lived on the fringes of the capitalistic nations—blacks, Indians, Eskimos, Polynesians—consumption was devastingly genocidal. Unprotected by medical strategies of any kind, the dark-skinned minorities died like butterflies in a mid-winter blizzard. On the other hand, anemia was different. It was and is a black man's disease of the blood, the result of his centuries-long battle against malaria in his African homeland. In building up an immunity against one dread disease, black people ironically inherited a capacity for incurring another dread disease. So anemia had deep roots in the black man's past—like his love of yams or his love for the chanting tribal drums.

On the other hand, lynching, the final word in the poet's triad of death, was different from the other two causes. It had no deep roots in the history of the black man's past; it was not transported from Africa; rather, it was a uniquely "American" practice that blended well with a brutally exploitative economic system. Essentially, the lynching of black males was the Southern white male's response to the black man's inferred sexual superiority; for, usually, the lynched black was castrated before he was burned or hanged, even if he had not been accused of a sexual crime. In this way, the guilt-stricken white South expressed its ever-lurking fear of the black man's imputed sexual vigor. To date, Margaret Walker has not published a poem elaborating on this particular topic of racial sexual rivalry in the South, but in a recent interview, she comments on the matter in an interesting fashion.[2] In her opinion, "sexual warfare" exists in the South because "there's a mirror image of racism in the South." The "mirror image of racism" the poet explains as follows: "What white men see in black men, black men see in white men.... The worst thing in the world [for the white man] was a black man with a white woman, and the worst thing in the world [for a black man] was a black woman with a white man." The bloody tide of lynchings that swept the South during the years following the Civil War and on into the mid-twentieth century indicates that the black man, powerless and politically helpless, lost the battle for sexual equality. And the poet is right; only black men die of lynching;

history does not record a single instance of a white man being lynched because he raped a black woman.

Two additional comments about the poem "For My People" should be made. First, according to the poet's own recollection, she needed just fifteen minutes to compose it on her typewriter.[3] The poem is thus comparable in composition time to Langston Hughes's "The Negro Speaks of Rivers," which Hughes states that he wrote while crossing the Mississippi River during a long train ride to visit his father in Toluca, Mexico.[4] Secondly, the poem is comparable to McKay's sonnet "If We Must Die" in its breadth of universal appeal; it struck a chord of vibrant response in pre–World War II America, and it became the rallying cry twenty-five years later during the strife-torn 1960s. If the test of a great poem is its universality of statement, then "For My People" is a great poem.

Although one cannot say that the rest of the poems in Margaret Walker's initial volume meet the same criteria for high poetic quality, they reflect the young poet's sense of "word power" and her sharp awareness of the importance of black orature. The poems in part 2, for instance, contain a series of black folk portraits—Poppa Chicken, Kissee Lee, Yallah Hammuh. In many of these, one can trace the influence of Langston Hughes's 1927 volume of poems, *Fine Clothes to the Jew*, which contained many poems portraying black folk and celebrating the black urban life-style. Indeed, both Poppa Chicken and Teacher remind one of Hughes's "Sweet Papa Vester" in that poet's "Sylvester's Dying Bed." All three are sweet men— men who pimp for a living and generally walk on the shady side of the street. There are differences, however, between the Hughes portrait and those by Margaret Walker. Hughes's portrait is comically objective; nowhere does the author obtrude an opinion in the brief story line; and everything, as in any good comic routine, is grossly exaggerated. As he lies dying, "Sweet Papa Vester" is surrounded by "all the wimmens in town"—"a hundred pretty mamas"—blacks and "brown-skins" all moaning and crying. On the other hand, both "Poppa Chicken" and "Teacher," written in a swinging ballad rhyme and meter, lack the broad comic touch one sees in the Hughes poem. In fact, Poppa Chicken is a "bad dude" and not to be taken lightly:

> Poppa Chicken toted guns
> Poppa wore a knife
> One night Poppa shot a guy
> Threat'ning Poppa's life.[5]

Teacher similarly has no comic stature. In fact, it is the poet's opinion that

> Women sent him to his doom
> Women set the trap

Teacher was a bad, bold man,
Lawd, but such a sap!
(p. 44)

Three other poems in part 2 of *For My People*, "Kissee Lee," "Long John and Sweetie Pie," and "Yallah Hammuh," reflect a Hughesian influence. Although all three are written in a swinging ballad rhyme and meter which Hughes never used in his black folk portraits, they all reveal a finely controlled and well-disciplined narrative technique; there is just enough compression of incident and repetitive emphasis to provoke and sustain reader interest. And all of the characters—Long John, Sweetie Pie, Kissee Lee, and Yalluh Hamma—come from the "low-down" social stratum where, Hughes believed, black men and women lived in accordance with a life-style that was to be treasured simply because it was distinctively black. Theirs is an environment filled with heroic violence, flashing knives, Saturday night liquor fights, and the magnificent turbulence of a blues-filled weekend of pleasure and joy. For instance, after Margaret Walker's Kissee Lee "learned to stab and run" and after "She got herself a little gun,"

... from that time that gal was mean
Meanest mama you ever seen.
She could hold her likker and hold her man
And she went thoo life jus rasin san.
(p. 38)

To the Kissee Lees of the world death comes soon and

... she died with her boots on
switching blades
On Talledega Mountain in the likker raids.
(p. 39)

The ballad "Long John Nelson and Sweetie Pie" presents another story which has been repeated many times in black folklore—the story of a very stressful romantic relationship that ends in disappointment, separation, grief, and death. There is the inevitable triangle involving Long John, who is ever a lover but never a laborer, Sweetie Pie, who cooks real good and eats far too well, and a "yellow girl," who has "coal black hair" and "took Long John clean away / From Sweetie Pie one awful day." The brief story ends when Sweetie Pie, her lover gone, wastes away and dies. To historians and literary scholars, it is a story of small, almost mean, insignificance; but to a black folk poet interested in the rich orature of her people, this little story opened another window on the world of the black experience.

Part 2 of Margaret Walker's first volume of poetry also includes poems about "Bad Ol' Stackolee" and "Big John Henry," black mythic folk heroes whose stories have been told and sung for generations. Since both men really lived and died, the poet in recounting their stories is dipping into authentic black folk history. John Henry, the steel-driving man who would not let "a steam drill beat him down," was employed in the Big Bend Tunnel in West Virginia on the C&O Line and lost his life in a tunnel accident in 1872. Similarly, Stackolee, born in Georgia shortly after the Civil War, became a Memphis gambler who was widely known for his big Stetson hat, his .44, and his ever handy deck of cards. When a fellow gambler named Billy Lyons objected to the way Stackolee shuffled the cards and, in a fit of anger, knocked off Stackolee's Stetson and spit on it, Stack promptly shot him dead with his .44. In her poetic version of the John Henry and Stagolee stories, Margaret Walker does not restrict herself to the known historical facts. She shifts through the accretion of myth and incident and, in swinging couplets, tells how "Bad Man Stagolee" shot, not Billy Lyons, but "a big policeman on 'leventh St." and how John Henry was a "sho-nuff man / Whut lived one time in the delta lan," in the Mississippi cotton country. Both men are larger-than-life heroes. For his murder of a white policeman, Stagolee is never caught and no one knows how he eventually died; all that is known is

> Bad-man Stagolee ain't no more
> But his ghost still walks up
>   and down the shore
> Of Old Man River round New Orleans
> With her gumbo, rice and good
>   red beans.
>
>   (p. 35)

On the other hand, the poet tells us how her John Henry died—"a ten-poun hammer done ki-llt John Henry." But the manner of his dying is not nearly as important as his symbolic fame as the preeminently gifted black laboring man. He stands for all black men who, amid great adversity, farmed and plowed, dug and hammered, lifted and strained throughout the South to build railroads, load steamboats, and tote bricks in "the bilin' sun." But Margaret Walker embellishes her John Henry with even more heroic attributes. He consorts with witches who

> taught him how to cunjer,
> And cyo the colic and ride the thunder.
>
>   (p. 49)

He can whistle like a whippoorwill and talk to the "long lean houn." In other words, in addition to being the symbolic black laboring giant, he has supernatural gifts that lift him far above humankind's mortal sphere.

One other poem in this section of *For My People* merits some comment.

"Molly Means" is a well-crafted poetical description of "a hag and a witch / Chile of the devil, the dark, and sitch."

> Imp at three and wench at 'leben
> She counted her husbands to the number seben.
> O Molly, Molly, Molly Means
> There goes the ghost of Molly Means.

(p. 33)

Apparently, Molly is a sorceress, in some way related to the New Orleans conjure women that Margaret Walker knew so much about. It is also apparent that the setting for Molly's witchery is rural, for farmers fear that she will blight their crops for

> Sometimes at night through shadowy trees
> She rides along on a winter breeze.

(p. 34)

What is interesting about the poem is that it was written in the mid-1930s, shortly after the period known as the Harlem Renaissance had drawn to a Depression-induced end, but in no way does the poem reflect, in theme or in style, the poetry of that period. Like the title poem of the award-winning volume, "Molly Means" speaks with a new voice in black American poetry. It is not a poem of racial or romantic protest, nor does it ring with social or political rhetoric. Rather, it is a poem that probes the imaginative vistas where witches and elfins dwell—a poem that demands "a willing suspension of disbelief." And, as indicated above, "Molly Means," in its balladic simplicity, is a far cry from the carefully cerebrated poetical statements coming from the poets of the academy during the mid-1930s.

In the 1940s and 1950s, Margaret Walker published a few occasional poems (later gathered for publication in a Broadside Press volume, *October Journey*, in 1973); but, in addition to attending to her responsibilities as wife, mother, and college professor, she devoted most of her "literary" time to researching historical and biographical data for her fictional *magnum opus, Jubilee.* When this novel was published in 1966, the South was already ablaze with the black protest against segregation and the century-long denial of the black man's civil rights. The events of that period—the bombings, the deaths, the marches, the big-city riots—stimulated the most exciting outburst of black poetry since the Harlem Renaissance. In the main, these poets, with some significant exceptions, were young urban revolutionaries who were conscientiously abrasive in their racial rhetoric. Not only did they insist that wrongs be righted, but they assumed a paramilitary posture and demanded that the guilty be punished by fire, by bullets, or by the sheer violence of their poetic rhetoric. Inevitably, the seething racial turbulence of the times provoked a poetical response from

Margaret Walker; and, because of her experience, background, and training—because of her familial gift of word power, her intensive apprenticeship in Chicago's literary workshop in the 1930s, and her mastery of the arts of black orature—her *Prophets for a New Day,* published by Broadside Press in 1970, stands out as the premier poetic statement of the death-riddled decade of the 1960s. The poems of this small volume reflect the full range of the black protest during the time—the sit-ins, the jailings, the snarling dogs, the 1963 March on Washington, the lynching of the three civil rights workers in Mississippi. All of the poems in the volume touch the sensitive nerve of racial memory and bring back, in sharply etched detail, the trauma and tension and triumphs of that period. "Birmingham" and "For Andy Goodman, Michael Schwerner and James Chaney" stand out as carefully wrought poetical reactions to a city and to an event that filled the world with horror and foreboding.

Both of these poems are unusual simply because painful emotions are not recollected in tranquillity but in moods carefully textured by the delicate filigree of the poet's imagery. For instance, in "Birmingham" the first part of the poem is filled with the persona's nostalgic memories of the beauty of the Birmingham countryside as the twilight settles over the red hills. In this section of the poem, the reader senses the God-wrought beauty that enfolds the city—a city filled with the evil that man has wrought.

> With the last whippoorwill call of evening
> Settling over mountains
> Dusk dropping down shoulders of red hills
> And red dust of mines
> Sifting across a somber sky
> Setting the sun to rest in a blue blaze of coal fire
> And shivering memories of Spring
> With raw wind out of woods
> And brown straw of last year's needle-shedding-pines
> Cushions of quiet underfoot
> Violets pushing through early new spring ground
> And my winging heart flying across the world
> With one bright bird—
> Cardinal flashing through thickets—
> Memories of my fancy-ridden life
> Come home again.[6]

Part 2 of the poem is concerned with death, and the images are of death and dying. The principal persona of the poem has returned in death to a city engulfed by death—a city "where a whistling ghost" makes "a threnody / Out of a naked wind."

I died today.
In a new and cruel way.
I came to breakfast in my night-dying clothes
Ate and talked and nobody knew
They had buried me yesterday.
I slept outside the city limits
Under a little hill of butterscotch brown
With a dusting of white sugar
Where a whistling ghost kept making a threnody
Out of a naked wind.

(p. 14)

In part 3 of the poem the persona longs to return to her "coffin bed of soft warm clay," far from the North's "bitter cold." For Birmingham and the South, drenched in the blood of countless black martyrs, is a good place in which to die and be buried.

My life dies best on a southern cross
Carved out of rock with shooting stars
    to fire
The forge of bitter hate.

(p. 14)

The lines dedicated to the memory of Goodman, Schwerner, and Chaney, the young civil rights martyrs murdered by klansmen in Mississippi's Neshoba County, are also rich in imagery and symbol. There is no confrontation rhetoric, but there is a very successful effort to filter through the nuances of memory and find the three young men again. First one remembers three faces—one "sensitive as the mimosa leaf," one "intense as the stalking cougar," and the third as "impassive as the face of rivers." And then one remembers that the summer of their death cannot last forever and that soon fall will come and what were three young men will metamorphose into three leaves, cut adrift from life and mixing helter-skelter with nature's superb fall potpourri of wind, water, and sunlight.

Three leaves...
    Floating in the melted snow
    Flooding the Spring
    oak leaves
    one by one
    moving like a barge
    across the seasons
    moving like a breeze across the window pane
    winter...summer...spring
When is the evil year of the cricket?
When comes the violent day of the stone?

In which month
do the dead ones appear at the cistern?

(p. 14)

At this point in the poem, the poet turns directly to the lives of the three
young men, to probe how a century of concern can be reduced to a quintessential moment in the "hourglass of destiny." Cut off prematurely, they will
never know the "immortality of daisies and wheat," "the simple beauty of
a humming bird," nor "the dignity of a sequoia"—never know the full meaning
of winter's renunciation nor spring's resurrection. And who murdered the
sensitive Goodman, the intense Schwerner, the impassive Chaney? In
answering, the poet exercises her poetic license to castigate with a forceful
alliterative phrase those who killed and entombed the three young men.

The brutish and the brazen
without brain
without blessing
without beauty . . .
They have killed these three.

Before closing the poem, Margaret Walker once again examines the startling contradiction between the South's languorous natural beauty and the
ugliness of black lynched bodies floating in muddy rivers or buried in
soggy graves shaded by fragrant magnolias and stately live oaks. The South
is full of paradoxes, but the juxtaposition of floral beauty and bloody
violence is the most puzzling. Nowhere is this more obvious than in
Mississippi. The poet writes:

The burned blossoms of the dogwood tree
tremble in the Mississippi morning
The wild call of the cardinal bird
troubles the Mississippi morning
I hear the morning singing
larks, robins, and mocking bird
while the mourning dove
broods over the meadow
Summer leaf falls never turning brown
Deep in a Mississippi thicket
I hear the mourning dove
Bird of death singing in the swamp
Leaves of death floating in their watery grave.

(pp. 20–21)

In the final section of *Prophets for a New Day,* Margaret Walker turns to
history and prophecy, linking today's black leaders, old and young, to the
biblical prophets of old. The volume's title poem begins

As the Word came to prophets of old,
As the burning bush spoke to Moses,
And the fiery coals cleansed the lips of
        Isaiah;
As the wheeling cloud in the sky
Clothed the message of Ezekiel;
So the Word of fire burns today
On the lips of our prophets in an evil age—
Our soothsayers and doom-tellers and doers
        of the Word.

                                        (p. 22)

The final lines of the title poem throb with the poet's indignation and outrage about the unfettered power of the beast of racial hatred that roams the land.

A beast is among us.
His mark is on the land.
His horns and his hands and his lips are
        gory with our blood.
He is War and Famine and Pestilence
He is Death and Destruction and Trouble
And he walks in our houses at noonday
And devours our defenders at midnight.
He is the demon who drives us with whips
        of fear
And in his cowardice
He cries out against liberty
He cries out against humanity.

                                        (p. 23)

The poems that end the volume of poetry present in brief portraits the "Prophets for a New Day"—Benjamin Mays (Jeremiah), Whitney Young (Isaiah), Martin Luther King (Amos), Julian Bond (Joel), and Medgar Evers (Michah). These poems with their strong religious content prove that Margaret Walker, in her latest poetry, has come full circle. She began with the Word and closes with the Word. To those who hope and believe she offers in the "breaking dawn of a blinding sun" a promise that "the lamp of truth" will be lighted in the temple of hope and that, soon one morning, "the winds of freedom" will begin "to blow / While the Word descends on the waiting World below."

Langston Hughes, in his review of Gwendolyn Brooks's *Street in Bronzeville*, stated that all good poets are more far-sighted and perceptive in discerning social problems and ills than are politicians.[7] Of Margaret Walker he would also have noted her great gift for prophecy and the marvelous word power that enabled her to burrow deeply into the rich orature of her people.

NOTES

This essay first appeared in *Black American Poets between Worlds: 1940–1960*, ed. R. Baxter Miller. Copyright ©1986 by the University of Tennessee Press. Reprinted with permission.

1. Paul Laurence Dunbar published his first volume of poetry, *Oak and Ivy*, in 1892, a few months after his twenty-first birthday.

2. *Mississippi Writers Talking*, John Griffin Jones, interviewer (University of Mississippi Press, 1983), 2: 140–41.

3. Ibid., 2: 133. The poet also states that she finished the poem in 1937 on her twenty-second birthday.

4. *The Big Sea*, pp. 33–34.

5. *For My People* (New York: Arno Press and the New York Times, 1968), p. 36. Subsequent references are from this edition and are noted parenthetically in the text.

6. *Prophets for a New Day* (Detroit: Broadside Press, 1970), p. 14. Subsequent references are from this edition and are noted parenthetically in the text.

7. *Opportunity* (Fall 1945): 222.

Castration Symbolism in Recent
Black American Fiction

Mah Ma-an don' luv me,
Treat me oh so mean.
Mah Ma-an don' luv me,
Treat me oh so mean.
He the meanest man
Ah have evah seen.

From "Fine and Mellow,"
a Billie Holiday blues song

When castration and death end Joe Christmas's tortured odyssey in Faulkner's *Light in August,* a scenario is enacted that had long been part of the racial culture of the American South. Faulkner makes it clear, in fact, that, given the mores of the region, Christmas's interracial sexual experiences have to end this way. Even Christmas knows this; for, when Percy Grimm advances with knife in hand, Faulkner's black-white man puts aside his gun and submits, almost lovingly, to his castration and death. Confused about his role, he had been a black stud for white women and a white stud for black women; and then, in his thirty-third year, he had fallen into the toils of Joanna Burden's panting eroticism and come to a predictably violent end.

Faulkner's castrated Joe Christmas is regrettable but understandable. He fits into the southern gothic tradition and, unfortunately, symbolizes the general tone of southern racial behavior. What one finds in recent black fiction, on the other hand, is quite different. There is no southern gothic tradition to provide the black author with a sheltering literary and cultural climate, and there is no volatile racial climate to justify black male victimization. In fact, the black male characters found in the pages of Gayl Jones's *Eva's Man* and *Corregidora,* in Morrison's *Sula,* in Walker's *The Color Purple,* and in Paule Marshall's *Praise Song for the Widow* never feel the organ-severing knife that sends a Joe Christmas hemorrhaging his way out of existence; but even an unperceptive reader senses that some rather severe psychological mutilation of the black male psyche does occur in these novels.

In a sense, Jones's *Eva's Man* is an exception to this generalization, for an act of sexual violence does occur in this novel—an act that is more physical than psychological. Published in 1976, *Eva's Man,* Gayl Jones's second novel, is a short, carefully structured work of fiction that relates the story of the sexual maturation, development, and downfall of Eva Medina Canada.[1] At the beginning of the story, Eva, a forty-three-year-old black woman, has been imprisoned for five years in what is called a psychiatric prison or a prison for the criminally insane. She has been found guilty of a sexually deviant crime deemed to be so heinous that she has been adjudged to be insane. Eva's life story and the events leading to the murder of her lover Davis Carter are presented in a series of artfully articulated flashbacks. So, even as we follow Eva in the series of scenes in Davis Carter's room just prior to his murder by sexual mutilation, the reader is told Eva's life story and how, as a young girl growing up in an apartment in Queens, she gradually moves from sexual innocence to sexual awareness in an emotionally charged environment that is fearful and threatening. At the age of twelve she is propositioned by Tyrone, her mother's young music-playing lover; at age seventeen she begins to have dates with her married uncle Alfonso who · also propositions her; and at age eighteen she is imprisoned in a reformatory because she stabbed a man named Moses Tripp who attempted to rape her in an alley. So there is no doubt that by the time Eva meets Davis Carter she has long been a victim of sexual abuse and harassment.

Jones tells the story of the sustained sexual encounter between Eva Medina and Davis Carter in sexually explicit language. In fact, the author makes it clear that Eva spends a full menstrual cycle in Carter's room. When she first meets him in the restaurant to share what becomes their favorite meal of cabbage and sausage, sexual activity immediately thereafter has to be postponed for three days because of her condition; and, when, during an act of fellatio she mutilates her lover and leaves him to bleed to death, she too is once again, as she says, "bleeding."

Jones provides no stated motive for Eva's act of sexual violence. The relationship between Eva and Davis appears to be harmonious. He complains of her silence and of the way she occasionally looks at him—"like you could just kill me baby" (p. 174). But they have no quarrel. So the reader is led to conclude that Eva's act is motivated by her subconscious response to men in general and not to Davis Carter in particular—a response to the years of sexual victimization that have left her humiliated, abused, and alone. Such a conclusion is suggested in one of the stream-of-consciousness passages in the novel when Eva says, "Yes, I was hurt by love. My soul was broken. . . " (p. 143). And, in another place, the author describes Eva's sense of loneliness and neglect: "She stands naked on the street. She asks each man she sees to pay her her debt. But they say they owe her nothing" (p. 144).

Two observations should be made at this point about Eva's act of sexual violence. First, Jones describes it in graphically realistic terms. Indeed, at times, her account of incidents surrounding the act are gruesomely explicit. At one point, the author notes that Davis Carter's severed organ was brought into the courtroom "wrapped up in a silk handkerchief, like a jewel" (p. 49). At another point, she writes about Eva's remembering having "a swollen plum in my mouth" and biting into "an apple of blood" (p. 129). Although many readers have found such explicitness offensive, it does underline the extent of Eva's sexual alienation. The author's realistic account also serves to remind the reader that, accompanying the sexual revolution of the sixties, there was an unprecedented rise in violent sex crimes throughout the nation and that Eva's crime reflected a national trend.

The second observation concerns Eva's behavior immediately after the act of mutilation. What she has done catapults her into a mind-boggling mood of euphoria. To celebrate the occasion, she rushes out of the room where she has spent a month as the willing prisoner of Davis Carter's love and goes to the restaurant where she and Carter had first met. Here she exuberantly bolts down a meal of her favorite cabbage and sausage and then, relieved and happy, she returns to the scene of her crime. One may conclude from Eva's behavior that her act has brought her long-sought release from the sexual tensions and uncertainties that have plagued her all her days. There is also the suggestion that her deed will benefit her mother, her grandmother Medina, and all black women who have to live in a male-dominated sex-saturated society. In any event, where in Faulkner's *Light in August* an act of sexual violence is rooted in an interracial social problem, in Gayl Jones's *Eva's Man* the act of sexual violence appears to be an intraracial personal problem. There is also some evidence that black men in general present a problem. Elvira Moody, Eva's cellmate who eventually becomes her lesbian lover, says of black men: "They ain't nothing but bastards. . . . If you don't get them, they get you, and if you do get them, the law get you. . . . All they think about is where they goin' to get their next piece" (p. 150).

Jones's earlier work, *Corregidora* (1975), sheds a little more historical light on the problem.[2] This time there is no absence of personal malice between a young black woman named Ursa Corregidora and her lover husband, Mutt Thomas. But there is more than the personal animus that exists between two lovers. The historical roots of the sexual conflict are clearly delineated. This novel asserts that the black woman's sexual slavery began with slavery—a time when the system granted every master and every white male overseer the unchallenged right to use and abuse every female slave on the plantation according to his fancy. Jones makes it clear that Mutt's abusive treatment of Ursa directly parallels the slave-master Corregidora's treatment of Ursa's grandmother and great-grandmother on the Corregidora plantation in Brazil. Not only had Ursa's grandparents been held in incestuous concubinage (Corregidora was the father of his daughter and his daughter's daughter [p. 116]), but Corregidora also sold their services as whores to any who would pay—any white man, that is. Since Ursa's great-grandmama and grandmama had repeatedly given explicit accounts of their sexual slavery, Ursa knew every detail of the humiliation endured by her people. There is no doubt that, in stressing the dismal history of the Corregidora women, Jones meant to establish a historical link between Ursa's sexual conflicts with Mutt and Tadpole and the conflicts of her immediate forbears with Corregidora.

In other words, when a drunken Mutt pushes Ursa down the stairs, causing her to lose her baby and her capacity for reproduction, Ursa's plight is a twentieth-century replication of the plight of her grandmother and great-grandmother. Once more a black woman is victimized by the insensitivity and thoughtlessness and sexual sadism of a man—this time not by a cruelly arrogant white slave-master but by a partially free and cruelly arrogant black man. Thus, Jones's central theme in *Corregidora* seems to be that the black woman of this century still has to cope with a kind of slavery—a slavery that still makes her the object of abuse by the macho male. For instance, Mutt's jealous rage about the customers who come to hear Ursa sing and then, according to the paranoid Mutt, leeringly lust for her "with they eyes," parallels Corregidora's jealous rage when Ursa's "Great Gram" is seen talking with "this black man about seventeen or eighteen." According to Great Gram's story, Corregidora runs the young slave off the plantation and then sends the dogs out to hunt him down and kill him. Says Great Gram: "... maybe he did the right thing to run away, because maybe if he had stayed there, the way Corregidora was looking when he seen us talking he might've had him beat dead" (p. 145).

Thus the question facing the Ursas of black America and throughout the diaspora is how best to cope with those black males who instinctively want to continue the black woman's sexual slavery. Jones does not provide an answer until the final page of her novel. Not surprisingly, it is the Eva Medina solution, not as boldly or graphically described as in *Eva's Man*, nor, it should be added, so murderously accomplished. Nevertheless, Jones seems to recommend either taking or threatening to take this action as a positive response for today's black woman caught up in the struggle for sexual survival throughout the Black Diaspora.

The scene is set in a hotel room where Ursa Corregidora, after a twenty-two-year separation, is reunited with her ex-husband, Mutt Thomas. To celebrate their reunion, she performs an act of fellatio and, in the process, thinks: " . . . it had to be something sexual that Great Gram did to Corregidora. . . . What is it a woman can do to a man that make him hate her so bad he wont to kill her one minute and keep thinking about her and can't get her out of his mind the next?" (p. 212). And even as Ursa remembers Great Gram's question, suddenly she also finds an answer to the question: "In a split second I knew what it was. . . . A moment of pleasure and excruciating pain at the same time, a moment of broken skin but not sexlessness . . . a moment that stops before it breaks the skin" (p. 212). In such a moment, Ursa argues, the man is abjectly powerless and the woman so uniquely powerful that she can say, in utter truth, "I could kill you," and, if necessary, promptly carry out her threat. The implication of this incident is that, just as the threat of castration had been Great Gram's response to Corregidora in slavery times, so the women of the post-slavery diaspora were and are similarly empowered to make such a threat and, if need be, like Eva, implement the same.

Two conclusions can be drawn from studying the patterns of sexual conflict in Jones's two novels. First, the roots of the black woman's sexual slavery are deeply buried in the physical violence and degradation of African chattel slavery. Here, too, are the roots of black concubinage, often incestuous and sadomasochistic. This lamentable side of black history in the diaspora has been widely documented. Dorothy Sterling, for instance, in a chapter entitled "Seduction, Rape, and Concubinage" in *We Are Your Sisters* (Norton, 1984), shows how black slave women, entrapped and exploited in a violent system, resorted to desperate stratagems to survive and retain their sanity and their womanly self-esteem. As Sterling reports, sometimes, in their travail, our sisters in slavery sang:

> Rains come wet me
> Sun come dry me
> Stay back, white man
> Don't come nigh me.
> (p. 26)

Obviously, a little song like this could not stop the savage whippings and the physical and mental and emotional indignities suffered by the black slave woman. For further documentation of her status, we have Frederick Douglass's tragic portrait of his mother (actually, his half sister as well as his mother), who was driven to an early death by cruel and inhumane treatment.

The second conclusion to be drawn from the Jones novels is that, with slavery's end, black men like the Mutt Thomases of the world began to imitate the sexual behavior of their former masters. Stripped of political and economic power and harassed by a still-dominant white majority, they sought to enjoy their new freedom in whatever limited sense they could under the circumstances. Within this context they sought to hold sexual mastery over their women, and to some extent, unless a former master intervened, the black freedmen enjoyed and exploited this power. So, over the years there occurred a mirror-imaging exchange of power, and in his sexual relations with his women the black man replaced his former master.

The result of this exchange of power has, a century after slavery's end, produced within the context of the feminist movement a fictional whirl-wind of protest over what history has wrought. Besides Gayl Jones's, there are many other voices raised in protest over the status of things—those of Toni Morrison, Alice Walker, Paule Marshall. Their message is clear and direct: Because of the wanton abuse of his assumed superior sexual status, the black male of the twentieth century has become a psychological and economic disaster who should be promptly denutted and cast aside on history's junkpile. And the prototypical male castaway can be found in abundant numbers on the pages of their fiction.

In Morrison's *Sula,* for example, the first male we meet is Shadrack, the community lunatic.[3] Shattered and disabled by a horrible World War I experience, he ought to be hospitalized in a total care institution. Instead, he, in a sense, symbolizes black male intelligence and behavior in the Medallion "bottom." Then there is Plum, Eva's drug-addicted son, scarcely worth the cost of the kerosene with which his mother set him afire. There are also Eva's husband, who deserted her under the most grievous circumstances, and Nel's husband, who first had a sexual liaison with her best friend and then deserted her. Finally, we have Tar Baby, a "high yella" alcoholic, and Ajax, the community stud, who speedily zips up and flees at the first sign that he might be responsibly involved.

Especially do the men of *Sula* appear to be a nondescript lot when they are compared with the women of *Sula*—with Eva, the fiercely indomitable matriarch for whom the act of mothering is a wholesome mixture of iron resolve, loving-kindness, and violent self-sacrifice; or with Sula herself, who strides through life with the magnificent indifference of an oversexed tomcat, careless of friend and kin alike; or with Nel, Sula's foil, who, endowed by slavery with a prostitute grandmother, strives first for respecta-bility and then for survival. The men do not even compare favorably with Hannah, who, until her death by fire, bestows sexual favors on all and sundry with charitable good grace. Even the Deweys, the succession of young boys who come to live under Eva's sheltering mantle, are so overindulged and spoiled by strong matriarchal women that they face futures which will be no better than the past and present of Medallion's black adult males.

The men of *Sula* face their greatest challenge, however, when they visit Sula in search of sexual favors and come away from that experience symbolically castrated. With a casual indifference that amazes them, she beds them and robs them of whatever vestiges of manhood slavery and slavery's aftermath have left them. Obviously, Sula's treatment of the men in her life is not as deadly as Eva Medina's treatment of Davis Carter in *Eva's Man* or what Joe Christmas suffers in *Light in August,* but it is psychologically devastating for the collective male ego. Only Ajax, the man she comes to love, escapes; but, as the author carefully explains, he had already been corrupted and, in a sense, symbolically castrated, by his root-making mother's over-protective love (p. 109).

If the men of *Sula* seem to be living on the edge of a slavelike no-man's-land, the men of Alice Walker's *The Color Purple* are dismally poor black peasants who in their treatment of the women in their lives behave like miniature black Corregidoras. Their behavior mirrors, in many respects, the besotted and inhumane life-style of former white masters and overseers. Ironically, they subject their women to the same abuse, cruelty, and insensitive neglect suffered in slavery times by their female ancestors at the hands of powerful masters and overseers. And, just as in slavery times when incestuous concubinage was roundly practiced, the young women of *The Color Purple* find themselves coping with the same humiliating custom. For instance, Celie, the central female persona, has by the time she is sixteen borne two children by her father and, while she lives under his roof, is constantly abused by him. She later learns that he is her stepfather, but the memory of the abuse she suffers at his hands stays with her to the bitter end. Indeed, so pervasive is the atmosphere of threat, intimidation, and terror in which Celie and her sister Nettie live that the reader is hard-pressed not to wish that Walker's harassed young women develop some strategem to fend off the rapacious males either by doing what Ursa Corregidora's Great Gram did to Corregidora or by implementing Eva Medina's somewhat fortuitous plan for the instant demise of Davis Carter.

Fortunately, neither Celie nor Nettie resort to desperate measures of this kind. Celie is rescued by her love for Shug, her husband's girlfriend; and Nettie escapes to Africa as a missionary and marries Samuel, a minister in the Sanctified Church and, by a fortunate happenstance, the stepfather of Celie's long-lost children. The two miniature black Corregidoras who had vexed their existence eventually fade into the background. Indeed, Alphonso, the stepfather by whom Celie bore two illegitimate children as a teenager, dies somewhat ignominiously while attempting to placate his new young wife one night. And Albert, Celie's husband, who had not only subjected her to physical abuse but attempted to rape her sister Nettie, eventually becomes Celie's friend and companion. Like the buzzard of folklore fame, he learned to "straighten up and fly right."

Sexual conflict in *The Color Purple* is thus stark and drear and rooted in the traditions and practices of slavery with its emphasis on male preroga-tives and patriarchal control. This is not true of Paule Marshall's *Praise Song for the Widow* (1983),[4] the final novel to be discussed here. In fact, sexual conflict is not a matter of primary concern in the novel. The core of the novel is Avey Johnson's reconnection with her racial past through her visit to the island of Carriacou and her participation in the "Beg Pardon" ritual dance. After this experience, the sixty-two-year-old widow from the affluent New York suburbs will never be the same. So *Praise Song for the Widow* says much of the influence of the African past on the black value system throughout the diaspora. But in preparation for the Carriacou experience, Avey Johnson suffers what can be termed a cathartic collapse on the island of Grenada; and, during the hours of writhing emotional turmoil, her own past as a young wife and mother is recalled in vivid detail. One has to be impressed by the skill and literary subtlety Paule Marshall uses in blending all of the various time sequences, for all of the facts and events remain clearly in place—the experiences on the tour boat, in Grenada, and on Carriacou, as well as the early days on Brooklyn's Halsey Street.

Necessarily, the focus of this discussion is on the one instance of overt sexual conflict between Avey and her husband, Jay, which she recalls during a paroxysm of grief in a hotel in Grenada. First, through her eyes we see a young Jay Johnson, a warmly gregarious extrovert who works hard, recites black poetry to his young family, enjoys black jazz and blues, and is sweet and loving to his young wife. Then, the reader follows the story of how changes were gradually wrought in Jay—how, in his zeal to please Avey and establish a firmer economic base for his family, he took on extra jobs, went to night school, earned a college degree, won his CPA license, and then moved his family from Brooklyn's Halsey Street to suburban North White Plains and became Jerome Johnson, successful accountant. As Avey recalls Jay's economic rise and the growth of her family's affluence, she also remembers the major crisis in her married life when, heavily pregnant with her third child, she quarreled bitterly and violently with Jay over an imagined and unproven charge of sexual infidelity. And she recalls how in the heat of the argument, she screamed, "Goddam you, nigger, I'll take my babies and go!" (p. 110), and how, instead of leaving her or hitting her or letting her leave, Jay stepped forward and, weeping copiously, embraced her and the children. And then she recalls that, after this screaming quarrel that wintry Tuesday in 1945, Jay ceased to be the old warm and convivial

Jay and became a hardworking Jerome Johnson, a bourgeois capitalist who was very critical of the slothful work habits of his less successful black brothers. Predictably, the hardworking Jerome Johnson who metamorphosed out of the easygoing Jay was soon dead of cardiac arrest, and Avey became an affluent widow who, whenever she wished, could enjoy her widowhood sashaying on luxury tour ships around the Caribbean.

The question arises, did Jay Johnson, in his driving ambition to become an economically secure Jerome Johnson, lose something precious? Did he sacrifice more than his racial *joi de vivre* or that special *esprit* long considered a special element in the black life-style? Did the quarrel on that snowy Tuesday night galvanize him to adopt a life-style that took away his black humanity? In other words, was he psychologically emasculated by that traumatic quarrel and the events that followed?

Obviously, what happened to Jay Johnson in *Praise Song for the Widow* has no roots in the slave experience. Rather it is part of the larger American scene in which people lose their souls in the drive for material success. But psychological castration is psychological castration, whatever the cause. Marshall's Jerome Johnson is obviously far removed from Jones's Mutt Thomas or Tadpole or from Morrison's Ajax or Tar Baby: He is intelligently ambitious; they are economic dodoes. But there is an even more significant difference. When he is challenged and threatened by his pregnant wife in that angry quarrel, Jay collapses in weeping submission. However, when *Corregidora's* Mutt Thomas is challenged by his pregnant wife, he knocks her down the stairs, killing the unborn child and maiming his wife for life. In the end, Ursa Corregidora makes it clear that, even after a twenty-two-year separation, for that act of brutal violence Mutt still deserves castration. Avey Johnson's case is different. Thrashing about in grief in her Grenada hotel room four years after her husband's death, she now realizes that in that bitter quarrel so long ago she inadvertently caused a change in her husband—a change that eventually resulted in the psychological castration of Jay Johnson. Her words are:

> She remembered that Tuesday in the winter of '45. Just moments before he had steeled himself and stepped forward, gathering her to him, she had sensed him, hadn't she, slowly backing away from her and Sis, easing toward the door to the hall behind him, a man eager to be gone.
>
> Perhaps he had left after all. While she had stood in the arms of the tearful man who had stepped forward, Jay might have slipped quietly out of the room . . . leaving Jerome Johnson to do what he perhaps felt he had neither the strength nor the heart for. . . .
>
> And in leaving he had taken with him the little private rituals and pleasures, the playfulness and wit of those early years, the host of feelings and passions that had defined them in a special way back then. . . . All these had

departed with him that Tuesday night. Her tears flowing, Avey Johnson mourned them. (p. 136)

It is obvious from the discussion presented above that some recent black American novelists have introduced male characters who, because of their penchant for sexual violence and because of their brutal insensitivity, deserve castration; and there are other male characters who, because of circumstances beyond their control, have been symbolically castrated. Whatever the case, these characters are depressing role models for young black male readers. Fortunately, the pen is mightier than the sword or the knife or whatever Eva Medina used, and what has been written is the fictional view of a world that a particular writer has elected to describe according to her value system and according to her fashion. Yet we must remember that fiction, like drama, presents "the abstract and brief chronicles of the time," and our writers of fiction can only write about what they have experienced, seen, or observed. Maybe at some time they too heard Billie Holiday sing:

> Mah Ma-an don luv me,
> Treat me oh so mean.
> He the meanest man
> Ah have evah seen.

NOTES

Reprinted from *CLA Journal* 29, no. 4 (June 1986): 400–413. Copyright The College Language Association. Used by permission of The College Language Association.

1. Gayl Jones, *Eva's Man* (New York: Random House, 1976). All further references to this work are from this edition and are noted parenthetically in the text.
2. Gayl Jones, *Corregidora* (New York: Bantam Books, 1976). All further references to this work are from this edition and are noted parenthetically in the text.
3. Toni Morrison, *Sula* (New York: Bantam Books, 1975). All citations of this work are from this edition and are noted parenthetically in the text.
4. Paule Marshall, *Praise Song for the Widow* (New York: G. P. Putnam's Sons, 1983). All citations of this work are from this edition and are noted parenthetically in the text.

In Search of the Unbroken Circle:
Black Nurturing in Selected Novels
of Toni Morrison

In *Cane,* the Harlem Renaissance's multigenre masterpiece, Jean Toomer describes how, not so long ago, "a song-lit race of slaves" sang their way through slavery's long night, "softly caroling" their messages of sorrow, hope, and despair. One song that they sang in their rhythmic and melodic African meter was a song about a circle that remained unbroken in the sky. Although, at first thought, this song seems to be one of Christian hope, actually it stresses the concept of African circularity—a concept with roots deeply embedded in Africa's tribal past and its emphasis on ancestor worship. For centuries, tribal *griots* had told their carefully preserved tales of the ancestors so that the living could hold hands with the ancestral dead and the circle be unbroken from then to now and henceforth forever. But those tribal members who, from the fifteenth century onward, were stolen from their homeland by the enslavers from the Euro-West and from the Islamic Middle East, lost their sense of tribal identity and saw their *griot* traditions destroyed. Instead of being able to continue to savor the spirit-easing joy of holding hands with their rich ethnic past, those who were enslaved in the New World found themselves entrapped in a social and labor system which literally triangulated them to death. Life's comforting tribal circularities were no more—no more departing and returning, no more separating and regathering, no more *griots* to help one find one's ancestors in the circles of the sky, and, hence, no more ancestors.

Not only did slavery rob the African of his deeply emotional link with his racial past and its stress on circularity, but it involved him in a system of forced labor that stressed linearity. Capitalism, the economic system governing the plantocracies of slavery, had linear goals and objectives. In other words, a linear, not circular, time frame governed the activities of the plantation—whether in Portuguese Brazil, Spanish Colombia, or English South Carolina. Planters and their overseers, in pursuit of maximum productivity and profitability, cared not for the slaves' grief over their lost Africanity. Their one pragmatic concern was to maintain an effective labor force through purchasing continually needed replacements, through monitoring female breeding cycles, and through efficacious use of the whip and other punitive devices. They cared not for the slaves' need to return, renew, revisit, nor even to remember. All they wanted was to work their labor force from dawn to dusk.

So in their longing for circularity, slaves, enmeshed in the triangularities of a brutal labor system, sang:

> Will the circle be unbroken
> In the sky, Lord, in the sky?
> Will the circle be unbroken
> When I die, Lord, when I die?

Of Toni Morrison's novels, three—*Sula*,[1] *Song of Solomon*,[2] and *Beloved*[3]—have plots and story lines that address the subject of black circularity and the spiritual nurturing needed to bolster one in the search for unbroken circles. Indeed, between *Sula*, which appeared in 1973, and *Beloved*, in 1988—a period of fifteen years—the author's emphasis on the subject appears to intensify. In *Sula*, for instance, Eva, the sturdy matriarch and nurturer, dominates the action only in the early part of the novel. She fades into insignificance after Sula, her nonnurturing, self-centered granddaughter, returns. Then in 1977 in *The Song of Solomon*, there is a marked increase of emphasis on modes and styles of black nurturing. Throughout the novel Pilate consistently plays the role of a nurturer; and, when Milkman, the young central persona and nephew of Pilate, makes his leap back into history in search of his family's completed circle, his search becomes the core of the action of the novel. In 1988, in *Beloved*, the entire plot is devoted to Sethe's desperate struggle to establish an unbroken circle with her past and provide a family-healing nurturing in her world—a world but one river away from the slave plantation from which she had escaped.

Indeed, one is challenged by the speculation that the time periods in which these novels are set determine the amount of plot time devoted to family nurturing and the search for ancestral circularity. In *Sula*, Eva's acts of family sacrifice and nurturing occur in the first generation after slavery. Such family nurturing is of no concern to Sula, Eva's nonnurturing granddaughter, who is three generations removed from slavery. Sula's concern is for Sula and for her needs and lustful gratifications. Ancestors and family and friends have no importance. Indeed, her complete repudiation of her grandmother's family-nurturing value system serves to strengthen by contrast her grandmother's image as a strong and caring matriarch. Also, one who dares to probe authorial intention can speculate further that, when Sula returns to Medallion after a ten-year absence and is greeted by flocks of defecating robins, the author is making more than a delicate suggestion that for Eva robins would sing and not rain defecation from the skies.

Similarly, in *The Song of Solomon,* Milkman matures and becomes responsible and accountable only when he flees from his present to search out his family's past, in a sense traveling back to events which occurred immediately after slavery and even crossing over imaginatively into slavery's time zone to imitate the ultimate in the search for circularity—a flight back to Africa like his slave ancestor, Solomon.

So *The Song of Solomon* ends, symbolically at least, in the same time zone in which *Beloved* begins: at that juncture in time when slavery's end was near and a quasi-freedom was about to begin, but at a time when slavery's ugly shadow was still everywhere. It was a time for black families, long broken and fragmented, to begin slowly to regather and rejoin and reunite and search, tediously, but with humble thanksgiving, for what might be the beginning of an unbroken circle. And, in that first generation of freedom, there was indeed a great search for kinfolks—for cousins and aunts and uncles and sisters and brothers. Bloodlines did not count; a friend could become an aunt or a cousin or a sister or a brother. All that mattered was that, once again, they could, with loving-kindness and close nurturing, rebuild long-broken circles.

In other words, Eva in *Sula,* Milkman and Pilate in *The Song of Solomon,* and Sethe in *Beloved,* although depicted in different stories with different plot lines, are linked by one major concern—the overwhelming urge to cement familial ties to assure that strong circles would be formed. This time the circles would not be the strong, steel-binding kind of tribal Africa, but they would be a giant step away from the chaos and disorder that existed during the centuries of slavery.

When we first are introduced to Eva in *Sula,* she is a product of slavery's chaos and disorder, living in that strange twilight when slavery was over and freedom had not yet begun. Deserted by her defeated and demoralized young husband, she is desperately struggling to keep her three small children from starving to death. At this time, there was no welfare or other form of support for starving black families, North or South. So to keep her family alive, Eva was reduced to the desperate remedy of temporarily abandoning her children to the care of a neighbor to go off to get a job on the railroad. When she returned to Medallion several months later, she was minus a leg but no longer penniless. In fact, because of the tragic accident she had suffered, she had received enough money from the railroad to keep her and her family from poverty's door for the rest of their lives and even down to the third generation—Sula's generation.

Thus, Eva's mothering began with an act of violent self-sacrifice—the kind of maternal self-sacrifice which had its roots in slavery, when survival and sacrifice were synonymous for black people. Eva used her money wisely and well, building a large, comfortable home on a high place in Medallion's "Black Bottom." There she reared her family and spread her matriarchal net beyond her doors into the black community. Not only did none of her own children ever leave Eva's house, but, after they were grown and began to have children of their own, she began to reach out and bring neglected or mistreated young boys into her home and make them part of a growing household. Each of these young men was given the name of Dewey. It was a name that Eva liked; so there was Dewey one, and Dewey two, and Dewey three. In addition to the Deweys, Eva's large household of sweet permissiveness also accommodated a man named Tar Baby, an alcoholic who had often been arrested, and anyone else who needed temporary shelter or food or counsel and consolation.

But the crippled matriarch also had to endure occasional pain and suffering that put her to the test. When her son Plum became a hopeless drug addict and good for nothing except to die, Eva performed another act of violent self-sacrifice and lovingly set him afire so that the horror of his life would end. Then, when her oldest, Hannah, the mother of Sula, accidentally set herself afire in the backyard, Eva propelled her wheelchair out of the second-story window of her bedroom in a futile attempt to fall on Hannah to smother the flames that were consuming her daughter's body.

Thus, throughout a life of suffering and tribulation, Eva, like Dilsey in Faulkner's *The Sound and the Fury,* endured. Also, like Dilsey, she was a resourceful and resilient matriarch, but there the comparison ends. Dilsey was trying to serve and save the Comptons; Eva was trying to build a circle of familial love and understanding. The burgeoning evil of the Compton household overwhelmed Dilsey; and at the end, as the sturdy matriarch made her way to the Easter service, she wept because there would be no resurrection for that benighted family. For Eva, on the other hand, life had been a continuing resurrection. Her compassion and concern went everywhere. It irradiated her household and Medallion's black community. In her portrayal of this character, Toni Morrison has, indeed, presented a black nurturer.

One additional comment should be made about Eva and the quality of her love and nurturing. It was African—disciplined and supportive but not verbally or emotionally indulgent. On one occasion, she had to explain this to her oldest and now fully grown daughter, Hannah, who quite innocently asked: "Mama, did you ever love us?" Eva was so offended by the question that she responded: "Now, give me that again. Flat out to fit my head." Hannah's response made matters worse. "I mean, did you? You know. When we was little." Eva, growing angrier by the moment, finally exploded and said to Hannah: ". . . . You settin here with your healthy-ass self and ax me did I love you? Them big eyes in your head would have been full of maggots if I hadn't" (p. 68). And then when Hannah made matters worse by asking if she ever played with them when they were little, Eva replied: "Play? Wasn't nobody playin in 1895. Just cause you got it good now you think it was always this good? 1895 was a killer, girl. . . . I set in that house with you and Pearl and Plum and three beets, you snake-eyed ungrateful hussy. What would I look like leapin' round that little old room playin' with youngins with three beets to my name?" (ibid.). When Hannah sassily responded, "I know 'bout them beets, Mamma. You told us that a million times," Eva went on: "Ain't that love? You want me to tinkle you under the jaw and forget 'bout them sores in your mouth? Pearl was shittin' worms and I was supposed to play rang-around the rosie? . . . what you talkin' 'bout did I love you girl I stayed alive for you can't you get that through your thick head or what is that between your ears, heifer?" (p. 69). Thus, Eva Peace's love was a love without frills. It was a nurturing love linked to the harsh realities of existence—a love that kept others alive and would eventually rebuild broken circles of familial love and concern.

When *The Song of Solomon* was published it was hailed as "the best novel of the Black Experience in America since *Invisible Man*"; it was a Book-of-the-Month Club selection and was awarded the "Best Novel of the Year" prize. Apart from all the praise and laudatory comment, it is a novel of enormous structural complexity. It contains a broadly coherent intermixture of plots and subplots all of which have interlinked flashbacks. The novel's inherent unity is established by the character of Macon Dead, Jr., better known by his nickname, Milkman. Whatever happens or whatever has happened is related to his past, his present, or his future. In fact, because the novel's primary concern is with the birth, growth, and maturation of Milkman, *The Song of Solomon* is in reality a *bildungsroman* or apprenticeship novel.

Pilate, Milkman's aunt, is the nurturer in this novel. Unfortunately, Morrison's emphasis on Pilate's eccentricities in behavior, dress, and appearance almost obscures her nurturing skills. When Pilate first appears in the novel, the reader quickly becomes aware of the fact that she is a very strange person. First, as the result of her family's practice of giving children biblical names, her illiterate parents had picked a man's name rather than a woman's name. This they had done with the help of a semi-illiterate midwife. Then, because her mother died in the birthing process, but literally before the baby was born, there was no umbilical cord to be severed, and Pilate was born without a navel. After she had become a sexually active teenager, this physical peculiarity became a handicap. It drove away lovers and provoked fear and apprehension among her superstitious friends, neighbors, and associates. They thought that, because she was not as other men and women, she must have strange powers which might affect the behavior and fortunes of others. And, as the story develops, Morrison demonstrates that she does have such powers. Fortunately, Pilate's powers have a positive and never a negative effect. They are used to nurture and protect and heal others, especially her family—a family stricken by emotional and psychological disorder and conflict.

The reader first sees evidence of Pilate's nurturing powers when, in an informative flashback, the story is told how, through her vast knowledge of sexually stimulating diets, she restores her brother Macon's sexual interest in his wife, Ruth. The result is the birth of Macon, Jr. In other words, Pilate has a power, not given to anyone else, to intervene in the affairs of others; but it is a power which she never uses with evil intent.

Pilate exercises her nurturing skills primarily as a mother and as a grandmother and for the preservation of her family. In her efforts in this regard, she is opposed by her money-grubbing brother Macon, who is motivated by three things: greed, a hatred for those blacks less fortunate than he, and a monumental disdain for all women, including his wife, his two daughters, his prostitutes, and above all, his sister, Pilate.

In several respects, Pilate is like Eva Peace in *Sula*. In her love of family, she is, like Eva, permissive and understanding. Her daughter Reba, like Eva's Hannah, lives "from one orgasm to another." Her love of Hagar, her granddaughter, drives her to abandon her wandering ways with migrant fruit and vegetable pickers and settle in her brother Macon's city, so that Hagar can become acquainted with the civilizing ways of city life. And when Hagar falls in love with Milkman, her cousin, Pilate is understanding. She sees no irregularity in their sexual relationship. As long as her granddaughter and her nephew are happy, she is happy. Nor does she intervene when the affair ends and a heartbroken Hagar prowls the city looking for Milkman with well advertised murderous intent. Like Eva, Pilate knows the vagaries of the human heart and that those whom she loves will suffer pain and sorrow.

Her nurturing powers come into full play in the second part of the novel when Milkman, abandoning his thoughtless ways, seeks to return to Danville, Pennsylvania, where his father and Aunt Pilate were born and the Dead family had its post-slavery beginnings. Initially, his motives are greedy and materialistic; he is in search of a bag of gold which both his father and his aunt thought remained hidden in a cave where they as children had to hide after their father was fatally shot by whites who wanted the richly fertile Dead farm. When he finds that there is no gold, Milkman then begins to trace his family's roots, traveling from Pennsylvania to a series of small Virginia towns. Since Dead was a name given his grandfather accidentally by an unknown Union soldier as the war refugee wagons rolled out of the southern war zones, Milkman, in his search, has little to go on, except a song:

> Jake the only son of Solomon
> Come booba yalle, come booba tambee
> Whirled around and touched the sun
> Come komka yalle, come konke tambee
>
> . . .
>
> O Solomon don't leave me here
> Cotton balls to choke me
> O Solomon don leave me here
> Buckra's arms to yoke me
>
> Solomon done fly, Solomon don gone
> Solomon cut across the sky, Solomon
> gone home.
>
> (p. 303)

It was a children's playing rhyme, like "Little Susie Walker," but it held a message about his family's slave origins. As the author states, after his discovery of his family's beginnings, Milkman, no longer obsessed with greed and love of property, "was as eager and happy as he had ever been in his life" (p. 302). The discovery of his roots in an obscure little Virginia town called Shalimar had converted him into a fairly likeable human being. He had found the long-obscured beginning of his family circle.

In the end, Pilate, ever the family nurturer, returns to Shalimar to bury her father's bones, which she had carried with her during her years of wandering with the migrant workers. Immediately after her father's bones are interred, a shot rings out and Pilate is soon dead. But just before she dies, she whispers to Milkman, in accordance with the creed that had guided her steps for more than sixty-five years: "I wish I'd knowed more people. I would of loved 'em all. If I'd knowed more, I would a loved more" (p. 340).

Beloved, Morrison's most recent, Pulitzer Prize–winning novel, is all about nurturing in slavery times and in those years of quasi-freedom when slavery still cast a long shadow over the ways of black folks. Familial circles have long been broken; and, at the novel's end, there is more emphasis on enduring and surviving than on rebuilding those circles. In fact, for the central persona of the novel, Sethe, the only home she had known until her escape at age nineteen was Sweet Home, the small slave plantation in Kentucky, about two days' traveling distance from the Ohio River and freedom. And whatever vestiges of family she had were the other slaves from Sweet Home—Baby Suggs, her mother-in-law, and Paul D., who, after his escape, had run for seven years and finally circled back into Cincinnati. The novel demonstrates that slavery put all forms of black nurturing at risk. Baby Suggs, for instance, bore eight children by eight different fathers but never got to know any of them except Halle, Sethe's husband. And she knew Halle for only the few years before he arranged to purchase her freedom. From that time on, she had not seen or heard of her one remaining child and assumed that he was dead. Sethe's attempts at family building and nurturing were even more tragic. Having married Halle, with her master's consent, and borne four children by age nineteen, she soon found her insatiable desire for freedom for her children and for herself an overwhelming complication in her young life. First, she was able to send to freedom her two young boys, Howard and Buglar; then she sent her yet unweaned daughter, Denver. Since the time of her children's escapes was a circumstance Sethe could not control, Denver's departure left her with breasts that were sore with unsucked milk. So an essential process in the mother-baby nurturing relationship was interrupted. But Sethe was not only a mother; she was a slave, and the system demanded that she be punished for aiding in the escape of her children or three potential hands who would spend their working days at Sweet Home. So she was beaten so savagely that her back was forever scarred by the lash marks of the whip. Then, insult was added to injury when she was literally "raped" of her milk by two young assistants of her master. They sucked her dry, leaving the young mother drained of an essential nurturing capacity. Her husband, Halle, forced to view the whipping and the following "milk rape," was driven mad by what he saw.

Sethe's life as a mother and a nurturer became even more complicated in freedom. After bearing her fourth child during her escape—literally at the river's edge—she was forced, in her desperation to keep her children from being returned to slavery, to kill her youngest child. Observers of the event stated that Sethe would have killed all four of her children to keep them from being returned to slavery, had not friends intervened.

From this calamitous event the central plot of the novel develops. The murdered infant returns some fifteen years later as a ghostly visitor; and Sethe, who had long been stricken by grief and guilt about her murdered child, turns to loving and caring for her "Beloved" with an overwhelming and obsessive intensity. The relationship between daughter and mother becomes strained and deteriorates, and Sethe ceases to be the nurturer under whose care a child matures and develops. Rather she is drained of her nurturing strength and emotionally enslaved by the experience. The enslavers at Sweet Home had raped her of her milk; Beloved, her enslaver in freedom, rapes her of her nurturing strength.

At the end of the novel, in the early 1880s, Sethe is alone. The ghostly Beloved has melted away; her two sons have long been gone, and Denver, her daughter, has gone off to work and lives elsewhere. Now there is no one to care for and nurture. Under the shadow of slavery, no family circles have been started or discovered or renewed.

So when Paul D., ever in search of a friend from Sweet Home, comes to visit, he finds a Sethe who longs for death. For more than twenty years she has been free of slavery's thrall, but she has remained a slave-born person who, despite her successful effort to rear her family in freedom, has never known the comfort and solace of warm family circles. Furthermore, because of the dire circumstances that beset her in freedom, she has exhausted her very rich nurturing energies on a teenage ghost—a ghost who, although vengeful and hostile, remains, ironically, her Beloved.

Thus, of the four Morrison characters considered here—Eva, Pilate, Milkman, and Sethe—Sethe, because of her close involvement in the slave experience and culture, is the least successful as a nurturer and builder and discoverer of family circles. This is in accord with the judgment of history. Slavery, a four-hundred-year adventure in Euro-Western capitalism, tore Africans away from their centuries-old tribal rituals and dehumanized them with rapes and whippings. Troubled and enmeshed in the harsh reality of being half slave and half free, Sethe had no time to sing. If she had, she would have probably asked in song:

> Will the circle be unbroken
> In the sky, Lord, in the sky?
> Will the circle be unbroken
> When I die, Lord, when I die?

NOTES

1. Toni Morrison, *Sula* (New York: Knopf, 1974). All references to this work are from this edition and are noted parenthetically in the text.

2. Toni Morrison, *The Song of Solomon* (New York: Knopf, 1977). All references to this work are from this edition and are noted parenthetically in the text.

3. Toni Morrison, *Beloved* (New York: Knopf, 1987).

PART 5

The Blues He Could Not Lose: Langston Hughes and His Work

Humanistic Techniques Employed in Hughes's Poetry

In one of his critical essays, *Tradition and Individual Talent,* T. S. Eliot concluded that there is a necessary creative tension between a given tradition and most writers who choose to write in that tradition. The tradition defines an approach and a set of guidelines that tend to restrict the creativity of a particular writer, and the writer in reaction seeks to assert his independence and modify the tradition. So tradition speaks to writer and writer speaks to tradition. At times, a writer affects a given tradition little or not at all. For instance, a nineteenth-century romantic poet like Philip Freneau did not change the tradition of romantic poetry at all. On the other hand, Algernon Swinburne, because of his literary and physical encounter with sadism and various kinds of eroticism, revolted against the tradition of Victorian neoromanticism, and the tradition was never quite the same after Swinburne.

The case of Langston Hughes is not exactly comparable, but there is substantial evidence that by 1926, with the publication of his *Weary Blues,* he had broken with one or two rather well-established traditions in Afro-American literature. By no means was he alone in this act of literary insurrection; Claude McKay, Jean Toomer, and other poets of the 1920s stood with him. In the first place, Hughes chose to modify the poetic tradition that decreed that whatever literature the black man produced must not only protest racial conditions but promote racial integration. There was little or no place in such a literary tradition for the celebration of the black life-style for the sake of the black life-style. Dunbar had, with obviously innocuous intent, attempted some celebration of the black life-style in the post-Reconstruction rural South, but his pictures of happy pickaninnies and banjo-plunking, well-fed cabin blacks did not square with the poverty and racial violence that seared the post-Reconstruction rural

Southland. In any event, by 1920 a poetry of strong social protest which attempted to plead cultural equality with white America had become a fixed tradition in Afro-American literature. It was thought that black America's writers could knock on the door of racial segregation and successfully plead for admission into a presumably racially integrated society. Of course, admission would not be gained unless these writers, painters, and sculptors had all been properly schooled in Euro-Western techniques and practices and thus fully qualified for acceptance. It might be pointed out in this context that to effect this end, even the so-called spirituals or sorrow-songs of the slaves were Europeanized—songs whose weird and sadly provocative melodies had had such a marked effect on northern whites when first heard on the Carolina sea islands in 1862. In 1916, Harry T. Burleigh, the organist at New York's ultrafashionable St. George's Episcopal Church, published his *Jubilee Songs of the United States* with every spiritual arranged so that a concert singer could sing it, "in the manner of an art song." Thus, the black man's art in song and story was to be used primarily to promote racial acceptance and ultimately achieve racial integration. And it was clear that it had to be a Europeanized art.

Necessarily excluded from consideration in any such arrangement was the vast amount of secular folk material which had been created through-out the years of the black man's persecution and enslavement in America. For during slavery black people had used song and story to achieve many social and political goals. They had covertly ridiculed "massa" and "missus" in song and story and had overtly expressed their disdain and hatred for the "niggah driber." And since slavery, they had sung the blues on water-front levees and in juke joints; they had built railroads and sung about John Henry and other laboring giants; they had been on chain gangs and as prisoners had been leased out to cruel masters to cut the tall cane on the Brazos to the tune of the slashing whip and under a blazing sun which they called "Ole Hannah." They had sung as they chopped cotton on tenant farms and scrubbed and ironed clothes in the white folks' kitchens. All of this orature, as some critics have called it, was, in the opinion of the monitors of Afro-American culture during the Harlem Renaissance, to be totally excluded from common view. Innocuous tidbits like James Weldon Johnson's "Sence You Went Away," one of the "croon songs" published in his 1916 volume *Fifty Years and Other Poems,* might be acceptable. But generally the richly complex burden of secular folk material—the songs and stories that came out of the sweat, sorrow, and occasional joy of black people of the lower classes—might impede integration and hence was to be expunged from the racial literary record.

The crystallization of a tradition that outlawed black folk literature and song inevitably fostered some attitudes which adversely affected the jazz and blues which were just beginning to be established in the early 1920s when Hughes first settled in New York City. For the indictment of folk material resulted in the cultural censure of the blues singing of Bessie and Clara Smith, the jazz playing of Duke Ellington, Louis Armstrong, and Fletcher Henderson, and the song-and-dance and vaudeville showmanship of Bill Robinson, Bert Williams, Eubie Blake, and Noble Sissell. Ironically, one of the cultural monitors of the period, James Weldon Johnson, had written that the cakewalk and ragtime were two of black America's principal contributions to American culture. Johnson, if you remember, had been a music man himself at one time in his career. But other strong-minded monitors of black culture ignored Johnson and deemed that the dancing, singing, laughing, blues-singing, jazz-playing black was too uncomfortably close to a despised folk tradition to project a proper integrationist image. In retrospect, one is forced to observe that in view of how deeply black jazz and music have influenced both twentieth-century American and Western European life-styles, this attempt to demean the image of the black entertainer and music man of the early 1920s is indeed one of the great ironies in Afro-American cultural history.

So Langston Hughes and other young poets of the early years of the Harlem Renaissance had to confront a point of view which had quickly crystallized into a binding and restricting tradition. Hughes also developed a dislike for the tradition of racial exoticism which, largely promoted by white patrons, began to be an absorbing concern of black writers by the mid-1920s. Although his resistance to racial exoticism eventually ruptured his relationship with his patron, Mrs. R. Osgood Mason, his fight against a tradition barring orature and the rich folk material of the lower classes of blacks became his major struggle. The discussion to follow will not focus on how he waged a successful fight to change that tradition. Rather my focus for the balance of this paper will be on the humanistic techniques which he used in his poetry to reflect and communicate the rich folk culture of black people.

Before making any specific attempt to describe Hughes's use of humanistic techniques in his folk poetry, one may make at least three generalizations about his folk poetry. First, most of his folk poems have the distinctive marks of orature. They contain many instances of naming and enumerating, considerable hyperbole and understatement, and a strong infusion of street-talk rhyming. Also, there is a deceptive veil of artlessness in most of the poems. Actually, there is much more art and deliberate design than one may immediately perceive. I should point out in this context that Hughes prided himself on being an impromptu and impressionistic writer of poetry. His, he insisted, was not an artfully constructed poetry. However, an analysis of some of his better monologues and his poems on economic and social class issues will reveal that much of his poetry was carefully and artfully crafted. The third generalization is that Hughes's folk poetry shares certain features found in other types of folk literature. There are many instances of dramatic ellipsis and narrative compression. Also we find considerable rhythmic repetition and monosyllabic emphasis. And, of course, flooding all of his poetry is that peculiar mixture of Hughesian irony and humor—a very distinctive mark of Hughes's folk poetry.

The foregoing generalizations have a particular relevancy when one studies some of Hughes's dramatic monologues. In most instances these are artfully done; the idioms of black folk speech and street talk abound and, very often, the final lines drip with irony and calculated understatement. An example is "Lover's Return":

> My old time daddy
> Came back home last night.
> His face was pale and
> His eyes didn't look just right.
>
> He says to me, "I'm
> Comin' home to you—
> So sick and lonesome
> I don't know what to do."

In the first place, there are two levels of monologue in this poem; the persona describes to the reader her elderly lover's return and then, in lines that the poet italicizes, there is an interior monologue in which the woman talks to herself. These italicized lines clearly reveal the heightened anxiety and inner emotional tensions that haunt the persona:

> *Oh, men treats women*
> *Just like a pair o' shoes.*
> *You men treats women*
> *Like a pair o' shoes—*
> *You kicks 'em round and*
> *Does 'em like you choose.*

This interior monologue contains a repressed truth, and one can imagine the tremendous psychological pressure such a truth has on the psyche of the persona. Moreover, the words in the interior monologue have a double-edged relevancy; they define the persona's particular dilemma and they also effectively generalize about a larger and more universal dilemma in the arena of sexual conflict. The full psychological impact of this monologue, however, is expressed in the last stanza of the poem when the conflict between outward compassion and inner condemnation is clearly delineated:

> I looked at my daddy—
> Lawd! and I wanted to cry.
> He looked so thin—
> Lawd! that I wanted to cry.
> But de devil told me:
> *Damn a lover*
> *Comes home to die!*

Inevitably, as the result of the carefully controlled narrative compression commonly found in the well-crafted dramatic monologue, many facts remain explicitly unstated. But Hughes calls upon the perceptive and imaginative reader to fill out the details of this miniature but poignant drama. The persona, deserted by her older lover many years ago, is now forced by an obviously unfair kind of social obligation to receive him once again. Her code of faithfulness and her sense of social propriety pull her in one direction. Her sense of fair play and justice pull her in another. In the end, the harassed persona is torn between a deeply instinctual inner desire to avoid pain and distress and a strong sense of obligation to honor an elderly lover "come home to die." Characteristically, Hughes defines the dilemma and then leaves the resolution carefully unstated. By so doing, he appears to be saying that the vulnerable, dilemma-ridden, anti-heroic persona is the kind of person who truly counts in the larger human equation.

Further examples of Hughes's humanistic techniques can be found in some of his blues poems and certain of his dialogue and debate poems. In his gutsy reaction against the tradition that censured the blues as offensive and devoid of cultural import, Hughes wrote a number of blues poems. In fact, *Fine Clothes to the Jew* (1927), *Shakespeare in Harlem* (1942), and *One-Way Ticket* (1949) have more than their fair share of such poems. Many are uncomplicated blues statements like:

> When hard luck overtakes you
> Nothin' for you to do.
> When hard luck overtakes you
> Nothin' for you to do.
> Gather up your fine clothes
> An' sell 'em to de Jew.

or:

> I beats ma wife an'
> I beats ma side gal too.
> Beats ma wife an'
> Beats ma side gal too.
> Don't know why I do it but
> It keeps me from feelin' blue.

In these poems there is a Hughesian blend of irony and humor but no psychological complexity. One contains some advice about how to handle hard luck with minimum psychological damage; the second poem describes the casual self-acceptance of a chronic woman-beater who apparently is unaware of the extent of his problem. But, in the blues poem "In a Troubled Key" there is a difference. The blues form is here:

> Still I can't help lovin' you,
> Even though you do me wrong.
> Says I can't help lovin' you
> Though you do me wrong—
> But my love might turn into a knife
> Instead of to a song.

The harassed woman is helplessly entwined in love, but here is the possibility that her patience will eventually become exhausted and instead of a song of love, there will be knife-work in the night. Similarly, the blues poem "Widow Woman" has an unexpected ironic ending. After promising to be ever faithful to a recently deceased "mighty lover" who had "ruled" her for "many years," in the last two lines she suddenly becomes aware of the full import of the freedom that is about to become hers. So the poem ends with the kind of ironic juxtaposition Hughes loved. The outwardly distraught widow stands sobbing by the open grave as she watches the grave-diggers throw dirt in her husband's face. But, inwardly, her heart soars joyfully at the prospect of freedom: " . . . You never can tell when a / Woman like me is free."

In addition to the humanizing techniques used by Hughes in some of his dramatic monologues, the poet also sometimes presented two personae in a dramatic dialogue form of poetry. In one or two instances, the dialogue broadens into a debate which the poet humanizes by carefully illuminating the two opposing points of view. For instance, in "Sister," one of the poems in *Montage of a Dream Deferred,* a dialogue occurs between a mother and her son about sister's involvement with a married man. The brother is embarrassed by his sister's behavior and asks:

> Why don't she get a boyfriend
> I can understand—some decent man?

The mother somewhat surprisingly defends her daughter; actually her Marie is the victim of the grim economic lot of the ghetto dweller. She "runs around with trash" in order to get "some cash." In other words, a grim and dehumanizing economic determinism is in control of the lives of all three—the mother, the son, and the daughter. The son, however, still does not understand; he asks, "Don't decent folks have dough?" The mother, out of the wisdom of bitter cynicism, immediately replies, "Unfortunately, usually no!" And the mother continues:

> Did it ever occur to you, boy,
> that a woman does the best she can?

To this the son makes no reply, but a voice, probably that of the poet, adds: "So does a man." In other words, Hughes is saying that, like the distressed, fragmented, and fallible personae of most folk poetry, human beings do the best that they can and their failures and defeats are actually the mark of their humanity.

Another poetic dialogue, entitled "Mama and Daughter," has a slightly different thrust and meaning. There is no polarizing conflict between the two personae, but obviously each is reacting quite differently to the same situation. The mother is helping her daughter prepare to go "down the street" to see her "sugar sweet." As they talk, the mother becomes increasingly agitated because she remembers when she, too, went "down the street" to see her "sugar sweet." But now, the romantic tinsel is gone forever from her life; her "sugar sweet" married her, got her with child, and then, like so many ghetto fathers, abandoned her to a life of unprotected loneliness. So a dramatic contrast develops between the naively hopeful daughter who is eager to join the "young man" she can't get off her mind, and the disillusioned mother who for different reasons can't forget her errant husband. When the mother expresses the hope that her husband—"that wild young son-of-a-gun"—will one day "rot in Hell," her daughter replies: "Mama, Dad couldn't be still young." The anger of the mother's final comment is the anger of all the abandoned women of all of America's urban ghettos. And what she leaves unsaid is more important than what she actually says:

> He *was* young yesterday.
> He *was* young when he—
> Turn around!
> So I can brush your back, I say!

In other words, love and sex have tricked the mother and left her lonely and full of bitter memories. And yet, the "down-the-street" ritual must be repeated for the daughter. Disappointment and disillusionment very probably await her later; but, to Hughes, disappointment and disillusionment await all lovers because these are, once again, the necessary and essential marks of the human condition.

There are three other poems by Hughes which provide interesting examples of his use of humanistic techniques. The first, "Blue Bayou," is a tersely wrought dramatic monologue in which the persona describes the circumstances leading to his death by lynching. In essence, it is an age-old southern tale of an interracial love triangle that, inevitably, turns out badly for the black man. What is striking about the monologue is the poet's use of the folk symbol of the "setting sun." In some of the old blues standards, the image of the "setting sun" is a recurring motif with various overtones of meaning:

> In the evenin', in the evenin'
> When the settin sun go down
> Ain't it lonesome, ain't it lonesome
> When your baby done left town.

or:

> Hurry sundown, hurry sundown
> See what tomorrow bring
> May bring rain
> May bring any old thing.

And at the beginning of "Blue Bayou," the "setting sun" could be a symbol of "any old thing." The persona says:

> I went walkin'
> By the Blue Bayou
> And I saw the sun go down.

Then, using the narrative compression and dramatic ellipsis usually found in the folk ballad, the persona tells his story:

> I thought about old Greely
> And I thought about Lou
> And I saw the sun go down.
> White man
> Makes me work all day
> And I works too hard
> For too little pay—
> Then a white man
> Takes my woman away.
>
> I'll kill old Greely.

At this point, the persona's straight narration ends. In the next stanza, sundown as a reddening symbol of violent death is introduced, and the italicized choral chant of the lynchers is heard:

> The Blue Bayou
> Turns red as fire.
> *Put the black man*
> *On a rope*
> *And pull him higher!*

Then the persona returns to state with a rising crescendo of emotional stress: "I saw de sun go down."

By the time the final stanza begins, "De Blue Bayou's / A pool of fire," and the persona utters his last words:

> And I saw de sun go down,
> Down
> Down
> Lawd, I saw the sun go down.

The emphasis in this last stanza is on the word "down." It is used four times in the last four lines, and in lines two and three "down, down!" are the only words used. And Hughes arranges the monosyllabic lines so that the second literally is placed "down" from the first. Thus ends this grim little tragedy of a triangular love affair that ended in a murder and in a lynching. Several additional critical observations may be made about this poem. First, it is interesting to note how Hughes manipulates the meaning of the setting sun. It is done with great verbal economy and tremendous dramatic finesse. At the beginning, when the persona views the setting sun, it is part of a beautiful Blue Bayou setting. But the persona's mood is blue just like the anonymous blues singer who shouts:

> In the evenin', in the evenin'
> When the settin sun go down
> Ain't it lonesome, ain't it lonesome
> When your baby done left town.

The persona quickly and succinctly relates what has happened to his baby, Lou. We do not know whether she left voluntarily with old Greely or had no choice. In any event, as the sun is setting, the persona decides to assert his manhood and kill old Greely. Then, a short time after the deed is done, the lynchers catch him by the Blue Bayou. Again the sun is setting, but now all nature begins to reflect and mirror the victim's agony. The bayou turns red with his blood; and then it becomes a pool of fire mirroring the flames that begin to burn his hanging, twisting body. Finally, the victim symbolically sees his own death as he repeats, "Lawd, I saw de sun go down."

Interestingly enough, it is through the actual use of his poetic technique that Hughes, the "artless" poet, conveys to the reader the brutal and agonizing slowness of the persona's death. Just as the setting sun in the American southland provides a scene of slow and lingering beauty as it sinks down, down, down over the rim of the earth, so the death of the victim is a slow and lingering agony as he sinks down, down, down into the pit of death.

It should also be stressed that, although this poem has a recurring blues
motif in its use of the setting-sun image, it has a finality hardly ever found
in the standard blues. In fact, all good blues reflect survival and recovery.
For instance, in "Stormy Monday Blues" it takes Lou Rawls six days to get
rid of his blues; then, after the "ghost walks on Friday," Saturday he "goes
out to play" and on Sunday he goes "to church to pray." In other words, in
the real blues the persona is always waiting hopefully to see "what tomorrow brings." But in Hughes's poem "Blue Bayou," the persona has no
tomorrow. Had the poem described a tomorrow, the reader would have
seen a bayou flooded with the bright colors of a beautiful sunrise; and,
mirrored in the bayou's sun-flecked waters, one would see the persona's
body slowly twisting in the early morning breeze. The stench of burning
flesh would be everywhere and no birds would sing to greet the multicol-
ored dawn.

A discussion of Hughes's humanistic techniques in poetry should include
two additional poems. These are "Jitney," an experimental poem celebrating a highly particularized mode of the black life-style, and "Trumpet
Player: 52nd Street," a poem that reflects the poet's consummate artistry in
one mode of genre description. Essentially, both are folk poems. "Jitney" is
an exuberant salute to the jitney cabs that used to wind up and down South
Parkway in Chicago and up and down Jefferson in Nashville, Tennessee.
They have long been supplanted by better modes of transportation but in
the 1930s and 1940s the jitneys were very much part of black Chicago and
black Nashville.

In his poem, Hughes attempts to capture the uniqueness of the experience of riding a jitney cab on two roundtrips between Chicago's Thirty-first
and Sixty-third streets. Like the cab, the poem snakes along; each stop—31st,
35th, 47th—occupies a single line, thus providing the reader with the sense
of movement in space. In other words, not only does the form reflect the
content in this poem, the form *is* the content.

The great merit of the poem is not its experimental form, however.
"Jitney" is a microcosm of a moving, surging, dynamic black Chicago. Thus
it is not so much a poem that celebrates a mode of transportation unique to
Chicago's black Southside; rather it celebrates the Southside folk who ride
jitneys and hustle up and down South Parkway to go to church, to go to the
market, to go to night school, to go to nightclubs and stage shows and
movies. Or sometimes, the time spent riding in a jitney becomes a peaceful
interlude in the hectic struggle to survive in a swiftly paced urban society—an
interlude to gossip or signify:

> Girl, ain't you heard?
> *No, Martha, I ain't heard.*

> I got a Chinese boy-friend
> Down on 43rd.
> 47th,
> 51st,
> 55th,
> 63rd,
> Martha's got a Japanese!
> Child, ain't you heard?

As people come and go, facts and circumstances obviously change; but apparently, the mood in a jitney cab is one of a warm, folksy friendliness—the kind Chicago's black residents remembered in their "down-home" days. Indeed, the poem suggests that in a large metropolis like black Chicago, one refuge from the cold anonymity of urban life is the jitney cab:

> 43rd,
> I quit Alexander!
> Honey, ain't you heard?
> 47th,
> 50th Place,
> 63rd,
> Alexander's quit Lucy!
> Baby, ain't you heard?
>   . . .
> If you want a good chicken
> You have to get there early
> And push and shove and grab!
> I'm going shopping now, child.

The pervasive mood of "Jitney," then, is one of racial exuberance and vitality. As the cab moves up and down South Parkway, the Southside folks who jump in and out and are busy about their business have no time to talk about deferred dreams. Obviously, Chicago's black citizens had as many dreams deferred as Harlem's black citizens; but the jitney provided neither the time nor the place for in-depth discussions of racial dilemmas. It is significant that by the time black urban America exploded into riot and racial confrontation, the jitneys of Chicago's South Parkway and Nashville's Jefferson Street had long since disappeared from the urban scene.

Finally, "Trumpet Player: 52nd Street" reveals a fine blending of the best of Hughes's humanistic techniques. In the musician's portrait, we see both a particular person and a folk symbol. For Hughes, who had started writing about "long-headed jazzers" and weary blues-playing pianists back in the 1920s, regarded the black musician as a folk symbol with deep roots in the racial past. Thus in the poem's first stanza we greet the symbol not the man. What the persona remembers, all black musicians have remembered throughout all of slavery's troubled centuries:

> The Negro
> With the trumpet at his lips
> Has dark moons of weariness
> Beneath his eyes
> Where the smoldering memory
> Of slave ships
> Blazed to the crack of whips
> About his thighs.

The instrument he is playing has no significance; it could be a banjo, a drum, or just some bones manipulated by agile black fingers; the memory is the same. And the memory makes the music different. Etched in pain, the sound is better, the beat more impassioned, the melody more evocative. And the music flows forth with greater ease, as Dunbar's Malindy proved in "When Malindy Sings." Actually these musicians have found the "spontaneous overflow of powerful emotions" that the youthful Wordsworth was in search of and actually never found, for too often in Euro-Western artistic expression traditional structures intervene and negate spontaneous creativity.

The poem also has its fair share of Hughesian irony. Where in ancient times man through his music sought the moon and the beautiful, ever-surging sea, now matters have changed:

> Desire
> That is longing for the moon
> Where the moonlight's but a spotlight
> In his eyes,
> Desire
> That is longing for the sea
> Where the sea's a bar-glass
> Sucker size.

So no fanciful escape from the hard facts of nightclub life is permitted. In other words, we can and must remember the past but we cannot escape the present, and through Hughes's gentle reminder one stumbles on one of history's great and overweening truths. If art does provide an escape from the present, it is but a temporary escape. But the memory of past pain and the awareness of the present's difficulties and deferred dreams are themes that make the *comédie humaine* so truly comic.

Finally, as the poem draws to a close, the poet actually presents the trumpeter himself:

> The Negro
> With the trumpet at his lips

> Whose jacket
> Has a *fine* one-button roll,
> Does not know
> Upon what riff the music slips
> Its hypodermic needle
> To his soul.

The figure of the hypodermic needle penetrating the soul of the music man suggests that the music provides only temporary relief from the difficulties of the present. In other words, jazz is a useful narcotic to allay the world's woes. But the poetic image of the hypodermic needle also suggests that jazz lovers can develop addictive personalities and become dependent on a little music that excludes the terror and woe of human existence. It is not only good for the soul but absolutely necessary for the psyche.

The final stanza of this extraordinarily well-made poem repeats what was said at the beginning of the poem about the historical role of the black maker of music:

> But softly
> As the tunes come from his throat
> Trouble
> Mellows to a golden note.

The music anesthetizes both performer and listener against remembered pain. In fact, the Fifty-second Street trumpeter with his "patent-leathered" hair and his jacket with "a fine one-button roll" disappears from view and a folk music man of ancient origin reappears. His role has long been to convert "trouble" into beautiful music. Many years ago James Bramston wrote that "music hath charms to soothe the savage beast." But Hughes humanizes the function of art and music. In "Trumpet Player: 52nd Street" the poet suggests that the black man's music nullifies the pain of the past and seals off the woe of the present. Admittedly, the poem, with its sophisticated imagery, is not probably orature of the kind found in the poems discussed above, but the black music man described therein has long been a focal figure in producing the songs and stories that black people have orated and sung down through the centuries.

There are many more instances of Hughes's use of humanistic techniques throughout the full range of his poetry. As has been indicated, however, this discussion has been limited to his folk poetry—to his orature. It is now clear that Hughes's devotion to this kind of poetry had two major consequences: He broke the back of a tradition which sought to exclude secular folk material from the canon of black literature. And, in his use of the language of the black lower classes, Hughes prepared the way for the use and acceptance of the revolutionary black street poetry of the late 1960s.

NOTE

This essay first appeared in *Black American Literature and Humanism,* ed. R. Baxter Miller (Lexington: University Press of Kentucky, 1981), 11–26. Reprinted with permission.

Hughes: Blues, Jazz, and Low-down Folks

Between 1921, the year in which Langston Hughes published his first poem in the *Crisis,* and 1926, the year in which he published his first book of poems, there were many changes in black America's literary and cultural climate. So sweeping and all-encompassing were these changes that the young poet whose "The Negro Speaks of Rivers" had charmed the black literary elite in 1921 found himself, five years later, almost a literary persona non grata. Actually, his book *The Weary Blues* did not result in his total rejection by the minions of black culture; *Fine Clothes to the Jew,* in 1927, did that. As a result, Hughes became in the late twenties a poetic pariah in the opinion of Harlem's leading critics. *The Weary Blues* in 1926 merely raised some eyebrows over the young poet's celebration of cabaret life and his less-than-casual preoccupation with blues and jazz. Some critics wondered what had happened to the splendid promise of "The Negro Speaks of Rivers." In that poem, a hitherto unknown nineteen-year-old from the Midwest had spoken with the poetic wisdom of the ages. He had given the Negro a creditable historic definition, tying him to ancient kingdoms and linking him to the onsweep of civilization. Indeed, the free verse lines of the poem have a certain Horacian dignity about them and are at once pleasantly instructive and instructively pleasant. As Jean Wagner notes in *Black Poets of the United States,* there is a broadly gratifying "racial romanticism" throughout "The Negro Speaks of Rivers," linking Hughes's poem to James Weldon Johnson's "O Black and Unknown Bards" and similar poetic pieces full of rhetorical force and racial edification. Moreover, the poem contains no painful specifics or disturbing reminders about centuries of racial injustice but proudly asserts that the Negro's soul "has grown deep like the rivers" of history. And too, there is timely mention of the African rivers, the Congo and the Nile, asserting the American black man's link to Africa, his romantic motherland, a land which in 1921 was so comfortably distant. So, on all grounds, Langston Hughes's "The Negro Speaks of Rivers" qualified as a preeminently acceptable poetic statement.

By 1925, the young poet, four years older and more widely traveled and much more attuned to literary and cultural trends, had changed his poetic style. His poem "The Weary Blues," which won first prize in *Opportunity's* first poetic competition in 1925, provided prima facie evidence that Hughes was no longer staring at distant vistas but was beginning to focus his poetic attention on scenes and settings that were less than palatable to the self-appointed monitors of Negro cultural development during the twenties. In retrospect, it is now clear that the changes which affected the style, content, and general literary attitude of his poetry were inevitable and irresistible. First, as Nathan Huggins has ably demonstrated in his *Harlem Renaissance,* naturalism touched all aspects of American literary expression in the post–World War I years, and black writers in Harlem were no exception. Moreover, Huggins offers the very plausible argument that some of America's then reigning literary critics believed that, if American literature were to have a significant rebirth, the newly emerging coterie of black writers would have to lead the way with their emphasis on a primitivistic naturalism that would somehow "shuffle off" the mortal coils that were stifling literary creativity. About this hope, Carl Van Doren was more than explicit: "What American literature decidedly needs at the moment is color, music, gusto. . . . If the Negroes are not in a position to contribute these items, I do not know what Americans are." No one endorsed this point of view with greater enthusiasm and esprit than did Carl Van Vechten, who, in Huggins's words, was the "undisputed prince" of all white literary figures associated with black Harlem during the 1920s. On the other hand, Allison Davis, in his article "Our Negro Intellectuals" in *The Crisis* (vol. 35, Aug. 1928), charged that it was the nefarious and invidious and sinister influence of Van Vechten that led some black writers astray and brought "black literary primitivism to its complete fruition." Actually, as Huggins points out in his evaluation of Van Vechten's importance to the Harlem Renaissance, the latter's own fiction—*Blind Bow-Boy* (1923), *Firecrackers* (1925), *Nigger Heaven* (1926), and *Parties* (1930)—places great stress on "intensification of experience for its own sake" which, in Huggins's opinion, reflected a Wildean "*fin de siècle* decadence."

But these are relatively esoteric concerns when compared with other developments which in the early 1920s were having a direct influence on young black writers like Hughes. Because these developments emanated from the black American masses, critics, looking at cultural developments through a "talented tenth" perspective only, either feigned a blissful unawareness of their importance or failed to understand that what the "low-down" folk were singing and saying could be grist for the black writer's mill. One important development in post–World War I America was jazz music—so much a cultural artifact of the twenties that F. Scott Fitzgerald labeled the gin-popping, Charleston-dancing decade "The Jazz Age." Before World War I, jazz music had been only a bawling infant in New Orleans's Storyville—an infant that somehow crawled its way along the Gulf Coast and up the Mississippi River to St. Louis and Chicago. At first, it was Ferdinand "Jelly Roll" Morton, as early as 1902, playing his "Jelly Roll Blues" and other teasing overtures to commercial sex in Storyville's whorehouses, thus giving the word "jazz" its initial somewhat pejorative meaning. Then, in 1914, Emmanuel Perez's Creole Band came up from New Orleans to open at Chicago's Grand Theater at Thirty-first and State. By the end of World War I, another New Orleans musician, Freddie Keppard, had brought his band to New York. And, when Louis Armstrong in 1922 came from Chicago to New York to join Fletcher Henderson's new big band, jazz had become more than a bawling infant; it had become a lusty adult.

What impressed Langston Hughes and others who were sensitive to black folk movements is that this new mode of music came out of the black experience. Admittedly, in the early twenties there were no neat socio-anthropological explanations of origin, source, and cause. All that anyone knew is that jazz had started in New Orleans and that its stress on polyrhythmic drumbeats and instrumental improvisation somehow reflected the music of the Congo Square dances at which black New Orleans—slave and free—had shouted, stomped, and danced at regular intervals from 1817 to 1885. Both Eileen Southern in her *Music of Black Americans* (1970) and Frederick Stearns in his *Story of Jazz* (1958) state that the cultural additives that helped jazz music get started were the introduction of European instruments and the tradition of the New Orleans funeral march, originally a joyous salute accorded a deceased brother or sister by one of the city's many secret societies.

Another cultural development that influenced Langston Hughes and his youthful contemporaries was the blues. Like jazz, it was rooted in the black experience and emerged as a mode of folk expression during the post-Reconstruction period. Although its four-line stanza in twelve bars, rhyming *aaba*, reminds one of the folk ballads of Western Europe, the call-and-response pattern, the falsetto "holla," and the flatted fifths and sevenths suggest a distant African origin. Apparently, the blues were born of the hard times of slavery but reached their broadest development right after slavery when the burden of individual responsibility in secular and worldly matters became almost too much for new freedmen to bear. Loneliness, frustration, the victimization of the powerless, and the vicissitudes of love were often the themes of the blues singer. Young men like Langston Hughes found the blues attractive because it was the kind of music that demonstrated the black man's emotional resiliency and his knack for singing his way through personal catastrophe. There is no evidence that the young poet ever heard Ma Rainey sing the blues with her touring Rabbit Foot Minstrels, but the title of his prize-winning poem "The Weary Blues" suggests that he had probably heard Bessie Smith sing her version of "The Weary Blues" which she had introduced in 1915 in Atlanta's famed 81 Theater. Certainly, Langston Hughes was one of the 100,000 persons who bought a copy of Mamie Smith's recording of "Crazy Blues"— the first known Columbia race record—which the celebrated song stylist cut on 10 August 1920.

A third cultural development which affected black literary expression in the twenties was the interest in Africa—Africa as the political motherland and Africa as the symbol of a purifying primitivism. Marcus Garvey's United Negro Improvement Association led the way in exploring a political return to Africa for black Americans; and, although opposed by Du Bois and his "talented tenth" cohorts, the articulate Jamaican captivated the minds of the black masses with his oratory and vision. Similarly, Alain Locke, the artist Aaron Douglas, and others led the way in exploring the esthetic meaning of Africa in the masterpiece of anthologies, *The New Negro,* published in 1925. Not only were the pages of this work festooned with African drawings, but in Alain Locke's essay "The Legacy of the Ancestral Arts," he explores the "vital connection" between the African artistic idiom and that of the American Negro. In the art of both there was, in Locke's opinion, an emphasis on the "decorative and purely symbolic material."

There is bountiful evidence that the early poetry of Langston Hughes was influenced by all three cultural developments—jazz, blues, and Africa as political refuge and artistic symbol. As indicated above, for his concentration on the themes of jazz and blues, he was severely castigated by most of the reigning Negro critics of the day. In the main, these critics assessed culture and the arts from a "talented tenth" perspective; apparently their objective was the development of Negro art forms that would pave the way for full integration into the mainstream of American society. It is interesting to note in this context that the Negro spiritual, in their view, was just such an acceptable art form; blues and jazz were not. The latter were the products of low-down folk who spoke a shamefully ungrammatical dialect, worked hard, and washed little; the spirituals, on the other hand, were the product of the blending of the songful religious zeal of slaves with Protestant hymnody. Not only did the Negro spiritual bring color and excitement and anthropomorphic intensity to an often colorless Judeo-Christian religion, but the music of the spirituals bore proof of the enduring creativity of "Black and Unknown Bards of Long Ago." Du Bois had written approvingly of the spirituals in his chapter on the "Sorrow Songs" in *Souls of Black Folk* in 1903, and his endorsement was the best kind of imprimatur. Then, in 1916, Harry T. Burleigh, the organist at New York's ultrafashionable St. George's Episcopal Church, brought out his *Jubilee Songs of the United States,* with every spiritual musically arranged so that a concert singer could sing it "in the manner of an art song." By the time James Weldon Johnson produced his two *Books of Negro Spirituals,* in 1925 and 1926, there was no doubt that the Negro folk spiritual had the full sanction of the Negro elite as a dignified and racially ennobling form of artistic expression.

Countee Cullen, Langston Hughes's fellow poet, was the first to raise a question about the jazz poems in *Weary Blues.* In his review in *Opportunity* (vol. 4, Feb. 1926), Cullen began by stating that Hughes is "a poet with whom to reckon, to experience, and here and there ... to quarrel." He conceded that the poems in *The Weary Blues* have about them an air of "utter spontaneity." But the poet, in Cullen's view, was "too much himself." *The Weary Blues* would have been a better volume of poetry had "Mr. Hughes held himself a bit in check," particularly with regard to the jazz poems at the beginning of the volume. Wrote Cullen: "I regard these jazz poems as interlopers in the company of the truly beautiful poems in other sections of the book. . . . I wonder if jazz poems really belong to that dignified company, that select and austere circle of high literary expression which we call poetry." Cullen was particularly upset by "The Cat and the Saxophone," an experimental poem in which two lovers converse against a background of cabaret music. Unfortunately, the lovers are not "talented tenth" types; they drink corn liquor, make verbal love in public, and end up dancing the Charleston, the famous dance initially popularized in 1922 in Miller and Lyles's musical show, *Runnin' Wild.* The background tune is "Everybody loves my baby, but my baby don't love nobody but me."

> EVERYBODY
> Half-pint,—
> Gin?
> No, make it
> LOVES MY BABY
> corn. You like
> liquor
> don't you, honey?
> BUT MY BABY
> Sure. Kiss me,
> DON'T LOVE NOBODY

daddy.
BUT ME.

Echoing Jeffrey's famous critical comment on Wordsworth's *Excursion*, Countee Cullen wrote of this poem: "I cannot say, *This will never do,* but I feel that it ought never to have been done." Cullen concluded that, although *The Weary Blues* was effective in spots, Hughes emerged as too much of a "racial artist" and his work reflected "too much emphasis . . . on strictly Negro themes."

Other reviewers of *The Weary Blues* were considerably more positive. Jessie Fauset, writing in *The Crisis* (Mar. 1926, p. 239), hailed Langston Hughes as a "citizen of the world" who had a gift for writing "more tenderly, more understandingly, more humorously" of life in Harlem than any other poet on the contemporary scene. In her view, his poem beginning "Does a jazzband ever sob?" "epitomized the essence" of Harlem cabaret night life. Quite understandably, she lavished considerable praise on "The Negro Speaks of Rivers," thereby seeming to imply some lack of enthusiasm for the jazz poems in the volume. Two other reviewers—DuBose Heyward in the *New York Herald Tribune* (1 Aug. 1926) and an unknown reviewer in the *London Times Literary Supplement* (29 July 1926)—were conspicuously silent about the jazz poems. Both hailed Langston Hughes as a valuable new poetical talent, with Heyward regretting that the young Negro tended to confuse "art with social propaganda" and the *Times* reviewer regretting that Hughes seemed to feel "caged" in Western civilization.

The dialogue about the artistic merit of Hughes's new poetic style and his concentration on jazz and blues was continued by the poet himself when he published an essay entitled "The Negro Artist and the Racial Mountain" in *The Nation* (vol. 122, 692–94) in June 1926. Ostensibly a solicited response to George Schuyler's "The Negro Art-Hokum," which *The Nation* had published the week before, Hughes's article developed into a long credal statement which bristled with defensive comments on the inadequacies of the "talented tenth" view of Negro art and culture. The principal point of Schuyler's article to which Hughes was asked to respond was that there were basically no differences between white art and culture and black art and culture. In his somewhat caustic and flippant manner, Schuyler had written: "Aside from his color . . . your Aframerican is merely a lampblacked Anglo-Saxon." Hence the assertion that the black man's art was peculiar or different was to be, in Schuyler's view, "rejected with a loud guffaw by intelligent people." At the beginning of his article, Hughes dismissed Schuyler's contention with dispatch. Not only was the "urge for whiteness" a very high mountain standing in the way of the development of "true Negro art," but "Nordic manners, Nordic faces, Nordic art, and an

Episcopal heaven" seem to be the primary concerns of upper- and middle-class Negroes who, like Schuyler, would "ape things white." Then, Hughes discussed the dilemma of a Negro artist who, like Jean Toomer, was caught between the white critic's demand for racial stereotypes and the black critic's demand for "respectable" plots, settings, and characters. The rest of the article was devoted to a well-articulated defense of the substance and style of his own poetry. In apparent response to Countee Cullen's comment that *The Weary Blues* was too racial and too jazz-oriented, Hughes asserted that his poetry was intentionally "racial in theme and treatment" and by deliberate design reflected "some of the meanings and rhythms of jazz." Jazz, he declared, was "One of the inherent expressions of Negro life in America: the eternal tom-tom beating in the Negro soul—the tom-tom of revolt against weariness in a white world . . . the tom-tom of joy and laughter, and pain swallowed with a smile." In reality, Hughes continued, Negro jazz was the product and the property of the "low-down folks" ("and they are in the majority—may the Lord be praised!"). If the "smug Negro middle class" could only turn away from the "white, respectable, ordinary books, and papers" and savor the joy and ecstasy of low-down folks, its members would be able to "catch a glimmer" of their own racial beauty. In conclusion, Hughes promised, with the somewhat abrasive bravado of youth, that young artists like himself would continue to "express our dark-skinned selves without fear or shame" and fully exploit the Negro's experience in all dimensions, regardless of white or black censure or praise.

Hughes's statement in *The Nation* had a Janus-like significance. It was not only a vigorous response to Cullen's less than laudatory review of *The Weary Blues,* but it also served as a fitting prelude to his next volume of poems, *Fine Clothes to the Jew.* The nature of the poet's self-defense also fixed the boundaries of future critical discussion of his works. From now on, the subject matter of his poetry and not the art of his poetry would be the center of the swirling controversy over his merit as a poet. Indeed, many years were to elapse before there was sound critical comment on how Langston Hughes handled language and imagery, or before there was an assessment of the esthetic quality of his work. During the twenties no one seemed to be interested in evaluating his technical craftsmanship as a poet. No one wondered what effect his self-proclaimed mode of spontaneous poetic composition had on his poetic form. His major critics were race and culture specialists who were quite incapable of assessing the finer qualities of his poetry. In this context it is appropriate to add that the critical controversy swirled around his use of jazz and blues and low-life incidents as poetic subject matter. No one discussed the merit of his many poems on Africa. Indeed, such a critical discussion had to wait until 1962 when Jean Wagner published his *Les Poètes Nègres des États-Unis* and commented extensively on the "African atavism" in Langston Hughes's early poetry. We now know that, given the racial esprit and cultural climate of the mid-twenties, Hughes was right on target with his Africa poems. When he wrote of "World-wide dusk / Of dear dark faces / Driven before an alien wind," he gave in summary the long, tedious history of the African Diaspora. And when he wrote:

> All the tom-toms of the jungle beat in my blood
> And all the wild hot moons of the jungles shine
>   in my soul.
> I am afraid of this civilization—

he was poetizing the message of Marcus Garvey, who had spoken of such fear and such hope to the members of the United Negro Improvement Association. Hughes retained a continuing concern for Africa right up to the time of his death, and it is unfortunate that during the 1920s critics tended to ignore this aspect of his poetical contribution.

At the end of "The Negro Artist and the Racial Mountain" Hughes promised to build a poetical temple for tomorrow and devote his talent to "racial self-expression without fear or shame." This he did in his second volume of poetry, *Fine Clothes to the Jew* (1927). The effect on spokesmen for the middle and upper classes of Negro society was something akin to mass apoplexy. The critical review of the work in *The Pittsburgh Courier* was headlined "Langston Hughes' Book of Poems Trash," and that in the *Amsterdam News*, "Langston Hughes—The Sewer Dweller." Chicago's Negro paper *The Whip* called Hughes "The poet lowrate of Harlem," and Eustace Gay of the *Philadelphia Tribune* wrote: "It does not matter to me whether every poem in the book is true to life. Why should it be paraded before the American public by a Negro author as being typical or representative of the Negro? Bad enough to have white authors holding up our imperfections to public gaze. Our aim ought to be to present to the general public . . . our higher aims and aspirations." What were the fierce improprieties of *Fine Clothes to the Jew* which provoked this furor? The simple fact was that about one-third of the poems in the volume were in form and fact blues poems and the balance were blues in spirit, if not in form. One example is the poem "Hard Luck," from which the volume received its title:

> When hard luck overtakes you
> Nothin' for you to do.
> When hard luck overtakes you
> Nothin' for you to do.
> Gather up your fine clothes
> An' sell 'em to de Jew.

Jew takes yo' fine clothes,
Gives you a dollar an' a half.
Jew takes yo' fine clothes,
Gives you a dollar an' a half.
Go to de bootleg's,
Git some gin to make you laugh.

This poem's celebration of the casual hedonism of the urban Negro embarrassed the Negro race's ambassadors of culture and refinement. How could they instill the proper attitudes toward the puritan work ethic when poets like Langston Hughes were singing the joys of economic improvidence? But if they were embarrassed by a poem like "Hard Luck," they were infuriated by a poem like "Bad Man"—simply because it presented a character who had been stereotyped by white America as a black Saturday-night crime statistic:

I beats ma wife an'
I beats ma side gal too.
Beats ma wife an'
Beats ma side gal too.
Don't know why I do it but
It keeps me from feelin' blue.

The Crisis mounted its attack on *Fine Clothes to the Jew* and Negro literature of that "ilk" in an article entitled "Our Negro Intellectuals," published in its issue of August 1928 (vol. 35, 268–69, 284–86). To write the article Du Bois, the *Crisis* editor, secured the services of Allison Davis, presently a distinguished social anthropologist and psychologist, but in 1928 a recent product of Williams and Harvard and a literary scholar and critic of impeccable reputation. The objective of the essay was not only to censure, with "learned rebuke," young Negro writers like Hughes and Fisher and McKay but to end forthwith the diabolical influence of Carl Van Vechten on those writers. Presumably, it was thought at the time that a brilliant Phi Beta Kappa scholar with a master's degree from Harvard could easily decimate Van Vechten, a writer from Iowa who had been wealthy enough to go to Yale. In his initial sentence, Davis arraigned the accused writers as follows: "For nearly ten years, our Negro writers have been 'confessing' the distinctive sordidness and triviality of Negro life, and making an exhibition of their own unhealthy imagination, in the name of frankness and sincerity, of war against hypocrisy. Sincerity is no defense . . . for the sensationalism of Dr. Rudolph Fisher's *High Yaller* or Mr. Langston Hughes' *Fine Clothes for the Jew.* " He then stated that Carl Van Vechten had induced young Negro writers to write about cabaret night life in Harlem and about Africa. Not only had Van Vechten's *Nigger Heaven* "warped

Negro life into a fantastic barbarism," but this white author had used the preface he wrote to *Weary Blues* to promote the cause of an "undiluted primitivism." Further, the aforesaid Van Vechten had "misdirected" Mr. Hughes, "a genuine poet who gave promise of a power and technique exceptional in any poetry." Davis did concede, however, that all that was wrong with the poetry of Mr. Hughes could not be placed at Van Vechten's door. The decision to write poetry exploiting "the meretricious themes of jazz" was the poet's own. Also, it was the poet himself who sacrificed "his indubitable gift" to a "dogma" that demanded a poetry that was "atavistic and colorful" but not truly imaginative. In conclusion, Davis expressed regret that Harlem's young writers chose to concentrate upon "immediate and crude emotions" rather than on the "essential Negro qualities of fortitude, irony, and an absence of self-pity."

Langston Hughes was quick to respond to Allison Davis's adverse criticism. In a letter published in the very next issue of *The Crisis*, the poet denied being "misdirected" by Van Vechten. In the first place, he asserted, many of the poems were written before he had made the acquaintance of Van Vechten. In the second place, those written after becoming acquainted with Van Vechten were "not about him, not requested by him, . . . some of them not liked by him nor . . . do they in any way bear his poetic influence." Flashing the same kind of authorial bravado previously displayed in his "Negro Artist and the Racial Mountain," he declared that, if the poems in *Fine Clothes* were "low down, jazzy, cabaretish, sensational and utterly uncouth in the eyes of Mr. Davis, the fault is mine—not Mr. Van Vechten's." Then, he closed with his now famous statement, so full of pointed innuendo: "I have never pretended to keep a literary grazing pasture with food to suit all breeds of cattle."

Fortunately, during this time, *Fine Clothes to the Jew* had some defenders and some enthusiastic advocates. One such was Margaret Larkin, who in a review in *Opportunity* (Mar. 1927) stated that the blues poems of Hughes's second volume of poetry were fraught with social meaning and that it was good to behold the emergence of "a poet for the people." Another critic who defended *Fine Clothes* was that urbane litterateur, Alain Locke. In a review entitled "Common Clay and Poetry" (*Saturday Review* 3 Apr. 1927, p. 712), he hailed the bluesy, low-down poems as proof that Langston Hughes was that kind of rare poetic genius who could "strip life to the buff and poetize it." Indeed, the poems were more than mere poetry—they were "vivid, pulsing, creative portraits of Negro folk foibles and moods." They were full of the "crying laugh that eases misery." They revealed how the "sordidness of common life" could be "caught up in the lilt of poetry." In fact, some of the poems, like "Song for a Dark Girl" and "Mulatto" were so "pregnant with social as well as individual tragedy" that they proved that

Hughes possessed a "tragic vision," rare in a poet of his comparative immaturity and inexperience.

Another writer who, in a sense, strode forward to defend Hughes was Charles S. Johnson. In an article entitled "Jazz Poetry and Blues," Johnson provided a "class-action" defense, as it were, of the new breed of Negro writer who had dared to write about the folk of Negro society—the "cabaret singers, porters, street walkers, elevator boys . . . hard luck victims . . . sinners, and hard working men." Interestingly enough, Johnson, who was the first editor of *Opportunity Magazine* and went on to become a top-rated sociologist and ultimately president of Fisk University, published his essay in *The Carolina Magazine* (May 1928, pp. 16–20)—a fact suggesting that the Chapel Hill publication was experiencing in 1928 a kind of creeping literary liberalism from which the NAACP's *Crisis* was temporarily immune. Also, it should be noted that Johnson's observations and comments indicate a quality of literary perceptivity not often found in sociologists who become university presidents. He wrote:

> The new racial poetry of the Negro is the expression of something more than experimentation in a new technique. It marks the birth of a new racial consciousness and self-conception. It is a first frank acceptance of race, and the recognition of difference without the usual implications of disparity. It lacks apology, the wearying appeals to pity, and the conscious philosophy of defense. In being itself it reveals its greatest charm. In accepting this life it invests it with a new meaning. "The Negro" of popular conception is not the educated person of Negro blood; he is the peasant, the dull, dark worker, or shirker of work, who sprawls his shadow over the South and clutters the side streets of northern cities. These are the forgotten lives that thread about within their circles, who run the full scale of human emotions without being suspected of feeling . Who would know something about the core and limitations of this life should go to the Blues. In them is the curious story of disillusionment without a saving philosophy and yet without defeat. They mark these narrow limits of life's satisfactions, its vast treacheries and ironies. Stark, full human passions crowd themselves into an uncomplex expression, so simple in their power that they startle. If they did not reveal a fundamental and universal emotion of the human heart, they would not be noticed now as the boisterous and persistent intruders in the society of lyrics that they are.

For its time and considering the intense intraracial discussions then taking place regarding appropriate approaches to Negro literature, Charles S. Johnson's essay is remarkably perceptive and prophetic. Certainly, it is an effective companion statement to Langston Hughes's bold announcement, two years earlier, that as a poet he would explore racial self-expression "without fear or shame," relating both how "the tom-tom cries" and how "the tom-tom laughs" and somehow capturing in poetry the incredible mixture of beauty and ugliness in the black experience in America, in Africa, and on the islands of the sea.

Inevitably, with the passing of time, tensions have subsided, perspectives broadened, and critics have become more understanding of what Langston Hughes was trying to do with blues and jazz in poetry. In 1947, in his essay on "The Harlem Renaissance" in the *Saturday Review* (vol. 30, 22 Mar. 1947, pp. 12–13, 44), fellow poet Arna Bontemps called Hughes the "chronicler of modern urbanization" and a "singer with an ear for street music and folk idioms." By this time, Gwendolyn Brooks had published her *Street in Bronzeville* (1945), Richard Wright's *Native Son* (1940) had become one of the most popular novels of the post–World War II years, and the problems of the urban black ghetto in American cities had become increasingly obvious. As a consequence, the blues and jazz poetry of Hughes acquired an even greater significance and relevance. Some ten years earlier, Benjamin Brawley in his *Negro Genius* (1937) had expressed his deep and abiding regret that *Fine Clothes to the Jew* had ever been published, for its poems reflected "the abandon and vulgarity" of the twenties. But Sterling Brown in his review of Brawley's book in *Opportunity* (vol. 15, Sept. 1937, pp. 280–81), ably defended Hughes's work and expressed his own regret about Brawley's rigidly Victorian approach to life and literature.

Further proof that the critical climate was improving was the appearance of Arthur Davis's very perceptive essay "The Harlem of Langston Hughes' Poetry" (*Phylon* 13 [1952]: 276–83). Davis notes that in Hughes's poems on Harlem there is a note of gay abandon, but there is also a note of urban weariness. Sometimes the dancing and the merry-making become a little desperate and frenetic. For this reason, if one listens closely, one can hear "a jazz band sob" in the early morning hours. Davis's conclusion is that, even in his early salutes to "Jazzonia," city of jazz, Hughes's poetry contains an undercurrent of tension and misery. The best jazz music is a tune "that laughs and cries at the same time." Indeed, Hughes's players and laughers and jazz buffs are all like his jester:

> Because my mouth
> Is wide with laughter
> You do not hear
> My inner cry
> Because my feet
> Are gay with dancing
> You do not know I die.

The implications of Davis's approach to Hughes's Harlem poetry suggest two conclusions. First, the poet was more than a facile versifier dealing only in matters of surface social significance and, second, Hughes apparently knew that Harlem had a deferred dream that might explode even when he was watching Midnight Nan do her dance at LeRoy's in the mid-twenties.

The most extensive critical assessment of Hughes's poetry for all periods of his writing career is found in Jean Wagner's *Black Poets of the United States* (1973). Published originally in French as *Les Poètes Nègres des États Unis* (1962), the text was translated into English by Kenneth Douglas, thus providing scholars in Afro-American literature with a critical study of major Negro poets from Dunbar through Sterling Brown. Wagner's study of Hughes is thorough, reaching into every nook and cranny of the poet's career; but, at the outset, the critic makes several generalizations that in a sense suggest a bias on his part that could militate against his providing a fair and judicious assessment of the poet's work. He finds four weaknesses in his poetry: "A sometimes excessive facility, an impulsiveness not always restrained by a judicious rein, a too frequent uncalled-for vulgarity for its own sake, and on occasion, the cultivation of originality at any price. . . . " These weaknesses, Wagner argues, "do not diminish the intrinsic worth" of the poet's achievement as the "most productive poet of the Negro Renaissance," but there is no doubt that they becloud the critic's judgment. One suspects that this general initial assessment of Hughes was motivated by the Harlem poet's failure to approximate in function or attitude or role what Wagner considered to be proper for the poet in Western society. Hughes was not, for instance, a fiery rebel who, standing on the hills of a superior wisdom, hurled diatribes of verse down on the erring urban masses. He was more of a spokesman and an interpreter for those masses and not enough of a gadfly critic and social irritant. Then too, self-torturing inner tensions were absent in Hughes; indeed, he appeared to be too easy-going and too well adjusted to be a genuine poet. His was no tortured genius, pitted against a massively hostile world; he did not burn enough with dis-enchantment. He was not a ferociously maladjusted, angry man. Nor was he a heroic loner or philosophic isolate. Actually, Hughes was a peripatetic cosmopolite—a man who made his convivial way to all shores and way stations and seemingly had more friends than enemies. One suspects that, given this kind of man, Wagner felt that the effervescent, well-adjusted Harlemite could not be the kind of poet the French critic admired.

Wagner also demonstrates an inability to comprehend all of the far-flung implications of living in a black urban ghetto. For instance, he belabors what he considers to be a significant difference between the urban "masses" and the "folk." He writes: "The folk have roots, ties to the earth, while the masses whose joys and sorrows, both material and moral, are depicted by Hughes in the sometimes shocking hues of the naturalist palette, and with whom his own origins ensured obvious affinities, for the most part are flotsam, uprooted human beings as yet ill-fitted for the harsh, unfamiliar urban environment to which the barriers of segregation and the economic necessities of the epoch had driven them." Needless to say, such a distinction is unnecessary in black America where the "uprooted" who fled to the cities had once been "folk" who had been too well tied to the earth. Because he makes this unnecessary distinction, however, Wagner fails to understand and evaluate Hughes's self-assigned poetic role as one obligated to record, in infinite poetic detail, how erstwhile rural folk adjusted and survived as semisophisticated urbanites in an America that was basically hostile to their race and kind.

Despite these limitations in critical orientation, Wagner labors to present a full poetic profile of Langston Hughes. Particularly does he make a total effort to discuss all of the implications of the poet's involvement with, and use of, jazz. In a section entitled "Rebellion: Through a Glass Jazzily," Wagner undertakes to show that Hughes's use of jazz was initially a mode of rebellion—"the tom-tom of revolt against weariness in a white world," as the poet himself had stated in his "Negro Artist and the Racial Mountain." But in his poetry, jazz is more than a means of rebellion; according to the poet, "The rhythm of life / Is a jazz rhythm." Jazz is the substance of life itself. From the "talented tenth" perspective the celebration of jazz was a mode of rebellion against the somewhat prudish bourgeois standards of racial self-improvement; but, in actuality, jazz was a way of life enveloping both white and black America. Wagner is on safer ground when he asserts that jazz in Hughes's poetry is a means of escape from the boring routine of getting and spending in a highly competitive urban environment. Even so, one must quibble with his language when he writes that "jazz . . . is a means of escape, another kind of addiction whose artificial paradises the poet equates with those obtained by the intravenous injection of a narcotic. For the popular masses in those immense ghettoes . . . the temple of jazz, the nightclub, is also the sanctuary of an illusion, where floodlights replace moonlight and the sea's swaying immensity shrinks to the dimensions of a few sips of liquor from a shot glass." This seems to be a verbal overreaction to Hughes's use of the jazz-as-escape theme.

Wagner also sees in the poet's use of jazz a plea for the "Negro's *carpe diem*": "Tomorrow . . . who knows? / Dance today!" And he notes the point, made so forcefully by Arthur Davis, that "the sound of jazz always has an admixture of despair." But Wagner carries this critical argument a step further and states that the Negro's use of jazz is another mode of mask wearing and is thus linked to Dunbar's poem "We Wear the Mask." Here one wonders if the French critic has not confused sheer urban fatigue with the black man's ancient need for guile and deception in times of racial conflict. Wagner also sees in Hughes's use of jazz a definable "erotic content." He notes that in one poem "the insidious rhythms of jazz are

accompanied by the erotic convolutions of the naked black dancing girl. . . . "
In a sense, this is the kind of "talented tenth" observation that would have
delighted a Benjamin Brawley, who viewed the jazz age as one of "abandon
and vulgarity." Actually, dancing has always been an art form, and art and
eros were associated long before the discovery of jazz. Moreover, there is
evidence of some critical misreading of the poem in question, "To a Black
Dancer in 'The Little Savoy' "; there may be some "erotic convolutions," but
the girl in the poem is not naked or, at least, evidence of her nakedness is
lacking:

> Wine-maiden
> Of the jazz-tune night,
> Lips
> Sweet as purple dew,
> Breasts
> Like the pillows of all sweet dreams,
> Who crushed
> The grapes of joy
> And dripped their juice
> On you?

As Blyden Jackson very wisely points out in his comments on Hughes in
Black Poetry in America (1974), Langston Hughes's poetry is a mélange of
sharply noted spontaneous impressions gathered from the black urban
scene. These impressions, communicated with a technical skill often obscured
by the poet's mask of casual creativity, in turn provoke equally sharp reader
reactions or impressions. In these lines, Hughes is provocative and suggestive,
and it is difficult for a reader like Wagner not to strip this "Midnight
Dancer" who has been anointed by the crushed juice of the "grapes of joy."

Wagner also recognizes that jazz not only affected the content of Hughes's
poetry but affected his poetic technique as well. Unlike Countee Cullen,
who questioned whether "The Cat and the Saxophone" was poetry, the
French critic sees the poem as an effective technical experiment "neither
more nor less blameworthy than some of E. E. Cummings's and Guillaume
Apollinaire's experiments, and with these it must no doubt be grouped."

Finally, Wagner views Hughes's use of jazz as a forthright expression of
Negro primitivism, and in this observation he finds full support in the
poetry. Jazz was "Harlem's heartbeat." The critic writes: "The actual substance of jazz is Negro life, especially that of the great black metropolis.
Between Harlem's heartbeats and the beat of the rhythm section . . . there
are natural affinities. . . . "

Wagner's analysis of the poet's use of the blues is presented in two
sections of his criticism, and in both sections he displays some naïveté

about the source and nature of the blues. In the first section, "The Social Setting of the Blues," effective analysis of the blues poetry is blocked by the intrusion of a lengthy, somewhat intense discussion of how and why Hughes tended to associate evil and trouble with black skin color. Admittedly, Wagner might not have known that "black-is-evil" had long been a sort of in-house racial joke among American Negroes, but one does wonder why he would go to some lengths to document a folk belief of this kind. Also, Wagner is distressed by the low-down nature of Hughes's blues world. He regrets that it is a "half-world peopled with unwed mothers and prostitutes, pimps, homosexuals and drug addicts, together with drunks, gamblers, bad men, and killers." Here again, Wagner reveals a lack of awareness of the essential folk origins of the blues in the Afro-American context. Nor does he appear to understand that in a black urban ghetto this "half-world" is very often the whole world.

The second section providing comment on the blues in Hughes's poetry is entitled "Religion and the Masses." After stating that the poet was not the kind of person who had "those crises of conscience" in religious matters "that seize upon certain delicate souls and shake them to their very depths," Wagner says that "as the poet of jazz," Hughes was particularly "well-fitted" to be "the interpreter of the orgiastic religion of black people of the lower classes." This latter conclusion is based on the critic's assumption that there is a "basic identity of nature and function" between religious exaltation and the exaltation inspired by jazz. In other words, Wagner sees an "identity between the profane and sacred modes of Negro lyric expressivity," and supports this point of view with documentation from the work of ethno-musicologists and jazz critics. Admittedly, this is a provocative assumption. Unfortunately, such an assumption leads Wagner to the erroneous critical conclusion that some of Hughes's religious poems in the "Glory Halleluiah" section of *Fine Clothes to the Jew* are "perfect" religious equivalents of the blues. One example given by Wagner of such a "blues" poem is "Feet o' Jesus":

> At de feet o' Jesus,
> Sorrow like a sea.
> Lordy, let your mercy
> Come driftin down on me.

Langston Hughes may have been an irreligious man who, in Wagner's words, tended to "reduce religious problems to social problems," but the poet would never have confused a religious moan with a blues "holla." In his article "My Adventures as a Social Poet" (*Phylon* 8, 1947), Hughes recalled an incident that reminded him of the yawning gulf between the secular and the spiritual which all poets must vigilantly respect. He stated that on one weekday night, when he was reading a poem about hard work and hard luck from the pulpit of an Atlantic City church, he was stopped by a note from the preacher who demanded that he not read "any more blues in my pulpit." Wagner is certainly right in his assertion that Langston Hughes was not, overtly at least, a profoundly religious man. But he is wrong in his assumption that the poet did not know the difference between a blues poem and a religious poem.

Two other writers have made comments on Langston Hughes's use of jazz and blues. One is George Kent, whose observations are to be found in his book *Blackness and the Adventure of Western Culture* (1972). In an essay entitled "Langston Hughes and the Afro-American Folk and Cultural Tradition" he makes several provocative observations bearing on the poet's blues poetry. First, Hughes was a poet who was "full of the folk"—one whose poetry continually explored "the rich density of the folk hope." He was a successful folk artist because he had "an instinctive . . . sense of the folk acceptance of the contradictory as something to be borne." For this reason, Hughes's folk poems and blues contain no resolutions and provide no solutions to life's dilemmas. All that one can do in a Hughes poem full of life's contrarieties is to conclude that life "jes be's that way." Like Arthur Davis, Kent also sees in Hughes's Harlem jazz poetry "increasing desperation and decreasing joy." This critic is most effective and original, however, in his discussion of the "blues devices" used in the poet's blues poetry. These are contrast, wit, folk imagery, and voice tones. Using these devices, Hughes wrote a blues poetry that enabled him to stay tuned in on the black urban experience in all of its dimensions. Kent concludes that some of the poet's best work is that which captures the spirit of the blues but dispenses with the so-called blues devices. In "Lover's Return," for instance, one finds irony, dramatic concreteness, and a folk acceptance of an unresolvable dilemma but none of the specific blues devices:

> My old time daddy
> Came back home last night.
> His face was pale and
> His eyes didn't look just right.
>
> . . .
>
> I looked at my daddy—
> Lawd! and I wanted to cry.
> He looked so thin—
> Lawd! that I wanted to cry.
> But the devil told me:
>> Damn a lover
>> Come home to die!

Kent and others argue that Hughes lacked the capacity to fashion a work of poetry having "the big vision"; but, as this poem demonstrates, a vignette giving only a small piece of the action is really all one needs to sense the full dimension of an overpowering human dilemma.

Finally, Blyden Jackson in his essay on Langston Hughes in *Black Poetry in America* has made some comments which deserve mention before closing this chapter on "blues, jazz, and low-down folk." First, he agrees with many other critics that Hughes was the master of both the blues form and "the architectonics" of the jazz poem. Three gifts enabled him to do this, according to Jackson. First, Langston Hughes had a ear for dialect and developed some mastery of both the dramatic monologue and dialogue as poetic forms. (Kent calls these forms "voice tones.") Second, he mastered the art of disciplined esthetic detachment from racial trauma. He could create art out of what Kent calls the "contradictory" without, as Jackson says, any "warm wallowing in his own emotions." Third—and this becomes very important in explaining Hughes's success as a jazz poet—he was a great impressionist. Within a few brief minutes he could verbally capture a scene or poetically editorialize on an incident; and then scene, poet, and incident would be gone, forever lost in the changing chimera of circumstance. The reader receives the poet's impression of

> The Negro
> With the trumpet at his lips
> Has dark moons of weariness
> Beneath his eyes.

He hears the "thump, thump, thump" as the jazz pianist pounds out "The Weary Blues" in a smoke-filled room. He sees those "six long-headed jazzers." All are fleeting impressions captured by the poet, and, as Jackson says, "impressions tend to lack depth." Moreover, when one puts them together, does one really have the truth or one man's ever-changing impression of the truth? Jackson concludes that Hughes's great weakness was that he could not or did not synthesize his multiple impressions into something big and comprehensive. But one can reply that the age of cabaret jazz of the twenties was a time of swiftly swirling events and dazzling movement. There was no time to put down the entire story, with a beginning, a middle, and an end. There was just time to record bits and pieces of the quickly passing scene as one poet saw that scene. Just as the blues were different for each person at any given time, jazz was somehow different each time you heard it. Only Langston Hughes, master impressionist, could effectively depict Negro America's first great period of blues and jazz and low-down folks.

REFERENCES

This essay first appeared as Chapter 2 in Richard K. Barksdale's *Langston Hughes: The Poet and His Critics* (Chicago: American Library Association, 1977). Reprinted with permission.

Bontemps, Arna. 1947. "The Harlem Renaissance." *Saturday Review of Literature* 22 March, pp. 12–13, 44.

Brawley, Benjamin. 1937. *The Negro Genius*. New York: Dodd, Mead.

Brown, Sterling. 1937. "Review of *The Negro Genius*." *Opportunity*, September, pp. 280–81.

Cullen, Countee. 1926. Review of *The Weary Blues*. *Opportunity*, February, pp. 73–74.

Fauset, Jessie. 1926. Review of *The Weary Blues*. *Crisis*, March, p. 239.

Heyward, DuBose. 1926. Review of *The Weary Blues*. *New York Herald Tribune*, 1 August, p. 4.

Huggins, Nathan. 1971. *Harlem Renaissance*. New York: Oxford University Press.

Hughes, Langston. 1926. "The Negro Artist and the Racial Mountain." *Nation*, June, pp. 692–94.

Jackson, Blyden, and Louis Rubin. 1974. *Black Poetry in America*. Baton Rouge: Louisiana State University Press.

Johnson, Charles S. 1928. "Jazz Poetry and Blues." *Carolina Magazine*, May, pp. 16–20.

Johnson, James Weldon, and J. Rosamond Johnson. 1925. Preface to *The Books of American Negro Spirituals*. New York: Viking.

Kent, George. 1971. *Blackness and the Adventure of Western Culture*. Chicago: Third World Press.

Larkin, Margaret. 1927. Review of *Fine Clothes to the Jew*. *Opportunity*, March, p. 84.

Locke, Alain. 1927. "Common Clay and Poetry." *Saturday Review of Literature*, April, p. 712.

Schuyler, George. 1926. "The Negro Art Hokum." *Nation*, May, pp. 662–63.

Southern, Eileen. 1971. *The Music of Black Americans*. New York: Norton.

Stearns, Marshall W. 1958. *The Story of Jazz*. New York: Oxford University Press.

Van Doren, Carl. 1924. "The Younger Generation of Negro Writers." *Opportunity*, May, p. 145.

Hughes's Poetry of the 1930s:
A New Song for an Old Hurt

There have been at least two broadly general critical assessments of the literary career of Langston Hughes during the 1930s which, although widely disseminated and authoritatively stated, are, in the light of objective evidence, wholly inaccurate. The first is found in an article, "The Negro in American Culture," by V. F. Calverton in *The Saturday Review of Literature* in 1940. By virtue of his record as one of the early anthologists of American Negro literature (1929) and his general support of Negro literary and cultural causes during the so-called "wet-nursing" years of the early 1920s, Calverton, by 1940, was fully sanctioned by experience and interest to be a spokesman for Negro literature and culture. And he was certainly authorized to have an opinion about Langston Hughes, however erroneous that opinion turned out to be. One may also state at this point that a full explication of the nature of Hughes's literary activities during the 1930s will probably reveal that this critic's disenchantment with the poet was doubtless more political than literary. In any event, Calverton begins his article by noting, with dubious critical intent, the divinelike status of the Negro writer of the 1920s; he was, in Calverton's view, "a literary son of God." Then, after bestowing lavish praise on McKay's *Harlem Shadows* for its rich "tropicality" and "pagan zeal," the critic dismisses Langston Hughes as follows: "Hughes, it must be admitted, has not been idle, but his work has not grown in importance. Rather it has stood still." He concludes by stating the hope that "newer" figures like Wright, Hurston, and Tolson will have "greater staying power and growth." His concluding observation confirms the validity of two ancient adages: first, all comparisons are odious, and second, literary critics rarely, if ever, have the gift of prophecy.

The second critical assessment of Hughes's literary career in the 1930s is found in Harold Cruse's *The Crisis of the Negro Intellectual*. Originally published in 1967, this somewhat opinionated appraisal of Negro literary, political, and cultural trends and movements in and around New York City has been an enormously popular work (by 1971 it had gone through its fifth printing). Although there is little or no literary criticism *per se* in the book, and most of the author's comments on Negro writers are *ad hominem* (or *ad feminam*) strictures, whatever critical pronouncements there are are delivered with an almost ferocious, sledgehammer directness. Of Langston Hughes, Cruse writes: "...Langston Hughes unfortunately...never developed much in scope beyond the artistic, aesthetic and intellectual limits of the 1920's. He was one of the aborted renaissance men...a man of culture without a cultural philosophy." As in Calverton's case, the critical generalization is not supported by any objective evidence. Nevertheless, unchallenged, both statements leave Hughes's literary reputation during the 1930s slowly twisting in the wind of critical disapprobation.

The evidence at hand in both Donald Dickinson's *Bio-Bibliography of Langston Hughes* (1967) and Therman O'Daniel's "Selected Classified Bibliography" (in *Langston Hughes: Black Genius,* 1971) directly disputes the assertions by Calverton in 1940 and by Cruse in 1967 that there was no real development in Hughes's literary career in the 1930s. Actually, the poet's literary output was extensive and richly diversified during this period. Between 1930 and 1942, not only did he publish six volumes of poetry and a plethora of occasional poems, but he produced a novel, a volume of short stories, seven full-length plays, and two one-act plays. Admittedly, not everything he wrote during this period was of uniformly high literary quality, but his *Not without Laughter* did win the Harmon Award for the best novel by a Negro in 1930. And at least two of his dramatic productions enjoyed the distinction of having long runs; *Mulatto,* a three act tragedy written in the late twenties, ran on Broadway and on tour for almost twenty months in 1935; *Don't You Want to Be Free,* a long one-act play, set a record for 135 performances at the New York Suitcase Theater in 1937. Moreover, some of the occasional poems published in *The Crisis* or in *Opportunity* reveal great poetical power and insight. Such a poem is a four-liner called "Today" published in *Opportunity* in October 1937:

> This is earthquake
> Weather:
> Honor and Hunger
> Walk lean together.

In a sense, this short poem is a companion-piece for an equally eloquent poetic statement entitled "History" found in *Opportunity* in 1934:

> The past has been
> A mint of blood and sorrow

This must not be
True of tomorrow.

The occasional poem, however, which is most important in considering
trends and developments in Hughes's literary career during the 1930s
is "A New Song." In many respects, it is the poet's credal statement
presented to explain any significant new directions in his writing career.
Evidently, Hughes deemed the poem to be a very important revelation
of his new purpose and insights, for he submitted it both to *Opportunity*
and to *The Crisis*. The former published it in its January 1933 issue
and the latter in its issue of March 1933. Cited here are some of the
lines which reflect what the editor of *Opportunity* called "a note of defiance
hitherto unheard among Negro poets except in the bitter tones of Claude
McKay":

> I speak in the name of the black millions.
> Let all others keep silent a moment.
> I have this word to bring,
> This thing to say
> This song to sing:
>
> > Bitter was the day
> > When I bowed my back
> > Beneath the slaver's whip.
>
> That day is past.
>
> > Bitter was the day
> > When I saw my children unschooled,
> > My young men without a voice in the world,
> > My women taken as the body-toys
> > Of a thieving people.
>
> That day is past.
>
> > Bitter was the day, I say,
> > When the lyncher's rope
> > Hung about my neck,
> > And the fire scorched at my feet.
> > And the white world had no pity,
> > And only in the sorrow songs
> > Relief was found—
> > Yet not relief,
> > But merely humble life and silent death
> > Eased by a Name
> > That hypnotized the pain away—
> > O, precious Name of Jesus in that day!
>
> That day is past.

I know full well now
Jesus could not die for me—
That only my own hands,
Dark as the earth,
Can make my earth-dark body free.
O, world,
No longer shall you say
With arrogant eyes and tall white head:
"You are my servant,
Nigger—
I, the free!"

That day is past.

This poem, like many others by Langston Hughes, speaks with two voices— the voice of the poet himself and the voice of the black Everyman of the far-flung reaches of the Black Diaspora. There is also the suggestion of a third voice—the voice of the Communist revolutionary. It is somewhat muted; but it is there, and the presence of this third voice serves to explain the unusual publication history of this very fine poem. The only time it was republished was as the title poem of the 1938 anthology, *A New Song*. Even then, as Jean Wagner clearly shows in his analysis of Hughes's poetry in *Black Poets of the United States,* subtle changes were wrought in the poem's wording so that its second version reflected an "irreproachable religious orthodoxy." This was done by omitting any references to the possibility that the poet in particular and American Negroes in general had turned away from Jesus and Christianity as refuges in times of trouble and woe.

There is now considerable evidence at hand that Hughes, in his own statements and correspondence, sought to de-emphasize his struggles during the 1930s with the black church and his involvement during that same time with international Communism. His comments in *The Big Sea* and *I Wonder as I Wander* are scarcely revelatory of any deep and abiding ideological commitment. Nor does his description of his encounter with evangelist Aimee Semple McPherson over the poem "Goodby Christ" in his article "My Adventures as a Social Poet" (*Phylon,* 1947) give any hint of the extent of his disaffection with orthodox religion during this period. Fortunately, Faith Berry's *Good Morning Revolution,* an anthology of the poet's "uncollected writings of social protest" published in 1973, supplies considerable material which, properly evaluated, can help to set the record straight. In her introduction, she makes the point that, although "Hughes' most outspoken ... poetry is from the 1930s," militant social protest is present in his poetry "as early as 1925." She also suggests, with considerable accuracy, that the poet's suppression of his Communist poetry does not reflect a cowardly attitude about a former ideological commitment but constitutes a very logical reaction to the almost neurotic polarization of American society into Communist and anti-Communist camps during the late 1940s and the 1950s. During that time, no publisher would have dared or been permitted to publish the writings of an author with proven Communist ties. It should be added in this context that any challenge to the accepted codes of religious orthodoxy could have had similarly devastating consequences on the perpetrator thereof, particularly if he were a black man attacking the black church. The reaction of Dr. Benjamin Mays to "Goodby, Christ," which will be noted below in greater detail, proves this point.

Good Morning Revolution furnishes clear evidence that by 1925 Hughes was a militant political radical. Indeed, this point is clearly stressed by Margaret Larkin in her article "A Poet for the People," published in *Opportunity* in March 1927. In her view, Hughes was, by virtue of poems like "Brass Spittoons," "Railroad Avenue," and "Porter," already a proven "proletarian poet"; for all of these poems reflect a deep and abiding concern for the welfare and status of the working man. As the poet stated in *The Big Sea,* his wealthy sponsor, now identified as a Mrs. D. Osgood Mason, was fully unaware of how completely her young charge had turned from poetry that celebrated black exoticism and primitivism to poetry of militant social protest; therefore she could not understand how, in 1931, he could write a poem full of satire and ironic fury about the construction of the then fabulous Waldorf-Astoria or write in that same year:

> I live on a park bench.
> You, Park Avenue.
> Hell of a distance
> Between us two.
>
> I beg a dime for dinner—
> You got a butler and a maid.
> But I'm wakin up!
> Say, ain't you afraid
>
> That I might, just maybe,
> In a year or two,
> Move on over
> To Park Avenue?

In "My Adventures as a Social Poet," Hughes stated, shortly after this poem was published, "I did not have a patron any more."

But there is more than militant social protest in "Pride," one of the poet's occasional pieces published in *Opportunity* in 1930; it smolders with the threat of revolutionary violence:

> Let all who will
> Eat quietly the bread of shame.

> I cannot,
> Without complaining loud and long,
> Tasting its bitterness in my throat,
> And feeling to my very soul
> Its wrong.
> For honest dreams
> Your spit is in my face,
> And so my fist is clenched—
> Today—
> To strike your face.

Significantly, none of the standard rhetoric of Communist propaganda appears in this poem, but its lines clearly reveal the poet's belief in the need for revolutionary change or, as he wrote in February 1931, a need to

> . . . cut the world in two
> And see what worms are eating
> At the rind.

So there is every indication that, by 1930, the year he published *Not without Laughter,* Langston Hughes had long been predisposed to support and endorse a program of radical social and economic change. His trip to Haiti and Cuba in 1930–31 and his return to an America engulfed in the shame of the Scottsboro trial were undoubtedly the catalysts that converted him into a poet of Communist propaganda.

Critical reactions to the poet's involvement in international Communism are mixed. Jean Wagner, whose study of Hughes includes the most extensive analysis of his Communist propaganda poetry to date, concludes that the poet's Communist poetry is "irredeemably false." Not only are these poems, in Wagner's view, innocent of "subversive import," but they reflect a "naïveté and childishness" which negate serious political intent. Wagner supports his conclusion by citing Charles Glicksberg's view that, in general, all American Negroes are so "deeply rooted in the American tradition" that they yearn, not for Communism but for fulfillment of "the promises of democracy." Glicksberg's opinion, stated in an article entitled "Race and Revolution in Negro Literature" (*Forum,* Nov. 1947), undoubtedly reflected the general post–World War II belief that Communism had indeed been a "light that failed," not only for Hughes and Richard Wright but for all other Negro intellectuals and writers as well. Generally, this is the point of view of Wilson Record, whose *The Negro and the Communist Party* (1951) has been termed the definitive study on the subject. Indeed, in a later article published in *Phylon* in 1956 ("Extremist Movements among American Negroes") Record states that the Negro's disaffection with the Communist party stemmed from his inability to accept "the separate Negro state in the

Black Belt proposal." According to Record, many Negro intellectuals, fearing the reimposition of social and economic segregation and separatism, abandoned the Communist cause for this reason. This interpretation is supported by James O. Young in his *Black Writers of the Thirties* (1973). In his view, "Although . . . the young radicals often sympathized with such Communist proposals as black-white labor solidarity and destruction of free-enterprise capitalism, they were never as far left as the 'reds.' They remained independent of the Party and were frequently critical of its policies" (p. 39). Young's conclusion is that none of the Negro thinkers who leaned toward the political left ever "condoned the idea of revolution."

But the opinions of Glicksberg and Record reflect after-the-fact generalizations published during a period of near political hysteria regarding Communism. Similarly, Young's comments attempt to deemphasize the Negro's role in leftist revolutionism and drape him in the robes of local patriotism. Persons nearer the scene of the Negro's involvement in Communism in the 1930s can possibly provide more reliable evidence about the participation of Negro intellectuals in general and about Langston Hughes's involvement in particular. According to Harold Cruse, for instance, the "leading literary lights of the 1920s" all went into Communism in the 1930s because they suffered from an "identity vacuum," caused by their failure as a "black intelligentsia" to develop a unifying cultural philosophy. Upon analysis, this typically Crusian generalization apparently applies only to McKay and Hughes, but not to Du Bois, Bontemps, Toomer, James Weldon Johnson, or Countee Cullen, all of whom remained aloof from the Communist lure. Given the context of his comment, however, one gathers that accuracy was not Cruse's concern here; rather, he wished to stress that he considered Communism a poor substitute for a unifying Negro cultural philosophy. On the other hand, both Nick Aaron Ford and Sterling Brown, now seasoned and retired professors of literature, were relatively young, on-the-scene critics of the Negro literature of the 1930s, and their comments are more specifically useful than Cruse's generalization. Ford in his *Contemporary Negro Novel* (1936) gives approving recognition of the trend of Negro novelists to lay aside "the pretensions of pure artistry" and take up "the cudgel of propaganda." Similarly, Sterling Brown, speaking before the National Negro Congress in 1937, claimed that "the Negro artist who will be worth his salt must join with those who are recording a world of injustice and exploitation—a world that must be changed." Earlier, George Schuyler in an article in *Opportunity* (June 1932) reviewing Roy Embree's *Brown America,* called for an end to the "exploitation" of Negro labor and an end to "petite Negro bourgeois professional folk" who aid in such exploitation. What was needed, said Schuyler, were Negroes "who are well-equipped leaders and organizers of the working class with proletarian instead of capitalistic psychologies." By 1935, Alain Locke in his annual review of Negro literature observes, with more than a tinge of regret: "... our art is ... turning prosaic, partisan, and propagandistic, but this time not in behalf of striving, strident racialism, but rather in a protestant and belligerent universalism of social analysis and protest. In a word, our art is going proletarian. ... " And because proletarianism in art and literature bred a naturalism which was somewhat offensive to the refined sensibilities of Mr. Locke, he added that in this new breed of literature "all the slime and hidden secrets of the river [of racial experience] are shouldered up on the hard, gritty sandbars and relentlessly exposed to view."

There are other indices of the extent of Negro involvement in political radicalism and Communism during the 1930s. First, some of the more influential publishing media of the day carried reports on this as a matter of newsworthy comment. *The Chicago Defender,* for instance, headlined an editorial "Why We Can't Hate Reds" and praised "the zealousness with which [the Communist Party] guards the rights of the [Negro] Race." And in an article in *Crisis,* "Negro Editors on Communism" (April 1932), Carl Murphy of the *Afro-American* was quoted as saying, "The Communists are going our way, for which Allah be praised." William Kelley of the *Amsterdam News* had a comment of similar import: "Since America's twelve million Negro population is so largely identified with the working class, the wonder is not that the Negro is beginning, at least, to think along Communistic lines, but that he did not embrace that doctrine en masse long ago." In May of that same year, John Gillard, in a *Commonweal* article entitled "The Negro Challenges Communism" (25 May 1932), observed: "On the surface it would seem that Russian red and American black is a coming color scheme. Why not? The Negro has a grievance. Christians refuse to heed it. Communism listens sympathetically. And when men are hungry and their children are fainting for bread, a promise seems better than a threat. Most of us who are not ourselves nursing the ills of poverty have a feeling of aloofness from the misery of our colored brother." Another, albeit somewhat negative, index of Negro involvement in Communism is found in the impassioned response of those conservative Negro leaders who abhorred and feared that involvement. In 1933 *Opportunity* ran two articles of this category. The first, by Asbury Smith, sought to answer the question "What Can the Negro Expect from Communism?" (July 1933). Unfortunately, the question is never fully answered, but Smith does state the three reasons why, in his opinion, Negroes should not join the party. These are: (1) "Class warfare" would not bring "economic justice"; (2) a dictatorship of the proletariat would result in a further and more intensive "restraint of democracy, censorship, and rule by fear and force"; and (3) the Negro en masse could not and would not abandon his religion and "share the

Communist hatred of the worship of God." His conclusion clearly reflects the racial hostility hovering in the American atmosphere: "If the Negroes accept Communism more rapidly than the whites, they will be oppressed with a cruelty and relentlessness unknown since Civil War Days." Kelley Miller in his article "Should Black Turn Red?" (November 1933) voiced a similar fear: " . . . not only would a communistic state in America put the Negro outside the pale, but the agitation for such a state on his part is fraught with grave peril to his race whose only hope for salvation lies in the fulfillment of the principles laid down in the Declaration of Independence and the Constitution of the United States."

In other words, Negro involvement in Communism and leftist political activity was a live and provocative issue in the 1930s. Admittedly, the rural masses of the agricultural South were never touched by the movement, but urban intellectuals, writers, and political polemicists were deeply involved. Langston Hughes was no exception. As Faith Berry's anthology, *Good Morning Revolution*, proves, the move to collaborate on matters of social protest with Communists in the 1930s constituted no giant ideological step for the poet. His poetry of the mid-1920s reveals a strong predisposition for programs of radical social and political change. For somehow, despite his avid concern for jazz and blues and cabaret nightlife and his vaunted reputation as the somewhat feckless folksinger of the urban masses, Hughes, early in his publishing career, demonstrated an abiding concern for social, political, and economic justice for these Negro masses. Even as he sang of Africa, "So long / So far away," and of "the low beating of the tom-toms," the seeds of political radicalism were being planted. They bore fruit when he returned from Haiti and Cuba in 1931 and discovered an America inflamed with the Scottsboro trial. His political sensitivities had already been ruffled by his temporary exclusion from Cuba by that country's immigration authorities. In his account of the incident in "My Adventures as a Social Poet" (*Phylon*, 1947), Hughes attributed the incident to the fact that he "had written poems about the exploitation of Cuba by the sugar barons." He also speculated that the "dictatorial Machado regime" might have objected to his translation of some of Nicholas Guillen's politically "radical" poetry like "Cane":

> White man
> Above the cane fields
> Earth
> Beneath the cane fields.
> Blood that flows from us.

But the imprisonment of eight young Negro boys, charged with raping two hoboing white prostitutes on a freight train near Scottsboro, Alabama, ignited within the poet all of the latent and smoldering fires of social, political, and racial protest. Typically, he wrote out his anger in poetry. The result was "Scottsboro," an occasional poem that appeared in *Opportunity* in December 1931 and has never again been reprinted, not even in the Communist-inspired *A New Song* of 1938:

8 BLACK BOYS IN A SOUTHERN JAIL.
WORLD, TURN PALE!

8 black boys and one white lie.
Is it much to die?

Is it much to die when immortal feet
March with you down Time's street,
When beyond steel bars sound the deathless drums
Like a mighty heart-beat as They come?

Who comes?

Christ,
Who fought alone.

John Brown.

That mad mob
That tore the Bastile down
Stone by stone.

Moses.

Jeanne d'Arc.

Dessalines.

Nat Turner.

Fighters for the free.

Lenin with the flag blood red.

(Not dead! Not dead!
None of those is dead.)

Gandhi.

Sandino.

Evangelista, too,
To walk with you—

8 BLACK BOYS IN A SOUTHERN JAIL.
WORLD, TURN PALE!

These lines reflect little evidence of the influence of Communist propaganda. Indeed, the poem's apparent objective is to identify the cause of the Scottsboro boys with those of the great martyrs of the world, living and dead; and the list is a distinguished honor roll, fully proving the passionate idealism of the poet's racial protest. Hughes's next publication on behalf of the Scottsboro boys, however, was fully in the Communist mold. *Scottsboro, Ltd.*, four poems and a play, was written and presented in early 1932 in order to earn money for the International Labor Defense, the organization within the party designated to defend the Scottsboro boys. Not only does the short play depicting the arrest, trial, and imprisonment of the youths end with "a great red flag rising to the strains of the *Internationale,*" but throughout the short work there are lines like the following:

> The voice of the red world
> Is our voice, too
> The voice of the red world is you!
>
> With all the workers,
> Black or white,
> We'll go forward
> Out of the night.

Alain Locke, who, during the 1930s, closely monitored Hughes's literary career through his annual reports on Negro literature in *Opportunity*, wrote the following evaluation of *Scottsboro, Ltd.* in January 1933: "Meanwhile, as the folk-school tradition deepens, Hughes, formerly its chief exponent, turns more and more in the direction of social protest and propaganda, since *Scottsboro, Ltd.* represents his latest moods. . . . The poet [in this work] is a militant and indignant proletarian reformer." Locke's comments implicitly suggest that Hughes's gradual poetical metamorphosis from folk poet to "indignant proletarian reformer" was unfortunate. As has been indicated above, however, the line between folk poet and social reformer was a very thin line for a poet like Langston Hughes. Moreover, in the spring of 1932, the poet had visited the Scottsboro boys in their prison at Kilby, Alabama, and recorded his reaction to that experience in an emotionally charged account ("Brown America in Jail: Kilby," *Opportunity*, June 1932). Immediately following the prison visit, he wrote out his anger about the gross injustice of Alabama law in a short piece entitled "Christ in Alabama." This poem, with lines beginning "Christ is a Nigger / Beaten and black," appeared in *Contempo*, a University of North Carolina student publication, just prior to Hughes's lecture at the university, also in the spring of 1932. The unfortunate result, as recorded in "My Adventures as a Social Poet," was that the poet's presence caused a near race riot. Shortly afterward, along with certain other American Negro writers and actors, Hughes was on his way to Russia, ostensibly to make a movie but actually in flight from a Depression-ridden, racially volatile America. So, by the time Alain Locke's comments appeared in *Opportunity* in January 1933, the poet was in Moscow and shiveringly preparing himself to write a volume of short stories eventually entitled *The Ways of White Folks*. According to a note in Jean Wagner's *Black Poets of the United States,* Hughes, before his departure in July 1932, had declared his belief that Communism "was the only force leading an active fight against the poverty and wretchedness of Negroes." It is widely known that because he found Communism's regimentation of artists and writers too restrictive, the poet never became a card-carrying member of the party; but, as will be noted in greater detail below, he never disavowed his belief that, during the Depression years, the American Negro had better friends in Moscow, Russia, than in Macon County, Alabama.

Predictably, during his stay in Russia and following his return to America via Vladivostok and the Pacific, Hughes poured out Communist propaganda poetry. One poem, "Good Morning, Revolution," promises social upheaval and radical change with these lines:

> Listen, Revolution,
>   We're buddies, see—
>   Together,
>   We can take everything:
>   Factories, arsenals, houses, ships,
>   Railroads, forests, fields, orchards,
>   Bus lines, telegraphs, radios,
>   (Jesus! Raise hell with radios!)
>   Steel mills, coal mines, oil wells, gas,
>   All the tools of production,
>   (Great day in the morning!)
>   Everything—
>   And turn 'em over to the people who work.
>   Rule and run 'em for us people who work.

And there is even more fierce resolve in a poem entitled "Revolution," published in *New Masses* in February 1934:

> Great Mob that knows no fear—
> Come here!
> And raise your hand
> Against this man
> Of iron and steel and gold
> Who's bought and sold
> You—
> Each one—
> For the last thousand years.
> Come here,
> Great mob that knows no fear,
> And tear him limb from limb,

Split his golden throat
Ear to ear,
And end his time forever,
Now—
This year—
Great mob that knows no fear.

These lines literally crackle with the promise of revolutionary violence and confirm that the Langston Hughes of the mid-1930s was, in his outspoken social and political militancy, a far cry from the image of the "cool" poet projected in the 1951 poem "Motto"—a poet who "never became a fanatical supporter of any one cause." These lines also contradict one of the conclusions in Davis's "Langston Hughes: Cool Poet" (1968), namely, that the poet "was never a fanatic and impassioned leftist." In the heat of his youth, like many other young poets, Hughes was deeply committed and in hot poetic pursuit of racial and economic justice. That his ardor for such causes "cooled" with the years was natural and inevitable. Certainly, Davis's 1968 assessment of Hughes as a somewhat detached and slightly amused observer of America's comedy of racial and social errors is fully accurate for the years immediately following World War II. But the poems and statements of the 1930s, which in so many instances were diligently suppressed by the poet, reveal a Langston Hughes who was an implacable and articulate advocate of revolutionary violence.

Hughes's 1953 statement before the Congressional Committee on Government Operations stressed that his support of the political left during the 1930s was motivated by Communism's interest "in the problems of poverty, minorities, colonial peoples, and particularly of Negroes and Jim Crow." The record indicates that he was also convinced that the Negro's problems were in a large sense economic and that one way to help the Negro laborer was to have him link arms and causes with the white laborer, not only in America but throughout the world. By the mid-1930s, the poet had traveled enough to know that the "Black Seed" of the African diaspora had been "Driven before an alien wind" and left to exist "in soil / That's strange and thin." The rich progeny of Africa was to be found in the Caribbean, on the islands of the Atlantic, and throughout the Americas; indeed, isolated pockets of "Black Seed" were scattered like "hybrid plants" throughout the world. And wherever blacks found themselves, they were economically destitute and politically oppressed. His poem "The Same," published in *The Negro Worker* in 1932, defines the problem and suggests a Communist solution:

It is the same everywhere for me.
On the docks at Sierra Leone,

In the cotton fields of Alabama,
In the diamond mines of Kimberly
On the coffee hills of Haiti,
The banana lands of Central America,
The streets of Harlem,
And the cities of Morocco and Tripoli.
Black:
Exploited, beaten, and robbed,
Shot and killed.
Blood running into

> DOLLARS
> POUNDS
> FRANCS
> PESETAS
> LIRE
>   . . .

The force that kills,
The power that robs,
And the greed that does not care.
Better that my blood makes one with the blood
Of all the struggling workers in the world
Till every land is free of

> DOLLAR ROBBERS
> POUND ROBBERS
> FRANC ROBBERS
> PESETA ROBBERS
> LIRE ROBBERS
> LIFE ROBBERS—

Until the Red Armies of the International Proletariat
Their faces, black, white, olive, yellow, brown,
Unite to raise the blood-red flag that
Never will come down!

Interestingly enough, this poem not only presents a ringing affirmation of the value of a Communist solution for the bitter economic plight of the colored peoples of the world, but it presents the other side of the coin of what came to be called "négritude," or an awareness of the worldwide cultural unity of the sons and daughters of Africa. Here Hughes's emphasis is upon black economic exploitation and need; later Senghor, Césaire, and Damas stressed the cultural unity that helped black people endure and survive the pain of that exploitation and need.

Langston Hughes's interest in Communism and its social and economic panaceas culminated poetically with his publication of *A New Song,* a small volume of poetry brought out by the International Worker's Order in 1938.

It contains a somewhat changed version of the original "New Song" published in 1933, as well as other earlier occasional poems like "Park Bench,"
"Pride," and "The Ballad of Lenin." In addition, there are new poems of
communist propaganda—"Chant for Tom Mooney," "Chant for May Day,"
"Song of Spain," and "Union," a poem in which the poet asks for "White
and black" to "put their hands with mine / To shake the pillars of those
temples / Wherein false gods dwell / And worn-out altars stand."

In general, literary critics of the 1930s responded only slightly or not at
all to Hughes's leftist and Communist propaganda poetry. Certainly the
muted critical response was nothing remotely comparable to the splendid
furor that followed the poet's publication of jazz and blues poems in the
1920s. Black critics of the day were particularly silent and unresponsive. Of
course, early in the decade Du Bois had departed from *The Crisis* and
therefore was not present to provide critical leadership in his attack on the
group of writers whom he dismissed as spokesmen for "the debauched
tenth." Brawley, a defender of the cause of the "talented tenth," continued
to publish his critical opinions, observations, and assessments, but his
efforts led him into troubled critical waters. In 1934, for instance, in an
essay called "The Promise of Negro Literature" (*Journal of Negro History*
19:54–56), he advocated that Negro literature return to old verities and
ancient truths: "The day of inflation, of extravagance, of sensationalism is
gone, and we must now come back to earth and to a truer sense of values."
This observation, made in the midst of the greatest depression the world
had ever experienced, bespeaks a serious misreading of literary trends and
events. Predictably, Brawley's *Negro Genius* (1937) fully demonstrates that he
was not *au courant* with literary events of the time. He excoriates Hughes
for the vulgarity of his jazz and blues poetry of the previous decade but
pointedly ignores any mention of the leftist poetry which Hughes had been
writing for several years. In his review of *Negro Genius* Sterling Brown notes
this fact as one of the weaknesses of Brawley's treatment of Hughes ("Hughes's
later poems of radical propaganda are neglected"), but Brown refused or
thought it impolitic to speculate about the competence of his then senior
Howard University colleague to evaluate "poems of radical propaganda." It
may have been that to Brawley these were not poems at all, for many of the
respected critics of the day stoutly maintained that propaganda was not
literature, and literature, hence, could never be mere propaganda. Brown
himself in his *Negro Poetry and Drama* (1937) does state, in his brief evaluation of the poetry of Hughes, that the poet's "most recent work is Communist propaganda" and that his "awakened interest in Communism has
resulted in such poems as 'Goodbye, Christ,' . . . 'The Ballad of Lenin,' . . . and
'The Ballad of Roosevelt.'" But possibly because of the pressures of time
and space or the limitations of his critical method, he added no critical

assessment of Hughes's poetry of Communist propaganda. Similarly, Saunders Redding in his urbanely critical account of the poetry of Hughes in *To Make a Poet Black* (1939) considers his folk and racial protest poetry only and makes no mention of the poetry of Communist propaganda. This lack of critical comment tends to confirm the suspicion that the canons of critical taste that placed some constraints on a Benjamin Brawley also limited the critical range of many another literary expositor. Indeed, one is led to speculate that if the poets and novelists of the 1930s could have stopped their abhorrent practice of confusing literature with propaganda, then Brawley's prayerful request that "writers come back to earth and to a truer sense of values" would have been granted.

Fortunately, one Negro critic, Alain Locke, had both the critical temerity and esthetic insight to question the critical canon that propaganda was not literature. He did not reach this plateau of belief easily or quickly, however. At the beginning of the decade, in his annual reviews of Negro literature in *Opportunity,* he lamented that Hughes was no longer the folk poet that he had been but praised the novel *Not without Laughter* because it palpitated "with the real spiritual essences of Negro life" and evoked "the folk temperament" as "truly and reverently" as his poetry had done earlier. But a lull in poetic creativity was to be expected, argued Locke, and he confidently predicted that Negro literature of the 1930s was to be a "literature of criticism and interpretation" rather than a "literature of creative expression." Or, as the critic somewhat flamboyantly expressed the matter, "the bouyant Renaissance" was about to be followed by a reinforcing "sober Reformation." By the middle of the decade, in an annual review provocatively entitled "The Eleventh Hour of Nordicism" (*Opportunity,* January 1935), Locke again lamented that "the poetic strain" in Negro literature "has dwindled in quantity and quality" and that the "occasional poems of Cullen and Hughes are below the level of their earlier work." But by this time he had developed a critical theory to explain the temporary demise of the poetic arts. He wrote: "Evidently, it is not the hour for poetry, nor should it be—this near noon of a prosaic, trying day." For, he continued, "Poets, like birds, sing at dawn and dusk; they are hushed by the heat of propaganda and the din of work and battle and become vocal only before and after as the heralds or the caroling serenaders." Fortified with this somewhat archaic and romantic notion of the poetical function, Locke then proceeded to condemn the poetry section of Nancy Cunard's *Negro Anthology* (1934), to which Hughes had contributed several Communist propaganda pieces, as nothing more than "hot rhetoric and clanging emotion." Similarly, Hughes's volume of short stories, *The Ways of White Folks,* Locke described as being "avowedly propagandistic and motivated by a radical social philosophy."

However, a change in his critical attitude is seen in his review "Jingo,

Counter-Jingo and Us" (*Opportunity*, January 1938). This essay, largely written in reaction to Benjamin Stolberg's article "The Minority Jingo" (*Nation*, 23 October 1937), starts with a discussion of the levels of jingoism in matters literary. In Locke's view, there was not only a "minority jingo," so clearly demonstrated in Brawley's *Negro Builders and Heroes* with its "artistically indigestible minority chauvinism" and "Pollyanna sentimentalism." But there were other kinds of jingoism—a majority jingo (to which a minority jingo always reacted), a proletarian jingo, a bourgeois jingo, a capitalist jingo, as well as jingoes of "the credal and racial varieties." As the article proceeds, it becomes clear that in Locke's view a jingo was no more than a propagandistic stance or point of view held by a given author. In the end, Locke argues himself into the conclusion that "good art" can develop from "sound and honest propaganda," but "dishonest propaganda" would always result in bad art or bad literature. Two other interesting conclusions are that the "Negro cause in literature" has been plagued by "bad art and the blight of false jingo" and that the "New Negro movement" of the previous decade was "choked in shallow cultural soil by the cheap weeds of group flattery, vainglory and escapist emotionalism." Thus in this review of the Negro literature of 1937, Alain Locke took two giant steps in critical belief: he recognized that propaganda can have a place in literature or art, and he finally was able to place the "fervent creativity" of the Harlem Renaissance in a more balanced critical perspective. Undoubtedly, these changes in his critical outlook enabled Locke to be more understanding of Langston Hughes's Communist and racial propaganda poetry and prepared him to greet the rising new genius of Richard Wright with greater critical sympathy and insight.

So using the critical criterion that honest propaganda can produce good literature, Locke approached Hughes's *A New Song* (1938). He found the little volume a far cry, qualitatively speaking, from what Hughes had produced earlier. The poet had used, said Locke, "a twangy lyre" in writing these poems of racial protest and Communist propaganda. Even armed with his more enlightened critical credo about propagandistic literature, Locke found nothing poetically inspiring in lines exhorting workers of "The Black / And White World" to arise, unite, and revolt. Nor did he consider poems like "Chant for May Day," with its rather ambitious orchestration for group recitation, of a very high poetic order. But Locke did make a critical exception of two poems in the slender volume; these were the "Ballad of Ozzie Powell" and "The Song of Spain." This last poem, although never included in any later collections of Hughes's poetry, had a special appeal to Locke and others who were sensitized to the political and social events surrounding the Spanish Civil War. Evidently, some of the emotional power of this poem stems from the fact that it contains Hughes's initial reaction to the war and to the death of fellow poet Federico Garcia Lorca in that war.

Few of the many later critical commentaries on Hughes's poetry contain specific observations about his leftist or Communist propaganda poetry. Undoubtedly, this trend was attributable to the temper of the times. With the Cold War, there was an inevitable cooling of interest in any kind of literature that was sympathetic with Communism or with the Soviet Union. This is even true of critical works with a Third World emphasis, such as *The Militant Black Writer* (1969) by Stephen Henderson and Mercer Cook. In this very provocative study of African literary protest and the black cultural and political revolution of the 1960s, stress is placed—and rightly so—on the role played by Langston Hughes in stimulating African literary protest and promoting the revolution of black consciousness in black America. In such a context, any discussion of the poet's earlier involvement with political radicalism would, in one sense, appear to be irrelevant. For what could the integrationist revolutionism of pre–World War II Communism have to do with the revolution for black separatism of the 1960s? The answer lies in ascertaining the cause and motivation for one's involvement in the promotion of a revolutionary cause. It is evident from the thematic thrust of his Communist propaganda poetry that Hughes's principal objective in the 1930s was to improve the lot of black people, not only in America but throughout the world. Viewed in retrospect, the enabling political machinery that he chose to use—international Communism—was of questionable value; but many during that time who were desperate for change saw this as the one viable means to achieve the kind of economic and social revolution needed to lift black people out of the abyss of colonial oppression. For this reason, it may be argued that the Langston Hughes of the 1930s—the Hughes who sang of the power of Lenin and of the glory of revolution—was a singularly dedicated militant black writer whose assault on American race prejudice was sustained, vigorous, and unrelenting.

Unfortunately, the one critic of Hughes's poetry who has discussed his leftist poetry in some detail does not agree with this conclusion. To Jean Wagner in his *Negro Poets of the United States* the Communist propaganda poetry of Langston Hughes was more rhetorical than ideological—more a participatory rite in a popular trend than a deep commitment to a revolutionary cause. Reflected in this judgment is the view shared by some that generally Hughes's commitment to causes was never deep and abiding but controlled by surface trends and popular vogues. François Dôdat, in an article on the poet in *Présence Africaine* (1965), articulates this opinion as follows: "This poet is not a thinker, but nobody would dream of reproaching him for it, because, on the contrary, he possesses an extraordinary faculty

for defining the confused sensations that constitute the collective conscience of simple minds." This observation damns the poet with a faint
praise that, in view of Wagner's predilection for poets who are prophets and
thinkers, would probably raise that critic's esteem for Hughes not one iota.
In fact, behind Wagner's conclusion that "in all this Communist propaganda one senses something *irredeemably false* [italics mine]" is the unquali-
fied assumption that all of Hughes's poetry in this vein was mere rhetorical
pose. One speculates whether Wagner makes this inference primarily
because the poet made no on-the-record, life-and-death commitment to
Communism. If he had, Wagner seems to ask, how could he have then
made his well-known comment about his inability to give up jazz in order
to promote world revolution? If the poet had been firmly and irrevocably
committed, he would not only have joined the party and become an
official, card-carrying member, but he would have "gone to school" in
the literature, philosophy, and political methodology of international
Communism. In other words, one is led to infer that to Wagner a commitment to party was like a commitment to religion—a commitment that
prohibited casual levity or occasional deviation from either the creed or
the discipline. Obviously, if a man has made no such commitment, no one
can take seriously his protestations for that cause or creed. Therefore,
Wagner observes: "It is a trifling startling to think that the U.S. Senate
should have called a committee of investigation into session to examine
these works [Hughes's communist propaganda writings] whose naïveté and
childishness far outweigh their subversive import."

Not only does this statement indicate that Wagner is himself very naïve
about the average senate committee's reputation for "investigative efficiency,"
but it also implies certain defects in his own critical method. In the first
place, his analysis of Hughes's Communist propaganda poetry does not
lead to, or support, his conclusion that the poems are naïve and childish.
In his discussion of the literature, Wagner stresses the poet's emphasis
on the need of a true union of black and white labor and on how
the "solidarity of the world proletariat" would, in Hughes's view, end the
ubiquitous exploitation of black labor. The critic also discusses the principal message of *Scottsboro Ltd.* —that with the help of Communists the
Scottsboro boys will ultimately be freed—but there is no hint in his comments that what the poet wrote on behalf of the Scottsboro boys was either
naïve nor childish. In the second place, the words "naïveté and childishness"
have little or no meaning in the lexicon of literary criticism. Not only do
they suggest a kind of hyperbolism or overstatement that good critics tend
to avoid, but it is difficult to conclude what Wagner means by his use of
these terms. Is his reference to the political simplicity of these poems? Or
are the poet's pleas for violent revolution the utterances of a political

unsophisticate who has no comprehension of the real sources of economic and political power? Unfortunately, there is nothing in Wagner's critical text to suggest an answer. In the third place, it appears that the critical method employed here is defective simply because Wagner permits a seemingly authoritative secondary source (Charles Glicksberg's "Race and Revolution in Negro Literature") to dictate his critical conclusion, even though there is nothing in his own analysis that leads to or supports such a conclusion. Finally, Wagner's critical method is suspect here because, by his own admission, his conclusion is based on inadequate evidence. In a footnote to his critical discussion (p. 436, n. 171), the critic states: "The poems just cited are probably not the only poems written by Hughes in this vein, and it should be possible to find others in various periodicals. But as it was our intention to throw light on one facet of the poet's work, not to take issue with the opinions held by the man, we did not believe any useful purpose could have been served by continuing our researches in this direction." This oddly illogical statement speaks for itself.

Over and beyond deficiencies in critical method, Wagner's discussion of Hughes's poetry of Communist propaganda justifies two other general observations about the value of his criticism. First, in taking Hughes's measure as a dedicated Communist revolutionary, Wagner is obviously using a Gallic yardstick. He wants tangible and incontrovertible evidence of some group alignment and involvement. Like the chroniclers of old who demanded of knights-errant proof of their "errantry," Wagner apparently demands specific proof of Hughes's Communist involvement, over and beyond any proof yielded by the words of a poem or a trip to Russia or a journey to the scene of the Spanish Civil War. Using the Gallic yardstick of formal and legalistic participation, Wagner seems to be saying that adherence to party regulation and compliance with party discipline, preferably at some personal sacrifice, are the only truly valid forms of proof of one's Communist involvement. If evidence of such activity is lacking, then one's expressions and actions on behalf of the party become "irredeemably false" expressions and actions. In other words, Langston Hughes enjoyed far too much individual flexibility, American-style, to meet Wagner's somewhat rigid and essentially Gallic (or European) criterion for true partisan commitment. Thus, what appears to be Wagner's rather patronizing devaluation of Hughes's Communist commitment undoubtedly reflects his own background and general orientation about the nature of political partisanship.

Nor does this French critic seem to have the background and orientation which enable him to empathize fully with the trauma experienced by the victims of American racism. In justifying his involvement with Communism, Langston Hughes explained (and Wagner has a note acknowledging such an explanation) that Communism's efforts to alleviate "the poverty and wretchedness of Negroes" was the source of its appeal to him. And he made it clear in his poetry, in his plays, and in his short essays that the dilemma of the Scottsboro boys, sitting on death row in Kilby Prison in Alabama, was not only an affront to Christians everywhere but proof positive that American racial justice was a mockery and a delusion. For some reason, on this matter Wagner the critic never fully heard and understood Hughes the poet. Possibly, cultural and racial differences were too great. Possibly, the critic had not read enough about what the poet said about Scottsboro. Maybe he had not read "Brown America in Jail: Kilby" (*Opportunity,* June 1932), the short statement giving the poet's impressions of his visit to "the Negro wing" of a "human zoo" where "like monkeys in tiered cages, hundreds of Negroes" were "barred away from life." Possibly, Wagner had not read the poet's account of his sensations upon entering "the solid steel door" of the death house of Kilby's Negro wing: "Dark faces peering from behind bars, like animals when the keeper comes. All Negro faces, men and young men in this death house at Kilby. Among them the eight Scottsboro boys. . . . Eight brown boys condemned to death. No proven crime. Farce of a trial. Lies. Laughter. Mob. Music. Eight poor niggers make a country holiday."

Hughes also presented in a speech before the American Writers' Congress in 1939 some of the problems that he had encountered as a Negro author in a segregated society, and what he wrote should have built bridges of understanding with literary critics who, like Wagner, were far removed from the American literary scene. One particularly effective point in his address was that the publishing business viewed the Negro as an exotic and therefore accepted from the Negro author only exotic material; as Hughes put it, "When we cease to be exotic, we do not sell well." Moreover, Hughes emphasized that in America the Negro author was denied "the common courtesies of decent travel" and routinely excluded from "jobs as professional writers, editorial assistants, and publisher's readers." So to be a Negro writer in the America of the 1930s was an economically hazardous and, at times, emotionally unfulfilling experience. For, as the poet had pointed out in his first speech before the American Writers' Congress, in 1935, the tasks confronting the Negro writer were heavy and arduous. First, he had to seek "to unite blacks and whites" in America, "not on the nebulous basis of an interracial meeting or on the shifting sands of religious brotherhood, but on the *solid* ground of the daily working-class struggle to wipe out, now and forever, all the old inequalities of the past." In addition, Hughes called upon the Negro writer to expose "the lovely grinning face of Philanthropy" which supports and sustains institutional racism and expose as well the "sick-sweet smile of organized religion which lies about what it does not know and about what it does know." If these responsibilities were not enough on the already overburdened Negro author, the poet also charged him to "expose also, the false leadership that besets the Negro people—bought and paid for leadership, owned by capital, afraid to open its mouth except in the old conciliatory way so advantageous to the exploiters. . . . And the Contentment Tradition of the O-lovely-Negroes school of American fiction, which makes an ignorant black face and a Carolina head filled with superstition, appear more desirable than a crown of gold. . . . And expose war. And the old My-Country-Tis-of-Thee lie."

In other words, critics who, like Wagner, have attempted to evaluate the poetic career of Langston Hughes from afar, as it were, have long had access to materials which define that writer's philosophy of authorship and describe the social, moral, and political climate in which he had to function as an author. How these materials are employed by a given critic are, of course, determined by that critic's own critical philosophy. The point of emphasis here is that Hughes's leftist poetry of the 1930s was not written in a cultural, political, or emotional vacuum; and, as Wagner's countryman Michel Taine once indicated, a literary work cannot be fully assessed without some knowledge of the man who wrote it, the milieu that shaped and molded the writer's experience, and the moment that sparked his creativity.

That Wagner failed at times to develop such a recommended well-rounded view of Hughes is indicated by his treatment of the "Goodbye Christ" episode in the poet's career. In 1932, just prior to, or immediately upon, his departure for Russia, the poet had written a poem bearing this title. In essence, it was a frank and direct attack on the Christian church and on organized religion in the United States, and it provoked such a controversy among both whites and blacks that it was never reprinted after its publication in *The Negro Worker* in November 1932. Indeed, so bitter and prolonged was the reaction from both the press and the pulpit that the poet felt compelled to issue an explanation of the poem's meaning in 1941, almost ten years after its publication. His short statement "Concerning 'Goodbye Christ'" has to be considered if one is to read and interpret the poem in the light of the author's intended meaning. Some of the lines that provoked a bitter reaction on all levels of the "establishment" are:

> Listen, Christ,
> You did alright in your day, I reckon—
> But that day's gone now.
> They ghosted you up a swell story, too
> Called it Bible—
> But it's dead now.
> The popes and the preachers've

Made too much money from it.
They've sold you to too many

Kings, generals, robbers, and killers. . . .

Goodbye,
Christ Jesus Lord God Jehova
Beat it on away from here now.
Make way for a new guy with no religion at all—
A real guy named
Marx Communist Lenin Peasant Stalin Worker ME. . . .

I said, ME!

Go ahead on now . . .
And please take Saint Gandhi with you when you go,
And Saint Pope Pius,
And Saint Aimee McPherson
And big black Saint Becton
Of the Consecrated Dime. . . .

Inevitably, this abrasively radical poem raised howls of indignation and
rage from religionists everywhere and from many of the so-called guard-
ians of the establishment. An enraged Aimee Semple McPherson, the
popular evangelist of the Temple of the Four Square Gospel in Los
Angeles, preached from her sanctified pulpit that Langston Hughes was "a
red devil in a black skin." There is no record of a response from "big black
Saint Becton," Harlem's popular and successful evangelist; but Dr. Benjamin Mays, serving as a spokesman for the black church, wrote in his *The
Negro's God as Reflected in His Literature* (1938), "The case of Langston
Hughes is clear. The absolute repudiation of Christ, God, and religion, and
the reliance upon Marx, Lenin, and Stalin is the extreme left to which the
negation of God . . . may lead." He added that Hughes's case seemed to be
typical of the "wave of cynicism, defeat and frustration in the writings of
young Negroes where God is discussed."

In his short statement explaining the genesis and meaning of the poem,
Hughes made essentially three points. First, he said that he found American-
style racial segregation and its violent consequences "unbelievable in a
Christian country." In 1931 he had made his first tour of the American
South and was appalled by all that he saw and experienced; and it seemed
to him that America itself, through its "apparent actions toward my people,"
was as a nation officially saying "goodbye" to Christ and his principles of
toleration, love, and spiritual friendship. Hughes's second point was that
the "I" in the poem is not the poet himself but a persona compounded of
"the newly liberated peasant of the state collectives" in Russia and "those
American Negro workers of the depression period who believed in the

Soviet dream." In other words, the "I" of the poem was designed to be a composite of white Communist laborer and black Communist laborer. In his explanation, the poet added that quite frequently, as in his blues poetry, he was not the "I" in his poems. One critic, Donald Gibson, explains this Hughesian practice as follows: " . . . Hughes assumes a multitude of personae. At one time he is the spirit of the race who represents the Negro or Blackman, then he is a shoeshine boy, a black mother . . . a black man without a job or money, a prostitute, a ghetto tenant. Sometimes he is a consciousness where role is incapable of determination. And sometimes he speaks . . . as the poet." Hughes's third point was that "Goodbye Christ" was the product of the poet's "radical" twenties; and, since that time, he had moved to a new level of belief which asserted "that no system of ethics, religion, morals, or government is of permanent value which does not first start with and change the human heart."

In his comments on "Goodbye Christ" Wagner appears to ignore Hughes's statement of explanation, although he admits to having received a copy of that statement (p. 438, n. 175). Instead he states his belief that the poem resulted from "a personal religious crisis" similar to the crisis which the poet had experienced at the age of thirteen in Lawrence, Kansas, and later described in *The Big Sea* (pp. 18–21). Wagner then equates Hughes's "spiritual frustration," evidenced in these crises, with that experienced by "many intellectuals in the 'talented tenth' who, resolutely determined on total emancipation, turned their backs both on the white man's Christianity, since they saw it as one of the last vestiges of enslavement that had survived the abolition of slavery, and the formalist religion of the traditional Negro churches, whose faded, simple-minded rituals did little to disguise the absence of a strong spirituality. . . . " In other words, Wagner's critical discussion of the poem drifts off the subject of the poem into a generalization of dubious relevancy and questionable validity. Certainly, he completely ignores Hughes's statement for the rationale of the poem. His conclusion about "Goodbye Christ" is even more surprisingly illogical for, once again, the statements that precede the concluding comment have no direct and discernible cause-and-effect relationship with such a conclusion. Writes Wagner: "But in Hughes' case these rebellious gestures [against the Church and organized religion] proved quite transitory. For these were gestures only, and not those crises of conscience that seize upon certain delicate souls and shake them to their very depths. McKay, Toomer, and Cullen did not hesitate occasionally to estrange their fellows in order to follow the paths of the spirit. But Hughes was not of that dimension. . . . " Not only is the comparison of Hughes with his fellow black poets unsupported and therefore both irresponsible and irrelevant (and even possibly "full odious"), but the reasons for summarily reducing "two religious crises" to the level of merely "transitory rebellious gestures" are never given. One suspects that Wagner has to cope throughout his Hughes study with a worrying hypothesis, namely, that Hughes was never a poet in the grand manner but only a facile versifier—one who lived only on the surface of events and hence could never truly suffer a deep emotional crisis. A critic with his neck in the noose of such a hypothesis has to select his evidence very carefully, lest the noose grow uncomfortably tight. For this reason, Wagner finds Hughes's explanatory statement about "Goodbye Christ" unusable, simply because it did not lead to his predetermined conclusion. This critical observation is supported by a note which Wagner appends to his comments. He writes: "He [Hughes] was fully justified . . . in noting the all *too* blatant divergency between the doctrine and the practices of his adversaries. But if he had not remained at the surface of these problems, how could he persistently have avoided proceeding to the sounding of his own conscience? All things considered, religious problems are reduced to social problems in his eyes, while the richness and the complexities of the inner life seem to have been a closed book for him." This note leads to Wagner's oft reiterated conclusion that Hughes did not have the inner dimensions which would have made him capable of a deep and abiding spiritual or emotional commitment. Such a conclusion, in the light of the poet's radical poetry of the 1930s, is quite untenable. During those years, the poet was committed as always to the cause of alleviating the economic and social distress of Negro people and fully convinced that Communism provided a feasible approach to attaining that objective.

In the 1953 statement which he read to the Senate subcommittee investigating his Communist involvement, Hughes said that his faith in Communism as an efficacious means of eradicating racial prejudice and economic inequality effectively dissipated with the signing of the Russo-German Non-Aggression Pact in 1938. The record indicates that this was true not only of Hughes but of many of his contemporaries who, at this point, became disenchanted with the *réalpolitik* of Communism. But further analysis of his poetry in the 1940s and 1950s will reveal that, although he changed his mind about Communism, his commitment to the cause of Negro rights and freedom remained unchanged.

REFERENCES

This essay first appeared as chapter 3 in Richard K. Barksdale's *Langston Hughes: The Poet and His Critics,* ed. Charles Sanders (Chicago: American Library Association, 1977). Reprinted with permission.

Berry, Faith, ed. 1973. *Good Morning Revolution.* New York: Lawrence Hill.

Brawley, Benjamin. 1934. "The Promise of Negro Literature." *Journal of Negro History* 19: 53–59.

Calverton, V. F. 1940. "The Negro in American Culture." *Saturday Review of Literature,* September 1940, pp. 3–4.

Cruse, Harold. 1967. *The Crisis of the Negro Intellectual.* New York: William Morrow.

Dôdat, François. 1965. "Situation de Langston Hughes." *Présence Africaine* 26:283–85.

Ford, Nick Aaron. 1963. *The Contemporary Negro Novels: A Study in Race Relations.* Boston: Meador.

Gibson, Donald B. 1971. "The Good Black Poet and the Good Gray Poet: The Poetry of Hughes and Whitman." In *Langston Hughes, Black Genius: A Critical Evaluation,* ed. Therman B. O'Daniel, pp. 65–80. New York: William Morrow.

Gillard, John. 1932. "The Negro Challenges Communism." *Commonweal,* 25 May 1932, p. 97.

Henderson, Stephen, and Mercer Cook. 1969. *The Militant Black Writer.* Madison, Wis.: University of Wisconsin Press.

Hughes, Langston. 1932. "Brown America in Jail: Kilby." *Opportunity,* June 1932, p. 174.

———. 1935. *To Negro Writers.* A Speech given at the first American Writers' Congress, New York, April 1935.

———. 1939. *Democracy and Me.* A Speech given at the Third American Writers' Congress, New York, June 1939.

Locke, Alain. 1933. "Black Truth and Black Beauty." *Opportunity,* January 1933, pp. 14–18.

———. 1935. "The Eleventh Hour of Nordicism." *Opportunity,* Part 1, January, pp. 4–10; part 2, February, pp. 46–48, 59.

———. 1936. "Deep River, Deeper Sea." *Opportunity,* Part 1, January, pp. 6–10; part 2, February, 42–43, 61.

———. 1938. "Jingo, Counter-jingo and Us," *Opportunity,* Part 1, January, pp. 7–11, 27; part 2, February, pp. 39–42.

Mays, Benjamin. 1938. *The Negro's God as Reflected in His Literature.* Boston: Grimes and Chapman.

Miller, Kelley. 1933. "Should Black Turn Red?" *Opportunity,* November 1933, pp. 328–32, 350.

Record, Wilson. 1951. *The Negro and the Communist Party.* Chapel Hill: University of North Carolina Press.

———. 1956. "Extremist Movements Among American Negroes." Phylon 17 (no. 1): 17–23.

Redding, Saunders. 1939. *To Make a Poet Black.* Chapel Hill, N.C.: University of North Carolina Press.

Schuyler, George. 1932. "Review of Edwin Embree's *Brown America.*" *Opportunity,* June 1932, pp. 175–76.

Smith, Asbury. 1933. "What Can the Negro Expect from Communism?" *Opportunity,* July 1933, pp. 211–12.

Wagner, Jean. 1973. *Black Poets of the United States: From Paul Laurence Dunbar to Langston Hughes.* Trans. Kenneth Douglas. Urbana: University of Illinois Press.

Young, James O. 1973. *Black Writers of the Thirties.* Baton Rouge: Louisiana State University Press.

Miscegenation on Broadway: Hughes's *Mulatto* and Edward Sheldon's *The Nigger*

On 4 December 1909, at Broadway's New Theatre, the curtain went up on a new three-act play written by Edward Sheldon. Although it bore the somewhat inflammatory title *The Nigger* and dealt with the intriguingly controversial topic of racial miscegenation, the play was apparently well received by the playgoing public—so well received, indeed, that it was published in book form by Macmillan in 1910, with a reprinted edition following in 1915.[1] In 1909, Broadway enjoyed a lively season, and the competition was vigorous and stimulating. *The Nigger's* big competition was *The Fortune Hunter* starring that scintillating star of the stage (and later the screen), John Barrymore. As far as race relations in America were concerned, 1909 was also an interesting year. For this was the year that a group of concerned white northern liberals—Oswald Garrison Villard, Joel Spingarn, Mary Ovington White—met to form the National Association for the Advancement of Colored People. Joining them in this enterprise was the young black scholar William E. B. Du Bois, whose Niagara Movement in 1905 and 1906 became a model for the NAACP. The NAACP's founders were motivated to organize their association because of the ever-increasing turbulence in race relations throughout the nation. They were particularly concerned about preventing further race riots like the one in Brownsville, Texas, in 1906 and the one in Springfield, Illinois, in 1908. So Sheldon's play's title blended with the racial climate of the times and evidently reflected white America's interest in this aspect of black-white relations.

Almost twenty-six years later, on 24 October 1935, Langston Hughes's *Mulatto* opened at Broadway's Vanderbilt Theater. Like Sheldon's play, Hughes's two-act play dealt with the theme of miscegenation and enjoyed a relatively long Broadway run (270 performances) and then successfully toured the nation for eight months. This was considered to be a fairly remarkable achievement for a play in the middle of the Depression. However, *Mulatto*'s publication history was quite different from that of *The Nigger*. Hughes's play was not published in English until 1963, twenty-eight years after its first Broadway run. Ironically, during this time, the play was translated into three foreign languages—Italian, Japanese, and Spanish—and the play was quite popular in Italy, Japan, and Argentina. But there was no American publication of *Mulatto* until Webster Smalley's edition of *Five Plays by Langston Hughes* was published by Indiana University Press in 1963.

Between 1909 and 1935, some conditions and circumstances in America had changed and some had remained agonizingly constant. America's racial climate had changed little. Blacks in the South were still voteless, powerless, and legally segregated; and blacks in the North lived, in the main, in poverty-stricken ghettos. In other words, although by 1935 Booker T. Washington had been dead for twenty years, the conditions about which he had prophesied that blacks and whites could be as separate "as the fingers on the hand" still existed. One interesting item of evidence attesting to this state of affairs was that, in 1935, Hughes was not given complimentary orchestra seats to attend the opening of his play at the Vanderbilt because the theater management had "reservations" about seating blacks in the orchestra section.[2]

Some things had changed. In New York City proper, blacks no longer lived in the Tenderloin and San Juan Hill areas in mid-Manhattan where they were to be found in 1909. After the infamous Tenderloin District riot in 1902, they had begun moving over into Brooklyn and then, after World War I, they had moved in great numbers into Harlem. By 1935, this area of Manhattan housed over 360,000 blacks and had become the most populous black metropolis in the world. In the early 1920s, it had truly been a heavenly refuge, but by 1935 the refuge was rapidly becoming a ghetto. Another interesting change of circumstances occurred on Broadway. In 1909, there were no black playwrights on Broadway, whereas in 1935 at least one enjoyed a somewhat tenuous status on the Great White Way.[3] Hughes's status is termed "tenuous" because the production and staging of *Mulatto* proved to be such a traumatic and discouraging experience for him. Indeed, the story of how *Mulatto* found its way to Broadway is evidence of the somewhat bizarre nature of a black playwright's lot in the 1930s.

According to Faith Berry, Hughes, just prior to his departure for the Soviet Union in June 1931, gave Blanche Knopf a manuscript copy of *Mulatto*.[4] At that time the author had no idea that four years would elapse before he could return to New York City and inquire about his play manuscript. He returned to the States in the summer of 1933, but he came back to California via Vladivostok, Shanghai, and Tokyo. In California, Hughes stayed with friends in Carmel in order to complete his first volume of short stories, *The Ways of White Folks*. From Carmel he traveled to Reno, Nevada, and thence, in December 1934, to Mexico to assist in settling the estate of his father, who had died in November. Unfortunately, once in Mexico Hughes found himself stranded; his wealthy father had left him nothing, and he found himself without funds to return to the States. So he stayed in Mexico with friends until May 1935. Even then, he did not return to New York to inquire about the *Mulatto* manuscript. Instead, he accepted an invitation from his friend Arna Bontemps to visit with the Bontemps family in Los Angeles in the summer of 1935. As a consequence, Hughes did not return to New York City until late September of that year.

To his amazement, he found upon his return that *Mulatto* was not only in rehearsal but was scheduled for an October 1935 opening. He also discovered something else. When he attended his first rehearsal, he found that Martin Jones, *Mulatto*'s producer, had drastically revised the brief two-act plot. For instance, where Hughes had Sallie, Cora's illegitimate mulatto daughter, leave to attend a northern college early in act 1, Jones, in order to retain a sex-cum-violence emphasis, cancelled Sallie's departure in act 1 so that she could be raped in act 2 to climax the racial violence at the end of the play. As a consequence, Hughes's emphasis on the tragic consequences of miscegenation was somewhat diluted in the acted version of *Mulatto*. For there is no doubt that Hughes had intended to probe the psychological impact of miscegenation in his play just as he had done in his poetry ("Cross," "Mulatto") and in his short story "Father and Son." In other words, his emphasis had consistently been on the vitiating aftereffects of miscegenation and its accompanying evil, black concubinage. The South's penchant for racial violence was certainly an important area of concern, but Hughes was primarily interested in the emotional stress and psychological insecurities of children born of forced interracial liaisons. In his view, they developed identity problems which, in turn, adversely affected their social behavior and their personal self-esteem.

Ironically, the changes introduced by Martin Jones in Hughes's play script to gratify the tastes of Broadway playgoers reflect, in some respects, the story line of Sheldon's *The Nigger*. That play, too, has an interracial rape scene and an off-the-set lynching. It also has an overly romantic love plot. The major difference, among several to be noted later, is that *The Nigger* is a somewhat tawdry melodrama with a happy ending; *Mulatto* is a tautly written drama with an unhappy ending.

A difference of less significance is that in Sheldon's play the social and moral collapse of the Old Plantation South is writ large. This is in contrast to Hughes's rather pointed analysis of a small unit of that South. Also, Hughes in his character portraits strives to avoid stereotyping his principal black characters. In *The Nigger,* on the other hand, all of the major characters are white stereotypical middle- or upper-middle-class landowners. Indeed, Sheldon's characters are almost nauseatingly "Southern" in their often mannered pomposity and their social posturing. They represent a storybook South that presumably ceased to exist after the Civil War. In contrast, Hughes's *Mulatto* presents only brief glimpses of the South and its regional idiosyncrasies. The play's focus is on the intense father-son conflict between Robert and his white father, Colonel Norwood, and on how deeply Cora was emotionally and psychologically lacerated by her experiences as Norwood's concubine.

The plot of Sheldon's play may be summarized as follows. The principal male character or protagonist is Philip Morrow, a young, well-bred southern aristocrat who presides over "Morrow's Rest," a stately antebellum plantation mansion that has been in his family for generations. "Morrow's Rest" is described as an old-fashioned "colonial mansion fronted by four great white Doric columns" and festooned by "luxuriant" honeysuckle vines and rambling crimson roses; and, of course, magnolia trees, heavy with fragrance, are everywhere. Completing the picture of tranquil beauty is a cluster of white rose bushes circling a moss-grown live oak. Sheldon seems to be saying that it is only in such a setting, reeking with heavily scented beauty, that heinous crimes can be committed and dark sins remembered. Philip Morrow's character foil is Clifton Noyes, a young man who, but for a lost wager, would have inherited a life of indolent gentility as the master of "Morrow's Rest." Instead, he has been forced to take the low road and become the owner of a whiskey distillery. And there is, of course, Georgiana Byrd, a beautiful but appropriately modest young southern belle who is charmingly gracious, ladylike, and, fortunately, unmarried. She exudes that rare quality of soft, virginal innocence and saccharine purity found in 1909 only among ladies who resided south of the Mason-Dixon line.

To complete the cast of characters, there are the "colored" servants—Jinny, "an ancient quadroon woman" who was Philip Morrow's mammy and Philip's father's mammy; Sam, the butler, who is also ancient, slow of foot, but loyal to Mastah; and Jim, Jinny's grandson. This last is shiftless, "no-count," obsequious, and, of course, immoral and given to strong drink. Eventually, he is lynched (in act 2) for committing the South's most outrageous and unpardonable crime—the rape of a pristinely pure white woman.

The action of the play reaches an exciting climax when Philip Morrow proposes marriage to "Georgie" on the eve of his election to the governorship of the state. Extensive plans are being made for the wedding when Clifton Noyes, "pale" with jealousy, reveals what Jinny, Philip's black mammy, already knows—that Philip's father's mother was really not white but a very light-skinned slave girl with whom his grandfather had had a "secret" affair just before he left to be killed in the Mexican War. Thus Sheldon revealed a South that northern playgoers in 1909 expected to find—a land full of dusky lovers and sexual guilt, or, as Langston Hughes wrote in "Mulatto," one of the poems in *Fine Clothes to the Jew* (1927):

> Silver moonlight everywhere
>
> . . .
>
> Sharp pure scent in the evening air
> A nigger night
> A nigger joy
> A little yellow
> Bastard boy.

Philip is naturally overwhelmed to learn the dark secret hidden in his family's festered past, for death is to be preferred to the curse of blood that is tainted by blackness. And when he is compelled by gentlemanly honesty to tell his beloved betrothed, she shrinks from him with loathing and disgust and runs screaming from the room. As a white southern lady, she suddenly cannot bear the touch of a lover who has suddenly become, because of his mulatto grandmother, "a nigger."

This highly dramatic scene occurs at the end of act 2, and act 3 is devoted to resolving the rather complex situation that has developed. The fact that a white southern governor has suddenly metamorphosed, through irrefutable historical evidence, from white to black is tragic, and something must be done to restore the protagonist's good fortune. This Sheldon does with all of the melodramatic finesse that was so popular on pre–World War I Broadway. First Georgiana changes her mind about her lover's racial background and announces that love will triumph over all—over race, over bad luck, over evil. She "bursts out": " . . . I jus love you so much, Phil, that I won't let anything come between us—not even—*that!* (p. 242)." And about "that," she goes on, "It's only such a little! Just a trace—that's all!" (p. 245). To this, Phil, the recently elected governor of a sovereign southern state, replies as a southern gentleman should: "Black's black, an white's white. If yo not one, yo the othah, Geo'gie" (p. 245). But when he states further that his racial identity should not remain a secret and that he will reveal all in a speech from his office balcony to a huge crowd gathered to honor him, Geo'gie is horrified: "Yo gon to stand up an say a thing like that—befo the whole city?" (p. 248). When Phil insists on full disclosure of his racial identity, Geo'gie finally relents and makes her final speech as a fully redeemed heroine should: "Theah's only one thing I know I understand and that is—I love you. . . . I don't care who you are or what you do—I don't care if ev'rybody in the world goes back on you, I'll stick all the closah, you can't get rid of me" (p. 251).

At this point, one can almost hear violins sobbing beautifully in the background. But Sheldon is not through; and, after a few moments of well-maneuvered suspense, he serves up, at the play's end, his melodramatic *pièce de résistance*. The crowd has gathered before the capitol building, and Phil goes out to announce to all and sundry that he is a "nigger." But the cheering crowd and the band's playing of the national anthem drown out his words. In vain, he raises his hands for silence, but "the band crashes through the national anthem and the roar of voices still rises from below" as the curtain falls.

So Sheldon's *The Nigger* suggests two truths about miscegenation. The first is that miscegenation could be borne and accepted especially if the race mixing had occurred during slavery time—a time when the superordinate white male master held full sway over his black female slaves to use and abuse as he wished. The second truth is that there always existed the possibility that white men of high position and status could have "tainted" blood as a result of a grandfather's sexual *mésalliance*. Undoubtedly, a play with these implications in 1909 reflected a northern liberal bias and could not have been presented in Charleston or Richmond or Atlanta.

As has been suggested above, Hughes's *Mulatto* differs from Sheldon's play in many respects. It is shorter, has a more restricted focus, and is concerned with the psychological consequences of miscegenation from the black perspective and not with the sociological consequences from the white perspective. Moreover, *Mulatto* is much more than a "sociopolitical statement," as Webster Smalley suggests.[5] The father-son conflict is intense throughout; in fact, the miscegenation theme is almost lost when Robert Lewis, the black illegitimate son, in a scene of Oedipal fury, slays his white father, Colonel Norwood. At this point, race seems to be of little concern.[6] Rather the emphasis is on an aborted filial love and a callous and inhumane rejection of the offer of that love.

So Hughes's play castigates a system that turned father against son, son against father, and made a mockery of the family as a unit. Slavery left blacks, once they were freed, poor, fearful, and illiterate; but, in Hughes's view, slavery's worst heritage was the psychological damage done to the mulatto boy or mulatto girl whose mother, like Cora in *Mulatto*, was forced to be her master's concubine. Hughes could have explored the full dimensions of concubinage in slavery, had he written a third act in which Sallie, Cora's daughter by Colonel Norwood, would also have been forced to become her own father's concubine. Had Hughes developed his plot in this direction, his play would have revealed how incest was the most sordid aspect of the sexual victimization and depravity inherent in American slavery.[7] But even without any mention of incestuous concubinage, Hughes's play does stress the fact that white men often felt constrained by custom and tradition from recognizing their mulatto children.

It is also appropriate in this context to state that Hughes's emphasis on the father-son conflict in *Mulatto* strongly suggests his own conflict with his father. The son of parents who divorced when he was a boy, Hughes had a harried childhood living with his poverty-ridden mother. When he went to live with his father in Toluca, Mexico, following his graduation from high school in Cleveland, Ohio, he found that he and his father were not compatible. According to the author's own report in his 1940 biography, *The Big Sea*, his father had become a hard-driving, profit-seeking business-man who had no patience with his poetry-writing son and no sympathy for the plight of his fellow blacks in the States. Thus, when the young Hughes, in compliance with his father's wishes, left Toluca to enroll, with considerable reluctance, as a first-year engineering student at Columbia University, the father-son relationship was tense and embittered. And when the year at Columbia proved to be an academic disaster, Hughes eventually got a job on an Africa-bound freighter and never saw or corresponded with his father again.

Another difference between Sheldon's *The Nigger* and *Mulatto* is that Hughes's play places considerable emphasis on the psychological dilemma of Cora, Colonel Norwood's concubine and the mother of his three mulatto children—William, Robert, and Sallie Lewis. The longtime partner of the Colonel's bed but never the wife of his bosom, Cora is torn between her mother's love for her self-assertive and aggressive son Robert and her respect for the Colonel, who is angered by his bastard son's attitude and life-style. In the Colonel's eyes, Robert does not behave the way a black bastard should behave; where he should have been obsequious and humble, Robert is aggressive and demanding. In fact, he demands the recognition that he is a Norwood who can walk in the Norwood front door and do anything that a white man can. Caught in a crossfire of anger between father and son, Cora tries unsuccessfully to serve as peacemaker. Then, when the actual physical struggle takes place between Norwood and Robert and the son strangles the father, Cora's first thought is to help her son escape the lynch mob that she is sure will be formed to track her son down. Scene 1, act 2, closes with Cora's highly emotional soliloquy in which she converses with the Colonel's corpse:

> Don't you come to my bed no mo'. I calls for you to help me now, and you just lays there. I calls for you to wake up, and you just lays there. Whenever

you called me, in de night, I woke up. When you called for me to love, I always reached out ma arms fo you. I borned you five chilluns and now one of 'em is out yonder in de dark runnin' from yo people. Our youngest boy out yonder in de dark runnin'. (*Accusingly*) He's runnin' from you too. You said he warn't your'n—he's just Cora's little yellow bastard. But he *is* your'n, Colonel Tom. (*Sadly*) And he's runnin' from you. You are out yonder in de dark, (*Points toward the door*) runnin' our chile, with de hounds and de gun in yo' hand. . . . I been sleepin' with you too long, Colonel Tom, not to know that this ain't you layin' down there with yo' eyes shut on de flo'. You can't fool me. . . . Colonel Thomas Norwood, runnin' ma boy through de fields in de dark, runnin' ma po' lil' helpless Bert through de fields in de dark to lynch him . . . Damn you, Colonel Norwood! Damn you, Thomas Norwood! God damn you! (p. 27)

As the play draws to a close and the sounds of the lynch mob pursuing her Bert grow louder, Cora, in another long soliloquy, bitterly recalls how her concubinage with the Colonel began:

Colonel Thomas Norwood! . . . Thirty years ago, you put yo' hands on me to feel my breasts, and you say, "Yo' a pretty little piece of flesh, ain't you? Black and sweet, ain't you?" An' I lif' up ma face, an you pull me to you, an we laid down under the trees that night, an' I wonders if yo' wife'll know when you goes back up da road into de big house. . . . An' ah loved you in de dark, down thuh under dat tree by de gate, afraid of you and proud of you, feelin' yo gray eyes lookin' at me in de dark. (p. 32)

And at one point, she observes: "White mens, and colored womens, and lil' bastard chilluns—tha's de ol' way of de South—but it's ending now (p. 30).

Mulatto ends when Robert takes his own life rather than be taken by the lynch mob. The last person on the stage is Cora. She stands quietly and doesn't move or flinch when Talbot, the white overseer, vents his frustration by slapping her. Her personal slavery as a white man's concubine has come to an end, and *Mulatto*'s message also seems to be that no black person is truly free as long as one black woman is kept as a white man's concubine.[8]

Obviously, Hughes's 1935 statement on miscegenation is far more psychologically penetrating and direct than Sheldon's 1909 statement. The principal cause for this difference is not that the intervening twenty-six years bred a greater awareness in the body politic of the social and psychological implications of miscegenation and black concubinage. Rather, the difference in approaches stems from the fact that Hughes's view is a racially interior view and Sheldon's is the racially exterior view commonly held by northern liberals in appraising southern mores and racial practices. Indeed, Sheldon, in the end, presents miscegenation as just another regional foible bespeaking the legendary moral turpitude of the sinful South. Hughes, on the other hand, had, like many of his fellow blacks, some experiential proximity to the problem. His father, like Colonel Norwood, had abandoned him for selfish and appetitive reasons. Moreover, Hughes had had a much-revered great-uncle, John Mercer Langston, who, like many other black race leaders of the nineteenth century (P. B. S. Pinchback, Francis and Archibald Grimke, Frederick Douglass, Booker T. Washington, William Wells Brown, and others) had a slave-master father (Ralph Quarles, a wealthy planter from Louisa County, Virginia). One can therefore conclude that because Hughes, in his own life and career, had been close to the problem, his play has an emotional tautness and psychological intensity lacking in *The Nigger*. Sheldon had aesthetic distance from his subject, but this very fact robbed his play of the emotional intensity that differentiates good drama from melodramatic entertainment.

NOTES

This essay first appeared in *Critical Essays on Langston Hughes*, ed. Edward J. Mullen (Boston: G. K. Hall, 1986). Copyright 1986 and reprinted with permission of Twayne Publishers, a division of G. K. Hall.

1. *The Nigger* (New York: Macmillan, 1910). (Subsequent references are from this edition and are noted parenthetically in the text.) Sheldon was a moderately popular pre–World War I playwright. His *Salvation Nell* (1908) and *Romance* (1913) enjoyed good runs on Broadway.

2. Faith Berry, *Langston Hughes* (New York: Lawrence Hill, 1983), p. 241.

3. Black musicals—*Clorindy, In Dahomey, Lode of Coal*—were very popular on and off Broadway at the turn of the century, and Wallace Thurman's *Harlem* had enjoyed a good season's run on Broadway in 1929.

4. Berry, *Langston Hughes*, pp. 240–41.

5. Webster Smalley, *Five Plays by Langston Hughes* (Bloomington: Indiana University Press, 1963), p. xi. Subsequent references to *Mulatto* are from this edition and are noted parenthetically in the text.

6. This is an interpretation that I think best coheres with the play's plot action. Another interpretation could be that Robert's action symbolizes a subconscious Freudian wish of all black males.

7. It is now general knowledge that incest of this kind was widely prevalent during slavery. Fiction writers as widely separated as Faulkner and Gayl Jones mention it in their writings, Faulkner in his stories about some of the slave families in Yoknapatawpha County and Jones in her account of the old Brazilian slaveholder, Corregidora. Also, in Dicken J. Preston's *Young Frederick Douglass: The Maryland Years* (1980), the author confirms that Captain Aaron Anthony, Douglass's white father, also fathered Harriet Bailey, Douglass's mother.

8. The sexual slavery of the black woman is described with brutal directness

in Gayl Jones's *Corregidora* when Ursa Corregidora recalls what her Great Gram had said occurred when she had been a slave on the Portuguese Corregidora's plantation in Brazil. A female slave had major functions—to "breed well or make a good whore. Fuck each other or fuck them." *Corregidora* (New York: Bantam Books, 1976), p. 145.

Langston Hughes and James Baldwin:
Some Observations on a Literary Relationship

Since one must now consider both the conventional wisdom of the pre-Rampersadian era and the dazzling *aufklärung* of the post-Rampersadian period in approaching any substantive discussion of the life and work of Langston Hughes, one can safely state that the portrait of James Baldwin remains fairly constant in both "time zones." The pre-Rampersadian view was that, of all of Hughes's black fellow writers, James Baldwin was the most consistently unfriendly and that his *New York Times* (29 March 1959, p. 6) review of Hughes's *Selected Poems* was the most hostile review that the author's work had ever received from a fellow black writer. This generalization excludes the slashing attacks on Hughes's blues and jazz poetry during the 1920s; these came from the news media and not from a fellow black writer. There are, however, two important post-Rampersadian addenda: first, Raoul Abdul, one of Hughes's secretarial assistants, once called Baldwin's very friendly greeting of Hughes in a Harlem restaurant in the early 1960s "the kiss of a Judas"; second, Baldwin admitted, sometime after the very damaging review was written, "I hadn't really read the book, to tell the truth. I wrote the review without fully understanding what I was doing or saying."

With that remark now a matter of record, the Hughes-Baldwin literary *mésalliance* becomes even more curious to explain and evaluate. Was it only a personal vendetta between two professional rivals? Or was it a younger man, obsessed with patricidal fury, attacking an obstensible father figure; for Hughes was twenty-two years older than Baldwin and the latter apparently hated father figures. Or were their differences originally not personal but generational and ideological?

The personal-vendetta hypothesis can be dismissed almost summarily. In the 1950s Langston Hughes was a man who, having "suffered the slings and arrows" of a somewhat "outrageous fortune" in the 1920s, 1930s, and

1940s, had donned "a mask of smiling affability," to use a Rampersadian phrase. His credo, as stated in *Montage of a Dream Deferred,* was

> I plày it cool
> And dig all jive
> That's the reason
> I stay alive.
>
> My motto
> As I live and learn,
>   is:
> *Dig and be Dug*
> *In Return.*

In other words, as Arthur Davis once described the Hughes of the 1950s, he had become a writer possessed of a "cooly ambivalent vision"—a man who scorned personal vendettas and embraced but two causes—the literary celebration of the urban black folk hero and the defense of blackness throughout the diaspora. In his pursuit of these two literary goals, Hughes was supported by some of the younger black writers who had just emerged on the post–World War II literary scene. This was even true of those who, like Gwendolyn Brooks, were successfully competitive in the pursuit of literary honors. In her autobiography, *Part One,* Brooks notes Hughes's "affectionate interest" in those young writers who came to him with manuscript in hand. And Lorraine Hansberry, the successful author of the play *Raisin in the Sun,* hailed Hughes as "not only my mentor but the poet laureate of our people." So, surrounded by a coterie of literary friends and associates, the Hughes of the 1950s sought no vendettas. He was too busy even to be overtly annoyed by Ellison's coolness after the latter's prize-winning *Invisible Man* appeared and shattered all best-seller records. Hughes in a letter to Arna Bontemps observed that Ellison now seemed to be more interested in what was going on in Hungary than what was happening in Harlem. Nor did he and his charming wife, Fanny, any longer visit the Hughes *ménage* on East 127th with their accustomed frequency.

Did James Baldwin then consider Hughes to be a hated father substitute? The evidence in hand does not support such a conclusion. Actually, Hughes never enjoyed anything like paternal proximity to Baldwin. He first became aware of the young writer after reading the latter's article on Harlem in *Commentary.* According to Rampersad, Hughes found the article praiseworthy and sent the young man a congratulatory note. To this Baldwin never responded. Later, he explained: "As for not writing to him, I just didn't know what to say. So I didn't say anything." There is abundant evidence, however, that Richard Wright was Baldwin's hated father substitute.

Wright had met the young writer in the winter of 1944/45 and became not merely his friend but his professional consultant. Through his assistance, Baldwin received his first major literary recognition—the Eugene F. Saxton Memorial Trust Award. He was also able, through Wright's immense influence, to publish in *The Nation, The New Leader, Commentary,* and *Partisan Review.* But over and above these accomplishments, Baldwin served an interesting literary apprenticeship with Wright. They had time to discuss the options facing a young black writer as World War II came to an end. What were the paths to literary glory? How does one find a best-seller audience? Once found, would it be white or black? And what about protest fiction? It worked with *Native Son* in 1940. Would it succeed as well in a postwar world in which there was more talk of racial integration?

So there is little doubt that Baldwin came to view Wright as a father figure and that, through the phenomenon of paternal surrogacy, came to distrust him and question his literary judgment and advice. In the view of some, that is the only way a young writer can break away from "paternal" influence and find his comfort zone of authorial independence. In any event, Baldwin issued his repudiation of his literary father figure with the publication of the essay "Everybody's Protest Novel." In fact, in order that Wright as father figure would understand the full force of the literary son's rejection of the principle of protest fiction, Baldwin published the essay three times—in *Partisan Review* in 1949; in *Perspectives USA,* a work edited for overseas distribution by Lionel Trilling in 1953; and then in *Notes of a Native Son* in 1955.

Undoubtedly, Baldwin was as much influenced by the integrationist *Zeitgeist* of the postwar era as by his anti-Wright feelings. Literary critics and prognosticators, full of a pervasive postwar cultural euphoria, predicted that the literary arts would be integrated just as the military services had been integrated. Hugh Gloster, for instance, in an essay entitled "Race and the Negro Writer," applauded what he termed "the gradual emancipation of the Negro writer from the fetters of racial chauvinism." Similarly, Saunders Redding, in an essay called "American Negro Literature," proclaimed his belief that the black writer had at last found a white audience, as proven by the success of Willard Motley and Frank Yerby. Also, he attributed the prize-winning achievements of Margaret Walker and Gwendolyn Brooks to the integrationist *Zeitgeist* that seemed to be in evidence in the late 1940s and early 1950s. Indeed, older poets like Hayden and Tolson had aligned themselves with the white academy, and a youthful LeRoi Jones chose to reside in the Village and not in Harlem. Baldwin, hoping that his novel-to-be would be a crowd-pleasing best-seller to an enlarged and integrated reading audience, undoubtedly wrote his "Everybody's Protest Novel" to please the white literary establishment. For had not the leaders of that establishment complained unendingly that black writers tended to confuse social and political protest with literature?

Hughes was fully aware that an integrationist *Zeitgeist* was in the air, but he was relatively unperturbed by it all. He had seen so many movements and trends come and go. When he read in *Perspectives USA* an article entitled "Two Protests on Protest" by Richard Gibson and James Baldwin, he fully assented to the possible legitimacy of their protests, even though Gibson recommended that blacks should read, not Chester Himes and Langston Hughes, but Eliot, Valéry, Rilke, and Mann. And he could understand Baldwin's rejection of *Uncle Tom's Cabin* and of Wright's novels of protest. After all, as he wrote to Arna Bontemps, young black writers did not have to stay in the same old pen; they had a right to try to "leap out," providing they did not land in some "lily pond." As Shakespeare had once said, "Lillies that fester smell far worse than weeds."

Hughes's tone changed, however, when he read Baldwin's *Go Tell It on the Mountain*. In the first place, as he wrote to Arna Bontemps, the novel contained the kind of protest Baldwin had been protesting against. His principal criticism, however, was against Baldwin's writing style; the novel was written in an elegant, soaring prose that was far above its humble subject matter. The person Baldwin had needed to help him write his story about black people and their religion was Zora Neal Hurston; for no one knew the language and folkways of blacks any better than Zora. Wrote Hughes in his letter of 18 February 1953 to Arna: "Baldwin over-writes and over-poeticizes in images way over the heads of the folks supposedly thinking them. . . . Which makes it seem like an 'art' book about folks who aren't 'art' folks." Hughes was also critical of the way that stress on religion in the novel only leads to frustration and sorrow. He complained, "Out of all that religion SOMEBODY ought to triumph somewhere in it, but nary a soul does." His conclusion was that "It's a low down story in a velvet bag." Although Hughes did not expressly say so, his objection to Baldwin's style was that it was a "white" style designed to impress a white audience.

There is no evidence that Baldwin ever knew of Hughes's low opinion of his very successful first novel, but he did read the latter's review of his *Notes of a Native Son*. It was entitled "From Harlem to Paris" and published in the *New York Times Book Review* in February 1956. In his critique, Hughes mixes praise and blame. First, Baldwin's literary style as an essayist is excellent. His "words and his materials suit each other." His "thought becomes poetry, and the poetry illuminates the thought." Indeed, as an essayist, Baldwin is "thought-provoking, tantalizing, irritating, abusing, and amusing," making him a far better essayist than a writer of fiction. In closing, Hughes says that the young writer still has a formidable hurdle to clear: he is still "half-American" and "half Afro-American." Once he fuses the two and develops a clearcut cultural identity, he will, Hughes concludes, become a great writer.

Hughes's criticism of Baldwin's fictional style and his concern for his fragmented cultural identity had absolutely no adverse effect on the younger writer's rise to literary fame and prestige. To use Irving Howe's phrase, Baldwin in the late 1950s and early 1960s courted the harlot *Zeitgeist* so effectively that his star rose in the world of literary achievement and recognition almost as high as Ellison's. In 1956 he even ventured to do what an Ellison dared not do—write *In Giovanni's Room*—a novel about white homosexual lovers. Ellison's triumph in 1952 with *The Invisible Man* and the great surge of white reader interest in Baldwin's fiction and essays proved that an integrationist *Zeitgeist* did exist. Obviously, it favored writers like Ellison and Baldwin and Tolson, but it had a damaging effect on both the reputation of Hughes and his relationship with younger black writers.

In 1958 when Hughes, in the midst of his many other writing and editing tasks, chose to cull from his poems of four decades his best and issue them in an edition entitled *Selected Poems,* he was not aware of how culturally irrelevant much of his poetry had become. Black blues poetry about black blues people who in their "simple" way survived in a ghetto filled with deferred dreams somehow had lost audience appeal in the 1950s. Rather, there was a readership for "arty" stories with integrated plots. Moreover, the period of the Harlem Renaissance, the setting for many of Hughes's "selected" poems, was for many of the young writers like Baldwin a mythic time in which nothing of great significance happened. So Hughes, in seeking to find a reading audience for his *Selected Poems,* confronted a group of generational and ideological skeptics. Many of them liked the man who chose to remain in the Harlem ghetto and live and work at 20 East 127th Street, but he had lost his relevancy in this time of lively new trends.

Thus it was that when the editor of the *New York Times Book Review* asked Baldwin to review *Selected Poems,* Baldwin accepted the somewhat lucrative offer but considered the collection of poems literally not worth reading. In an integrationist *Zeitgeist,* such poems had no cultural relevancy. So Baldwin, a master of style and image, wrote a review lacking in both critical substance and integrity of statement. There was nothing personal in his failure to read the volume that he attempted to review. It was just that a busy and totally *engagé litterateur* had little or no time for what he considered to be cultural irrelevancies. And thus it was, too, that, at the beginning of his review, Baldwin said of Hughes's selected best poems, "A more disciplined poet would have thrown most of these poems in the waste basket." For not having read the poems, he chose, like some of the postmodern structuralists, to be dismissive rather than critical.

As we now know, the integrationist *Zeitgeist* was soon spent, and Julian Mayfield in an article entitled "Into the Mainstream and Oblivion" provided a forceful argument that the mainstream was a "nowhere." All of us also know that Baldwin, too, changed. By 1963, his answer to Hughes's question "What happens to a dream deferred?" was *The Fire Next Time.*

NOTE

This lecture was delivered at the Langston Hughes Conference held at City University of New York in 1988.

Langston Hughes and Martin Luther King, Jr.: The Poet, the Preacher, and the Dream

This paper seeks to examine how two prominent black men of America's twentieth century—one a poet and the other a preacher—never walked in each other's shoes but ultimately courted and articulated the same dream. Both died in an assassination-riddled decade, the poet from postoperative toxicity in a Harlem hospital in 1967 and the preacher of an assassin's bullet on a balcony in the Lorraine Hotel in Memphis in 1968. The poet had lived sixty-five years full of far-flung travel and literary adventure; the preacher had lived only thirty-nine years, with the final ten of these (as he might have stated) standing on the volcanic heights of an America teetering on the edge of the seething cauldron of racial conflict. At the death of the preacher, a martyr's mantle was quickly in place and his violent death was mourned throughout the world. For the poet, fame has come more gradually. The Langston Hughes Society has been formed in his honor; it publishes *The Langston Hughes Review*, encourages Hughes scholarship, and fosters the teaching of Hughes in schools and colleges. But for the poet there is no commemorative national holiday, simply because the fashioner of a dream rarely acquires the fame and recognition granted the articulator and practitioner of a dream.

When Martin Luther King, Jr., was born in 1929, James Langston Hughes had not only jettisoned his first name but was well launched in his career as an African American writer and literary spokesman. In 1925, he had won the Opportunity Poetry Prize for his "The Weary Blues," and by 1929 he had not only published two volumes of poetry, but he had won the Wytter Bynum prize for undergraduate poetry and was nearing the completion of his first novel, *Not without Laughter*. Following its publication in 1930, he received for that work the Harmon Gold Medal, the first prize in the Harmon Foundation's annual competition for achievement in African

American arts and letters. Using the prize money (four hundred dollars), Hughes traveled in the spring of 1931 to Haiti and Cuba. Upon his return to the United States, he found a nation aflame with the Scottsboro case; and it was at this point in his career that he began his long and determined assault on American racism. In a sense, he became the prophet for a preacher who would not be called forth for yet another twenty-five years to preach against that same racism. Coincidentally, for both men the fight against racism started in Alabama.

The poet's first words about Alabama were words of anger over the near lynching of eight Negro youths in Scottsboro. In "Christ in Alabama" he wrote:

> Christ is a nigger
> Beaten and black
> Oh, bare your back!
>
> ...
>
> Most holy bastard
> Of the bleeding mouth,
>   Nigger Christ
> On the cross
> Of the South.
>
> (*Scottsboro Ltd.*, 1932)

Then Hughes sought to distance himself from a church-going, hymn-singing South that reveled in festive black lynchings and castration rituals, and he wrote "Goodbye Christ":

> Listen, Christ,
> You did alright in your day, I reckon,
> But that day's gone now....
> You ain't no good no more.
> They've pawned you
> Till you've done wore out.
>
> (*Negro Worker,* 1932)

And with the dark mood still upon him, he speculated that, in view of the mounting tides of racial injustice that Justice was not only blind but

> Her bandage hides two festering sores
> That once perhaps were eyes.

Then, as the angered and disillusioned poet drifted, along with so many others in Depression-ridden America, into a defensive political and social leftism, he began to sense the international dimensions of racism and what Du Bois had designated would be the primary concern of the West in the twentieth century—the color line. Using the mask of the black Everyman, Hughes wrote:

It is the same everywhere for me—
On the docks at Sierra Leone,
In the cotton fields of Alabama,
In the diamond mines of Kimberly,
On the coffee hills of Haiti,
The banana lands of Central America,
The streets of Harlem,
And the cities of Morocco and Tripoli,

Black:
Exploited, beaten and robbed
Shot and killed.

(Negro Worker, 1932)

But, even as the poet in the early 1930s railed against racial injustice and the failure of Western Christianity and the violence of an exploitative Third World colonialism, he also became the Dream-Keeper who expressed his faith in his dream of a better tomorrow. In the 1920s he had written:

We have tomorrow
Bright before us
Like a flame.

Yesterday—
A night-gone thing,
A sun-down name.

(Crisis, 1924)

And, in *The Dream-Keeper,* a slim volume of his poems published in 1932, the poet stated unequivocally:

Hold fast to dreams
For if dreams die
Life is a broken-winged bird
That cannot fly.

So, even as the nightmare of Scottsboro was upon him, causing him to write in anger "8 Black Boys in a Southern jail / World, turn pale," he continued his courtship of the dream of a better world and a better America.

Thus, Hughes's political and social leftism was only a thin facade covering Hughes the social and political dreamer-idealist. His poem "Let America Be America Again," published in his *A New Song* in 1938, offers further proof of his belief in the validity of the dream:

Let America be the dream the dreamers dreamed—
Let it be that great strong land of love
Where never kings connive nor tyrants scheme
That any man be crushed by one above. . . .

When this was written in 1938, the youth who would become the preacher was 9 years old. Already there were indications that his life would be different in many respects. Whereas, by 1938, the poet had traversed the world's major routes of travel and carried his message, the preacher-to-be found his life rigorously circumscribed by a racial segregation that narrowed the scope of his cultural and social experiences. There was no High Museum or its equivalent in his life in Atlanta, Georgia. He did not have access to the city's Carnegie Library nor to any of its entertainment and cultural activities. He knew of Auburn Avenue and Ebenezer Baptist where his father and his grandfather preached, and he knew of the colleges in southwest Atlanta from which his parents had graduated. And he knew of the Scottsboro boys still held in Alabama's Kilby jail and of Angelo Herndon's troubles with Georgia racist law. But the ripening years would have to come and pass before, as preacher, he would be able to articulate the poet's dream about a new and spiritually refurbished America.

With World War II's beginning in 1939 and America's involvement in the conflict in 1941, Hughes's travels ceased, and he settled down in Harlem to become black America's major literary spokesman. The many changes in the world's political climate at this time gradually muted his leftist anger; and by 1943, in his patriotic poem "Freedom's Plow," he again courted his idealistic dream about America. Published in *Opportunity* in April 1943, this longish poem was written as a declamation piece for Paul Muni and had been featured on one of the radio programs sponsored by the Vocational Opportunity Program in March of that year. In this poem, Hughes again wrote of his dream:

> America is a dream.
> The poet says it was promises.
> The people say it is promises—that will
> come true
>
> . . .
>
> America!
> Land created in common,
> Dream nourished in common,
> Keep your hand on the plow! Hold on!

With the war's end in 1945, the poet joined in black America's fight to gain freedom from segregation and Jim Crow laws; and in 1947, 1949, and 1951 he published more poetry affirming his belief in the validity of his dream of freedom for America and its black minority. For instance, in *Fields of Wonder* in 1947, he wrote:

> Now dreams
> Are not available

> To the dreamers
> Nor songs to the singers. . . .
>
> But the dream
> Will come back
> And the song
> Break
> Its jail.

Then, in 1949 in *One-Way Ticket,* using a more provocative imagery, Hughes expressed the quintessence of his dream for a revitalized and renewed America. This time he returned to Alabama, where, in the early 1930s, he had had his first serious encounter with southern racism. This time the dream was conveyed in the context of the orchestrated music of an Alabama dawn—a time when the gently nuanced beauty of the sky at daybreak blended with the warm and fertile verdure of the countryside and with, he wrote,

> the scent of pine needles
> And the smell of red clay after rain.

But the poet saw and heard something else in the music of his dream— something more than the beauty of rising swamp mists and gently falling dew. He saw in his dream a colorful and glorious intermixture of

> long red necks
> And poppy colored faces
> And big brown arms
> And the field daisy eyes
> Of black and white black white black people.

And, in his musical dream, the poet promised to

> put white hands
> And black hands and brown and yellow
>   hands
> And red clay earth hands in it,
> Touching everybody with kind fingers,
> And touching each other natural as dew
> In that dawn of music when I
> Get to be a composer
> And write about daybreak
> In Alabama.

In this poem, Hughes presents his dream of a racially integrated America—a carefully composed and divinely orchestrated blending of all of the racial colors in a glorious "daybreak" and new day in the Southland. As history

has since proven, the dream proved to be a poetic prophecy—a prophecy
for a young preacher-to-be who, in 1949, had just started his graduate study
at Crozier Theology School and within seven years was to settle in
Montgomery, Alabama. Almost as soon as he was settled in as minister
at Montgomery's Dexter Avenue Baptist Church, the preacher began to
hear the softly echoing strains of a "dawn of music" which would bring a
momentous "daybreak" in race relations in Alabama and throughout the
South.

One-Way Ticket was Hughes's last book of poetry in the 1940s, a decade
which was probably his most productive decade as a poet. With the 1950s
there were many changes. The poet, spurred by the success of the Simple
stories, devoted more time to comic fiction and urban folk drama. But,
most important, he lost his focus on the dream on which he had concentrated his poetical energies for almost two decades. Undoubtedly, the
tensions brewing in Harlem and in other crisis spots in black urban
America had something to do with the radical alteration of the dream.
Indeed, this is the message of *Montage of a Dream Deferred,* his new-style,
bebop jazz poem published in 1951. With violence simmering just under
the surface throughout black urban America and with widespread frustration about unfulfilled postwar expectations, all dreams about a thoroughly
democratized and free America had to be modified, postponed, changed,
or, as the poet said, "deferred." But, even as he announced that, because of
America's racial climate, dreams had to be deferred, the poet asked in his
poem entitled "Harlem":

> What happens to a dream deferred?
>
> Does it dry up
> like a raisin in the sun?
> Or fester like a sore
> And then run?
>   . . .
> Or does it explode?

The full answer to the poet's prophetic question came in the 1960s when
America's black urban ghettos exploded in rapid succession—Watts, Detroit,
Newark, Patterson, Philadelphia. Interestingly enough, by the time the
poet's question had been answered and his prophecy fulfilled, the preacher,
now grown, matured, and firmly astride his "unicorn of deliverance," had
set the South aflame. Black colleges and universities, so long mired in
passivity and social inaction, had come alive in a united spirit of revolt
against racial segregation. And the black church came out of its century-
long apathy to declare its militant revolt against a past and present filled
with racial dishonor. The preacher had wrought these changes in the South

in less than a decade. But the preacher's greatest moment of achievement, in the view of many, was in August 1963 when, from the steps of the Lincoln Memorial, he articulated his version of the dream for America. The preacher's declaration came approximately twelve years after the poet had declared that the dream, at least for black urban America, had to be "deferred" until the times were more propitious.

One might add whence came the preacher's optimistic endorsement of the dream so long after the poet had turned away from the dream? There are doubtless many explanations for the preacher's optimism. First, as a result of his training and study, he was not only well read in Christian philosophy and Ghandian social ethics, but he was emboldened by a sort of Old Testament faith that moral and social justice would prevail and, in the words of Amos, roll down from the mountains in a mighty stream. Second, he was emboldened by his success against segregation in places where blacks had never before been successful—Montgomery, Birmingham, and Albany, Georgia. Particularly stimulating was his success in Birmingham, the bastion of white supremacy in the South. After leading the black children of Birmingham against Bull Connor's dogs and hoses on Good Friday in April 1963, he had been arrested, imprisoned, harassed, and threatened with death but was rescued by a timely call from the White House.

Thus it was that, four months later, the preacher stood before a crowd of thousands on 28 August 1963 and said:

> I say to you . . . I still have a dream. It is a dream deeply rooted in the American dream that one day this nation will rise up and live out the true meaning of its creed: "We hold these truths to be self-evident; that all men are created equal."

> I have a dream that one day on the red hills of Georgia, sons of former slaves and sons of former slave-owners will be able to sit down together at the table of brotherhood.

> I have a dream that one day, even the state of Mississippi, . . . will be transformed into an oasis of freedom and justice.

> I have a dream my four little children will one day live in a nation where they will not be judged by the color of their skin but by the content of their character.

> I have a dream today!

> I have a dream that one day, down in Alabama . . . little black boys and black girls will be able to join hands with little white boys and white girls as sisters and brothers.

> I have a dream today!

We do not know the reaction of the poet as he listened to his dream described so forcefully and dramatically in the preacher's rich oratorical style. Certainly, during all of his years of "dreaming" he had never climbed even a small mountain of visible popularity. Now on this August day, one hundred years after the Union victory at Gettysburg, as the self-styled "Dream-Keeper," he was undoubtedly cheered that thousands the world over were listening to the dream. We can also assume that he, like many other Americans, was enormously cheered when, as a result of the March on Washington and the great "I Have a Dream" speech, some of the dream was translated into reality when the great civil rights bills were passed and made into law. And we can also assume that the poet felt a prideful glow when the preacher who had sought through a program of nonviolent social change to implement the dream was awarded the Nobel Peace Prize in 1964.

In the historic afterglow of the events of the "Fatuous Fifties" and the "Searing Sixties," inevitably comparative judgments are being made: A discriminating few, believing that the medium is the message, prefer that a dream be couched, not in crowd-swaying rhetoric, but in the subtle poetic imagery of an Alabama daybreak, when there is a musical mingling of "kind fingers" on "white hands / And black hands and brown and yellow hands / And red clay . . . earth hands." They prefer a rapturous chorale of "long red necks / And poppy colored faces / And big brown arms / And the field daisy eyes / Of black and white black white black people."

Decades after the respective deaths of the poet and the preacher, how do we now assess the dream and the dreamers? We now know that, just as the dancer can never become the dance, the dreamer can never become the dream. Once evoked or expressed, the dance and the dream drift off into a timeless life of their own, shorn of man's creative chemistry and no longer circumscribed by time, space, and place. Not so the dancer and not so the dreamer. Each remains in time's relentless grasp, subject to gravity's pull and to death's dissolution. It is interesting to note that, just as Hughes in 1951 abandoned his humanistic dream of a happily integrated America and announced that all such dreams must be deferred, the preacher by the mid-1960s began also to modify his dream. The racial turbulence of that decade permitted no more optimistic dreaming of an integrated America. Indeed, at that time a nightmarish confusion stalked the land and once again fulfillment of the big dream of a united society had to be deferred. Burning urban ghettos, raging student unrest, a bloody and futile overseas war, the militant cries of the Black Power advocates—all underlined the need for new strategies and pragmatic solutions. So, just as Hughes in *A Montage of a Dream Deferred* talked about breaking through the ghetto's finely wrought economic barriers, the preacher and his strategists turned their attention to addressing some of the economic problems entrapping black people in ghettos in America. Like the poet fifteen years earlier, Martin knew that there would not be and could not be a racial daybreak in Alabama or anywhere else, unless there was economic justice for the black worker everywhere in America. And that is why the preacher was in Memphis helping to try to solve the plight of the striking black sanitation workers on that fateful day in April 1968.

There is no evidence that either Hughes or King, in seeking new directions, ever fully abandoned his dream of an integrated America or ever stopped hearing the faint music of a racial daybreak in Alabama. Even as death came to the poet in a Harlem hospital in 1967 and to the preacher in a Memphis motel in 1968, each believed, deep in his heart, that everyone should

> Hold fast to dreams.
> For, if dreams die,
> Life is a broken-winged bird
> That cannot fly.

NOTE

This lecture was presented at a Martin Luther King, Jr., birthday commemoration at Rust College, Holly Springs, Mississippi, in 1988.

PART 6

Conclusion

The Graduate Experience from a Minority Perspective

Over fifty years ago, I entered graduate school. Since America was still in the grip of an intense economic depression, the word "minority" had at that time at least three shades of meaning: First, it applied to the slim numbers of students who, out of a larger number of students, chose or were chosen in those times of economic blight to go to graduate school. The American "graduate school" was still something of a novelty developed in academe under the aegis of a postgraduate program at Johns Hopkins modeled on something observed in the German university of the late nineteenth century. So as an entering black graduate student, I was a minority member of a minority group of students who were lucky enough to go to college in a time of severe economic depression. In fact, the word "minority" primarily referred during those days to a girl who, accosted in the wrong manner by an older man, could charge that man with statutory rape. The street term for a young girl, attractive enough to be so accosted, was "jail bait." The legal term was "minority female."

So when I entered Syracuse University Graduate School in the fall of 1938, I was not officially a member of a minority racial group. I was, instead, known pretty widely as the graduate school's only "colored" student. Generally, there were two reactions, or two schools of thought. The first was the "what's-he-doing-here-anyhow!" school. The second was the "watch-him-closely" school. Members of this school believed that if I was crafty enough to be "scholarshipped" in, I was smart enough to be institutionally destructive while there. After World War II, this broad suspicion became even more widespread; everyone who had entered a prewar graduate program and had been quietly colored was now classifiable as an undetected black spy—a favorite J. Edgar Hoover mode of "subject" classification.

Fortunately, I was blissfully unaware of the sociopolitical interest generated by my presence in Syracuse's graduate program. As I recall, I was not at all pleased that I could not find on-campus housing, but I did not let my unhappiness with "ghetto" housing get in the way of my studies. Like other "colored" students (four were enrolled in the fall of 1938), I lived in the older area in which Syracuse's Jews had lived earlier in the century. What bothered me was the program itself. All of my courses could well be described as "esoteric." I had had six years of one so-called dead language—Latin—but a year of Anglo-Saxon, another Germanic language, was difficult to understand. Those who study the history and development of the English language discover, to the functional detriment of Anglo-Saxon, that the putative source language of English does not have too much to do with the origins of English words and phrases. Many, many "English" words and phrases are derived from medieval French words and phrases; for following the Norman conquest of England of the eleventh century, there was a rather longish period of substantial French cultural and linguistic influence. For this reason, courses in Anglo-Saxon play no logical role in rendering a graduate English student more knowledgeable about anything, with possibly two exceptions. First, you read Beowulf's story in the language of the Icelandic hero and his hard-pressed kinfolks; and secondly, you learn about man's inhumanity to man in terms of litotes—the strongly figurative language of melancholy and distress used to describe puny man's fight against the great monsters of the deep. But acquiring a knowledge of Anglo-Saxon and developing some skill in reading it was a useless phase of English graduate study. And so I concluded then that when one organized a graduate program in anything, one had to have what I called the A–S equivalent—a requirement that permits you to know something that no one else would ever, ever know. For I found that, even as we were being required to take Anglo-Saxon at Syracuse, Harvard's English department was requiring its doctoral candidates to take Middle High German, Middle English, and Old Gothic. The rationale for such a requirement was that a well-prepared graduate student knows not only what no one else will ever know, but he is in command of essentially useless knowledge and must be able to extract some ego strength in our very pragmatic society for just knowing this.

My next graduate experience occurred when, armed with what was known as a GREB grant (Graduate Record Educational Board grant), I entered a large midwestern graduate school for the beginnings of doctoral study. Two points are of interest here. My source of financial aid was Rockefeller money; the phrase GREB made Rockefeller seem less insidious as a philanthropist. Second, the timing of my grant was very bad; World War II was raging on all continents and islands of the sea. I almost believed that I received the grant simply because everyone else was at war somewhere. In any event I persevered as a class-attending peacemaker as long as I could; this time I kept my mastery of Anglo-Saxon a close secret but took a class in German taught by a German *emigré* from the University of Leipzig who had both a close-clipped beard and a dueling scar. Since the course was taught in German and I therefore knew little, the course compared favorably with my earlier course in Anglo-Saxon.

That was in 1942; by the spring of 1943 I too was off to war. But I left with a title that only the fortunate few used. I was a "humanist"—a term that had a curious import during the war years. Not only did it mean you were an intellectual person, but an intellectual person concerned about values—not like the scientists who were fashioning bombs and gas ovens. And so I learned that, should I ever have an opportunity to run a graduate school, I should operate it so that its students should be inflated by knowing something not generally known and that all associated with the enterprise would develop a "humanist" view or become "humanists." I should also point out that, even in 1943, no one was yet sufficiently sophisticated in ethnic intercourse to call me a "minority" person. In fact, I am afraid that "ethnic intercourse" meant in 1943 what it now means among the morally unenlightened—sex between two persons from different ethnic backgrounds, or "twilight integration."

My attendance to warlike matters merely postponed my further involvement with a graduate school. This time, in 1946, using government funds known as the GI Bill, I enrolled for doctoral study. It seemed as though everyone else who had been in the service had the same idea. Almost immediately I knew that those seeking higher degrees were no longer a sanctified few or a carefully selected minority. Rather, with the Depression almost a faint memory, America's ethnic masses poured into graduate school. Everyone had, if not enough, some money. In a lot of instances, spouses worked, and graduate schools were no longer the haven of an elite. The man who had been a nameless "grunt" in the armed forces became a nameless graduate student, and the sacrosanct temple of academia—the graduate school of old—disappeared forever. With its disappearance also disappeared all that was highfalutinly meaningless in graduate work. Right away, I missed the bored intellectual who was not really appreciated by his social class and I found the new graduate school bureaucracy spiritually depressing and psychologically deflating. Indeed, the prewar graduate school had been a rather comfortable place in which one could dawdle, taking a course now and then and doing the reading that came easily to hand. Moreover, in those days there were "rules" limiting the coming and going of women. Now they were everywhere—in the libraries, on the quads, and even in the classes. The war, it seemed, had somehow lost track of its major objectives—the defeat of the Axis powers, Germany,

Italy, and Japan—and caused, instead, a radical alteration of the American graduate school.

Most graduate schools now had rules and regulations and a dean to see that these rules and regulations were obeyed. Departments carefully evaluated students, determining whether all applicants met admission criteria and whether needed tests like something called the GRE general or GRE subject matter or Miller's Analogies bore the proper scores. And, as the Cold War with the Soviet block or the Warsaw nations became colder, graduate schools in major research institutions became carefully monitored research factories. As a consequence, the graduate student could, if he were not careful, become a member of a research team or group and come under surveillance that was only a little less restrictive than he had suffered in the military during the war.

Also, ethnic minorities came into view. Suddenly, there were Jews and Croats and blacks and Hispanics and Thais and Nigerians and Malaysians and Haitians—all spewed forth by an unsettled postwar world. Of course, blacks stood out from the rest; they were the only large minority group then existing in the United States and not restricted to reservations who were segregated and legally discriminated against. So now I was not only a graduate student who was a veteran, but a graduate student who was a black minority veteran.

The life of a graduate black minority veteran was a strange one, indeed. For academic reasons, we enjoyed some on-campus social visibility. Professors, mostly male, sucked on their pipes and wore well-fitted masks of indifference to campus and departmental racial policy. All black minority veterans who were students knew that we had a strange statistical prominence but we did not know why. Some of us thought that it had something to do with the recently organized United Nations. None of us knew then that the strangely paranoid man who ran the FBI lived in mortal fear of every academically trained black veteran and organized his Bureau accordingly. None of us knew then that coping with a well-organized black "revolution" bolstered with effective Communist support was high on the FBI agenda. All we knew then was that we moved in a strange statistical glow—a glow that bothered Irish politicians and members of the Mafia. The latter two groups were interested in amassing power, and they could not understand why they had lost control or never had control of the black segregated minority, especially those black graduate student veterans who moved around in someone's statistical glow.

As I pursued my personal academic goals, I was not really bothered by my apparent statistical importance, although, when I applied for a loan from the prestigious and wealthy Harvard Foundation, reference was made to Harvard's concern for my on-campus behavior as a statistically important person. I, of course, did not know of what the loan-giver spoke. Was I to enter into a special contract with him? Was I, in order to qualify for the loan, contract to indulge in a certain kind of racially decorous behavior on campus? And I had a lot of other questions: What was racially decorous behavior? Who would monitor my behavior away from campus? What did my behavior as a grown man have to do with my academic integrity, anyhow? The English department, had it not, certified that I had long been a person of considerable academic integrity. Defeated by my questions, the loan-giver forgot the provost's concerns and gave me the money; but, by this time, there was just a little odor associated with the statistical glow.

I was caught in the glow's full glare when I had reached the job-search phase of my graduate career. Ironically, we had all just been morally boosted by Truman's declaration about creating a totally desegregated armed forces, when I received an incredible teaching offer from Duke University, a southern institution of great wealth and prestige. At first, I thought that Duke, buoyed by Truman's action with the armed forces, was trying to use my appointment as a means of blasting through the walls of academic segregation. My advisor, a rather crusty liberal from Vermont, advised me, however, that in many respects the South was still fighting the Civil War and that evidently an error had been made. In any event, he would call. His call to Newman Ivy White did indeed confirm that a fairly egregious error had been made. The distinguished Duke professor had confused me with the scion of a rather famous white Mississippi family—a family whose members had had some intellectual ambitions once upon a time. This was an error resulting from slavery's rather aggressive paternalism and mode of name transfer. After all, a white Mississippian named Barksdale could have gone to Harvard from Vanderbilt and been selected to teach Victorian literature at Duke University. In fact, given the nature of post–Civil War life in America, the chances for a southern white named Barksdale being in the Harvard Graduate School as against a northern black named Barksdale are at least two to one.

By an ironic circumstance, when I did get a position in 1949, I ended up at what was then North Carolina College at Durham, the home of Duke University. Despite the fact that NCC was on a different side of the North Carolina city, many of the Duke English faculty with Harvard roots were very kind to me during my stay at Durham. Many of them were disturbed that they worked at a segregated institution in a segregated state. They all, they said, felt powerless before the law.

In the meantime, segregation's statistical glare was becoming too uncomfortable to bear. In the early 1950s, the authorities at the state's flagship university at Chapel Hill began to harass the rather recently appointed president of NCC to fulfill his appointment promise to relieve the university at Chapel Hill of any blacks seeking to enroll in its graduate programs. Almost immediately, the recently appointed president seized upon my services, and I was, almost quicker than a flash, appointed vice-chairman of the Graduate Council, an on-campus officer of a quickly formed graduate program. The chairman of the Graduate Council was the then dean of Chapel Hill's graduate school. Immediately I had a problem. Could I serve as chief officer of a graduate program developed solely to accommodate segregation's needs? I had had no choice in the Duke employment dilemma. Did I have any choice in this situation? Without thinking the matter all the way through and coming firmly to grips with all of the implications of my accepting employment in a completely segregated institution in a completely segregated state, I resigned my position as vice-chairman of the Graduate Council. The recently appointed president was very unhappy over my decision to play the role of a disloyal employee. Although he did not fire me for insubordination, he, instead, let me know of his displeasure by denying all of my travel requests and all of my supply requisitions. The glare of the statistical light of segregation had not only become uncomfortable; it had become almost scorchingly hot.

I began to realize that it was just not enough to know some Anglo-Saxon and be a humanist. It was also necessary to survive. And so, in 1953, when I was offered the deanship of the segregated graduate school in a segregated North Carolina College, I accepted it with all of the psychological disabilities thereunto appertaining. By a twist of fate, a year later, in 1954, the NAACP won the *Brown v. Topeka Board of Education* legal suit before the Supreme Court of the United States. Many of us, at that time, thought that this action by the court predicted the immediate death knell of segregation at all levels of education. The Mississippi Barksdales, I assume, knew better.

I quickly found out that running a graduate school was quite different from being a graduate student. In the first place, graduate students, viewed from above, have little or no dignity. They seem to be almost eternally traumatized by life and circumstances. No one, I found, was ever in search of further learning. Most were motivated to pursue graduate study in order to improve teacher certification rank and thus improve salaries. I also found that there usually was little or no time to indoctrinate anyone with the virus of humanism. In fact, I found that in a state in which everyone kneeled before the gargantua of segregation, "humanism" was not a word that had any meaning. It was like something taken from Anglo-Saxon.

Fortunately, before my academic career formally drew to a close, I had two more experiences with graduate programming which were less flatly pragmatic. No one spoke or read Anglo-Saxon, but one occasionally heard something good about humanism. Undoubtedly, the times had a lot to with the development of a refreshed and refreshing academic climate. In the first place, a young Baptist minister began a fight in the South against segregation. After ten years of aggressive battle on the highways and byways and through the institutions of church and state, segregation was no more. Inevitably, Dr. King's victory substantially improved the conditions for learning among both blacks and whites throughout the South; and, by 1967, the year in which I accepted the graduate deanship at Atlanta University, the discomfiting glare of segregation was gone, J. Edgar Hoover was on his death bed, and I could, every now and then, get a whiff of southern humanism. Everything, it seems, had improved. The students who sought graduate degrees were younger and not so economically driven and intellectually haggard. And financial aid was a bit more plentiful. Foundations provided assistance to those graduate programs that wanted to be competitive in buying good graduate students with competing grant offers. And also, through segregation's once closed door came emissaries from large northern institutions to steal a bout with the southern sun, play a little golf, and then try to court your best master's-level students with good offers for doctoral study. In fact, I became a busier negotiator of projects and proposals than I was a graduate dean. Would Atlanta University's Graduate School of Arts and Sciences accept this $50,000 or that $50,000? Particularly did the offers escalate in 1968, the year of Martin Luther King's assassination. A guilt-stricken nation sought to abase itself with libations and offerings at the altar of racial forgiveness.

Coping with surfeits of every kind, I tried to be selective and take offers designed only for program improvement and program enhancement. Working under very harassing conditions with the Peace Corps, for instance, we cooperated with that organization in establishing a degree program which started before the Peace Corps volunteers traveled and ended after they had returned from their overseas post. With consistent and unflagging assistance from the National Endowment, we set up an unprecedented cooperative degree program with the Institute of Liberal Arts of Emory University, enrolled students in the program, and oversaw their comings and goings over the twenty-two-mile route between Emory and Atlanta University. And when the Ford Foundation, still pouting because Atlanta University had turned down a 1965 centenary fund offer which would have united into one the five institutions in the Atlanta University Center, offered Atlanta University's Graduate College of Arts and Sciences $7.5 million for improvements in its social science program, I, as dean of that college, assented vigorously. The president dissented just as vigorously, arguing that neither Ford nor any other foundation had the essential right to select for remediation its areas of need. Ford, however, was just as persistent, taking its fight to fund a new doctoral program in the social sciences all the way to the university board's executive committee. The board, of course, sided with Ford. Thus, quickly, out of plenitude came confusion and an embarrassment of riches. And just as quickly all became history. I departed for a professorship in a midwestern research institution. The president of Atlanta University soon retired, and Ford Foundation personnel changed so radically that I doubt if anyone stayed abreast of the newly funded doctoral program in the social sciences. Now, over twenty years later, Atlanta University no longer exists. In a somewhat desperate quest for survival, it has joined hands with Clark College and is now Clark Atlanta University.

My final stint in graduate administration was the period in which I served as graduate associate dean for student services at the University of Illinois at Urbana-Champaign. Fortunately, I did not have to duplicate the high-wire act of Atlanta. In fact, Atlanta's experience taught me the difference between administration and development. In Illinois's program, there was more specialization. The research department's staff developed various kinds of funding programs. Specifically, I helped students cope with the many problems graduate students can have; like students in North Carolina's segregated program and those in Atlanta's program, the essential student problem at Illinois was inadequacy of funding. The principal advantage at Illinois is that all graduate staff persons have some access to the extra funding generated by a portion of the university's indirect-costs money allocated to the graduate college. From this fund we were able to draw money to support student travel to appropriate professional meetings, and we were, upon a student's written request, able to draw small amounts of money to meet that student's emergency needs. We also had assistance programs specifically organized to help minority students. Although we never had a healthily large number of minority students enroll in a major number of the graduate college's eighty-seven departments, we provided the sixty or sixty-five minority students who did enroll with preenrollment grants, providing for each minority student a nine-month stipend of about eight thousand dollars a year, plus full tuition and fees. Unfortunately, Illinois's program of minority graduate recruitment was never fully competitive with programs at other Big Ten institutions, like Ohio State or the University of Wisconsin at Madison.

Since I retired from the graduate college in 1982, graduate minority enrollment has continued to fall. Studies indicate that this is a broad national trend. Indeed, once again, we have well-financed funding programs available but fewer and fewer minority applicants. And, once again, social, economic, and political conditions which help to set social tone and atmosphere affect graduate school enrollments. It seems that, after the so-called Reagan years, American society is fatigued and not in search of the brave new worlds we sought in the 1940s right after World War II. Also despite the many elections of blacks and other minorities, considerable racial defeatism is in the air. With segregation no longer a formidable barrier to social and racial intermixture there is a surprising amount of racial unease everywhere. Indeed, as we prepare for a minorities-dominated twenty-first century, America's white majority is filled with a confidence-shaking fear. Chances are that in the next century they will be outbred and outproduced and outspent, and only on the university campus will they try hard to keep their genie of racial superiority in the bottle. Indeed, the graduate school and not the halls of Congress will be action center. There someone might remember a little Anglo-Saxon and also fashion a new humanism for the broadly diverse culture that will be America's.

NOTE

This lecture was presented at the University of Oklahoma in 1989.

A Note on the Author

RICHARD K. BARKSDALE is professor emeritus of English and former associate dean of the Graduate College at the University of Illinois at Urbana-Champaign. Over his forty-year career he has published widely in scholarly journals such as *Phylon, College Language Association Journal, Western Humanities Review,* and *Black American Literature Forum.* He is the author of *Langston Hughes: The Poet and His Critics,* and coedited, with Keneth Kinnamon, *Black Writers of America.*

ACL 2227

10/14/92

PS
153
N5
B29
1992